May I Have A

Word

With You?

Also by Vanessa Davis Griggs

Countless Blessings (E-book and limited edition flipbook with *Steely Gray*)
Steely Gray (E-book and limited edition flipbook with *Countless Blessings*)

Forever Soul Ties
Redeeming Waters
Ray of Hope
Destiny Unlimited

Wings of Grace (Sequel to *Promises Beyond Jordan*)
Promises Beyond Jordan
The Rose of Jericho

The Blessed Trinity Series
The Other Side of Divine (Book 9)
The Other Side of Dare (Book 8)
The Other Side of Goodness (Book 7)
The Truth Is the Light (Book 6)
Goodness and Mercy (Book 5)
Practicing What You Preach (Book 4)
If Memory Serves (Book 3)
Strongholds (Book 2)
Blessed Trinity (Book 1)

May I Have A Word With You?

Devotional

Vanessa Davis Griggs

Free To Soar
Birmingham, AL

Free To Soar
P. O. Box 101328
Birmingham, AL 35210

Vanessa Davis Griggs
www.VanessaDavisGriggs.com

10 9 8 7 6 5 4 3 2 1

ISBN-978-0-9673-0035-1

Printed in the United States of America

Dedicated to my mother, Josephine Davis,
and in memory of my father, James Davis Jr. both
who made sure I was introduced to the Word of God early
in my life. My mother, by reading the entire Old Testament before
I made my debut into this world. And my father, who took me to the
church house (in a big old bassinet no less) when I was two weeks old.

Acknowledgments

All praises to God the Father, God the Son, and God the Holy Spirit for all that I am and all that I ever hope to be. For loving me so much that You would choose me, in every sense and connotation of the word. Thank You for strength and all that You've given me along this journey we call life (here on earth) as well as life in Heaven to come.

I give thanks and honor to my mother, Josephine Davis and my father James Davis Jr. (who transitioned from this life on April 30, 2018). Thank you both for giving me life, love, and for planting seeds of love and belief in the power of God and having God in my life. Thank you for being the ones who introduced me to Jesus, my Lord and Savior, Who loved me so much that He gave His life so that I could not just have life but life more abundantly.

To my husband Jeffery; my children Jeffery, Jeremy, and Johnathan; daughter-in-law, Sonceria; my grandchildren Alexandria, Asia, Ashlynn, Jada, and Jasher: there are no words to convey the love and joy I have in my heart for all of you. To my first ever family, which has grown tremendously from myself and my four siblings: Danette Dial Brown (brother-in-law Herbert), Terence Davis (sister-in-law Cameron), Arlinda Davis, and Emmanuel Davis (Cumberlan) along with all of my nieces and nephews, God has truly smiled on us. I have some of the best aunts (Ruth Washington, Rachel Shockley, Mary Mack, Clara Lee, the late Naomi Sessions), uncles (Joseph Lee, James Lee, and the late Abraham Lee), and cousins (I can't even name them all) in the world! In memory of my late grandmothers who absolutely impacted my life: Peggy Hamilton Lee Wiseman and Lucille Davis.

To Catrina Jackson, my friend and one I'd be more than proud to have had as a daughter; Bonita Chaney, my friend and prayer warrior; Vanessa L. Rice who has been hanging with me since reading my novel *Promises Beyond Jordan* and us meeting early on in Tuscaloosa, AL; Linda H. Jones to whom words can never convey the love I have for you. To my friends and other special people: Rosetta Moore, Shirley Walker, Zelda Oliver-Miles, Eden Carlton, Cheryl Sloan Wray, Brenda Taylor Jones, and Hannah Black; you are so loved and beloved.

I am forever grateful to all who have been in my corner (some of you from the very beginning), and equally grateful for the new people who are just discovering me and my books. To all who have ever extended an invitation for me to speak or visit events as a special guest (churches, schools, businesses, book clubs, conferences, etc.): Thank you for allowing me to use my other God-given gift as a speaker, presenter, or your special guest author. To my Facebook friends: I love so many of you (note I didn't say all - LOL) and love being able to pray with you and speak words of encouragement over and to you.

My sincere thanks to you who have chosen this book; and for another opportunity to share with you what God has given me. Please know how much God loves you. And that He didn't bring us this far to leave us. I am always in awe of what God is doing. And I say this with the utmost confidence: I don't know what the future holds, but I know WHO holds the future!

Again, I thank you for things done both large and small to help spread the word about what God has given my hands to do (including my novels). Thank you for choosing my books. I consider it an honor when you do, and I do not take it for granted. Please know that I love and appreciate you very much! Oh, and the BEST is *STILL* yet to COME!

Vanessa Davis Griggs

www.VanessaDavisGriggs.com

Table of Contents

Introduction

$\mathcal{M}$ay I have a "Word" with you? actually comes from the sentiments expressed in "Let me talk to you" or "May I speak with you?" It's a desire to chat with someone about something important. Another familiar expression might be, "Let me holla at you." But the polite people generally ask permission first, respectfully saying, "May I have a word with you?" before sharing what they desire to say.

For me, there's nothing more glorious to share or talk about than the Word of God. Hence: May I have a "Word" with you?

God's Word is rich and more powerful than a two-edged sword. The Word of God (the Bible) deals with *every* area of our lives: spiritually, physically, mentally, socially, emotionally, *and* financially. No matter what's going on; no matter what we may be going through: There's a *word* in God's *Word* for us. My prayer is that you'll be encouraged, enlightened, inspired, and blessed beyond measure as you realize you're not alone regardless of what it might feel like at the time. God has a purpose for your life. God is there through it all—the good, the bad, *and* the ugly.

When things are up; during our down times; when things don't make sense; when the numbers just don't add up no matter how many times we re-add them; when we're expecting multiplication only to discover instead that it's division (and long division at that) with several rounds of having to carryover; my heart and prayer is that we know: God always has a **Word** for us.

A lot of what you'll find here are writings I once shared in a column (by this same title) between the years of 2007 and 2011 in *The Birmingham Times* newspaper. They have been compiled here, and in many cases revised and updated as needed. In those instances where it may seem something is being repeated, read on because there's another message for you there.

Hi there! My name is Vanessa Davis Griggs. It's a pleasure to make your acquaintance.

May I have a "Word" with you?

An Open Book Test

All of us are familiar with school and having to take tests (whether we've done it or are doing it now). Sometimes, tests are scheduled; sometimes, there's a pop quiz (meaning one we weren't expecting). Second Timothy 2:15 says, "Study to show thyself approved unto God, a workman that needeth not to be ashamed, rightly dividing the word of truth."

First off, we need to study *before* the test. In life, there will be things that show up; and we discover: It's only a test. James 1:2-3 reassures us, "My brethren, count it all joy when ye fall into divers temptations; Knowing this, that the trying (testing) of your faith worketh (produces) patience." Understand that there will be trials and tests in life.

It matters not whether the test comes from the world, Satan, or from God, the fact remains: God has provided you with the answer to every question, problem, or equation you may encounter. The answers are in the Book—the Bible. But unlike some testing where we must memorize as much as possible and are only allowed to use what we can recall from what we've read or heard; we have the pleasure of being able to search the Book for our answers, if needed, *during* our test.

It's an open book test.

Yes, it's great when we already know the answers and can just whiz through our testing time. In fact, that's highly encouraged. But should we need to look in the Book during the test, it's not considered cheating when it's an open book test.

Some may say, "Wait a minute; God doesn't test us." We must understand that any good teacher will give a test to see where the student is and what needs to be worked on to ensure the student is prepared. Those of us who are living by faith would never know how strong our faith is if there weren't any tests along the way to show us how powerful and how much faith we have. James 3:14 says, "What doth it profit, my brethren, though a man say he hath faith, and have not works? can faith save him?" If we have faith and our faith is never tested, then how do we really know we have it?

Okay, back to our test. Let's say the question is: "What should you do when you've done all to stand and you just want to quit?" For the answer, turn to Ephesians 6:13(c)-14(a): ". . . and having done all, to stand. Stand." Question 2: "You're worried about things and you don't know which way to turn. What should you do?" One answer can be found in Philippians 4:6: "Be careful for nothing; but in every thing by prayer and supplication with thanksgiving let your requests be made known unto God."

What if you're having negative thoughts, and they're causing you to feel bad and/or defeated? Then turn to Philippians 4:8, "Finally, brethren, whatsoever things are true, whatsoever things are honest, whatsoever things are just, whatsoever things are lovely, whatsoever things are of good report; if there be any virtue, and if there be any praise, think on these things."

Do you have people in your life who are trying to take you down? Well, the answer for that is as close as Isaiah 54:17, "No weapon that is formed against thee shall prosper, and every tongue that shall rise against thee in judgment thou shalt condemn. This is the heritage of the servants of the Lord, and their righteousness is of me, saith the Lord." Feeling sick? Isaiah 53:5 (d) "...with his stripes we are healed."

What to do when you find you need help? For that answer, turn to Jeremiah 33:3, "Call unto me, and I will answer thee, and show thee great and mighty things, which thou knowest not." Feel like you're all alone and going against the world all by yourself? Feel like no one is on your side, and you're wondering what you should do? Look up Deuteronomy 31:6, "Be strong and of good courage, fear not, nor be afraid of them: for the Lord thy God, he it is that doth go with thee, he will not fail thee, nor forsake thee."

May I have a "Word" with you? Second Timothy 3:16 clearly states, "All scripture is given by inspiration of God, and is profitable for doctrine, for reproof, for correction, for instruction in righteousness: That the man of God may be perfect, thoroughly furnished unto all good works." When tests and trials come, don't worry. We already have the answers.

And if we don't know them from memory, well guess what? This is an open book test—the answers are in the Book—the Bible!

Class, let's take out our Book (Bible) and begin.

Echoes

*I*saiah 55:11 states, "So shall my word be that goeth forth out of my mouth: it shall not return unto me void, but it shall accomplish that which I please, and it shall prosper in the thing whereto I sent it." There is an importance in words and words spoken.

Most of us are familiar with echoes. An echo is when one says something (most time yelling it out or using some type of mechanical device) and whatever is said comes back . . . returns exactly as it was sent out.

The Bible tells us that God's Word shall not return unto Him void. Look at this! God speaks His Word and it returns (echoes) back to Him just as He said it. This is a wonderful Word for all of us. God speaks it, and it echoes back even to Him just as He said it. That means, when God says, "You're more than a conqueror" then it comes back, "You're more than a conqueror."

When dealing with echoes, it doesn't matter what we say, it will come back to us just as we said it. That means if we say, "I am so dumb," the echo will declare "I am so dumb." If we say, "I can't do this" the echo will say, "I can't do this." It will not argue with us about it. If we say, "With Christ, I can do all things if I believe" what will return back will be "With Christ, I can do all things if I believe."

Now, let's take this a step further. Let's not merely consider the words we speak as echoing back to us in sound. Let's consider that whatever we say echoes back to us manifested. Imagine yelling out, "I am blessed beyond belief!" and having those words echoed back, then physically manifested in our lives.

So from here on out, let's consider that whatever we're putting out there by the words of our mouth that it will return back to us a Spiritual Echoes. Question: Are our spoken words spoken building us up or are they tearing us down?

Two powerful things happen with echoes. One: when we speak the positive things from our mouth, it makes us feel good. But to hear the words echoing back gives an even greater feeling. The other thing is that speaking positive things to others and having them say the words out loud, causes them to feel empowered.

The trick is not merely speaking the words, but feeling them when they're repeated back to us. If we're the type who goes around saying, "I can't do anything right," how does that make us feel? Not too great. Then to add insult to injury, because we spoke it and put it out there, now it's required (there are certain laws that govern things regardless of what we think, like the law of gravity, for instance) to come back to us.

This alone should be enough for every one of us to be careful to speak only what we desire to come back to us. Echo these words now. "I *can* do this!" "I *am* smart!" "I *am* wealthy beyond imagination!" "I *am* blessed, and I *am* a blessing!"

God has given us tremendous gifts: the power to think, to believe, and to speak. God has given us the power to get wealth. And wealth is not always money, either. We can be wealthy in health, wealthy in knowledge, wealthy in family and friends, wealthy in joy and peace. And yes, wealthy in our finances.

Words are powerful. There was a time, not so long ago, when people hailed the power of positive thinking. Yes, the Bible does say, "As a man thinketh, so is he." First, there is the thought, so thoughts are very important. But the real power lies . . . is unleashed when we begin to speak it. We can think a thing. We can believe something all we want. But speaking what we believe and speaking what we think—out loud, that's when true power is released. Therefore promote the power of positive speaking.

May I have a "Word" with you? God's Word that goes forth out of His mouth will *not* return unto Him void, but it *shall* accomplish that which God pleases, and it *shall* prosper in the thing God sends it to accomplish. Spiritual Echoes!

"Hello! Is anybody out there?!" Commit to say what God says!

Nevertheless with God is More Than Enough

*a*nd Simon answering said unto him, Master, we have toiled all the night, and have taken nothing: nevertheless at thy word I will let down the net." Luke 5:5. How many of us are doing something today that we know God told us to do? How many of us look at what we've been told to do and wonder if we're crazy to either do it or to keep doing it when it doesn't look like it's working out the way we envisioned when we began it?

Look at the word nevertheless: never the less. But *never the* less with God is *more than enough.*

Yes, God told you to do something. You were excited because He showed you the end at the beginning. You saw where God was going with it. You put your hand to the plow, set out on the journey, stepped out on faith, and the next thing you know nothing seems to be working quite like you envisioned it. Those folks you thought would be excited about what God called you to do don't show up or support you when you're doing what you were instructed to do.

Then there are the obstacles that pop up on every corner, one thing after another. Obstacles, honestly, one would think God would have cleared from your path before you ever got there. But they are there, nevertheless, trying to stop you.

Nobody said that our road would be easy, but sometimes we can't help but to look up to Heaven and say, "Come on, God. Can I get a break down here right about now?" Somebody knows what I'm talking about. You've worked hard at this thing. You've been faithful, learned your craft. You've worked it, toiled day and night. You're tired; ready to put away the net. But God has use for what you have. *Nevertheless*!

As in this passage of scripture in Luke 5, Simon (we know him as Peter) was a fisherman. He knew his craft. He'd worked all night long. Jesus asked to use his boat as a platform to effectively teach the people. After Jesus finished speaking, he said to Simon, "Launch out into the deep, and let down your nets for a draught." Can't you just see Simon (Peter) who knew what he was doing? Peter, knowing that one had to fish at night in that particular fishing place to catch anything which he'd already done and had come up empty-handed. Now he was being told what to do by someone who wasn't a fisherman.

But this was Jesus telling him to do something. Peter told Jesus they'd toiled all night and had nothing to show for their effort. Then Peter said, "Nevertheless at thy word I will let down the net." Right where Peter was, he decided to be obedient to the Word. "And when they had this done, they enclosed a great multitude of fishes: and their net brake. And they beckoned unto their partners, which were in the other ship, and they should come and help them. And they came, and filled both the ships, so that they began to sink." Luke 5:5-7. When it comes to God nevertheless is always more than enough!

May I have a "Word" with you? God has told you something to do. It looks like you have less to work with, less help, less resources, and have had less results in the past. Continue to be obedient even though it may look like you're failing. Do what God is telling you because God is telling you to do it. Nevertheless with God is always more than enough. Simon was obedient to what Jesus told him and there ended up being so much that it filled two ships to where they began to sink.

When we're obedient to God, there won't be room enough for us to receive all that God has in store for us!

As Though They Were

There's a scripture (Romans 4:17) that tells us to, "Call those things that be not as though they were." Being a present tense person means saying "I am. . . " and filling in what you believe "I am" or "I have" already. Don't dwell so much on the past because we can't change what has already happened. We can replay it in our mind. We can learn from it, but there's nothing we can ever do to change it.

Herewith is this wonderful Word from God: Call those things that be not as though they were. "I am" is present tense, "I will" is future tense, and "I was" is past tense. The present means it's happening *now* which is not a bad thing at all. Learn to appreciate the *now* because truthfully, *now* is the only time we can truly experience.

The others (past and future) are either gone or not here yet. When anything is spoken about in future tense it means it hasn't happened and who knows if or when it ever will. The words *were* and *was* are past tense verbs. Using past tense indicates it's already done and whatever *it* is, *it* can't be changed. "As though they were." What a powerful Word from God!

In essence, God is saying whatever you ask me for *now* and believe that you have received it *now*, then right *now* start acting like it's done. "Call those things that be not as though they were!" Are you shouting yet? With God, it's already done! It's a "were," past tense . . . can't be changed from having been done.

19

"I believe I *have* received the desires of my heart!" See, it's already mine. You may not be able to see it, but call those things that be not (things people can't see with their natural vision) as though they were (already done as can be seen using spiritual vision).

See how God operates His Kingdom—on earth as it is in Heaven. "Let there be light" and there was light. God spoke it and it was so.

At the time we speak it, do we see it? Not yet. But guess what? It's already done in the spiritual realm. So call those things that be not as though they were. Be confident and bold enough to say, "I am what God says I am!" At the moment of saying it, believe that it's done . . . past tense. Because as far as God is concerned: It is.

So why use the present tense of the verb (I am) instead of the past tense (I was)? Because once you are, you are. Nobody can take it away after it's done.

May I have a "Word" with you? What do you desire? Then what are you saying? Are you calling forth what your natural eyes see? Or are you calling those things that be not as though they were?

Act like it's done; act as though it is! Right now. Call those things that be not as though they were.

According to Your Faith

What are you believing God for? What have you asked God to do in your life? Has it come to pass yet? If it hasn't and it's been a while, could the problem be with you?

I'm sure you don't want to hear this. But in Matthew 9 verses 27-28, Jesus is being followed by two blind men who were crying and saying, "Thou son of David, have mercy on us." And when Jesus came into the house, the blind men came to Him and Jesus asked them, "Believe ye that I am able to do this?" And the blind men said, "Yea, Lord." Matthew 9:20 says, "Then touched he their eyes, saying, According to your faith be it unto you." And verse 21 says, "And their eyes were opened."

According to Jesus' own words, what we believe Him for is being regulated by our faith. "According to your faith be it unto you." Faith is not always the spiritual thing we associate the word faith with. In other words, we can have faith for bad things. Case in point: a person who is broke. Someone who believes she's broke, and consequently, speaks and acts like it, then what is believed becomes a reality. "According to your faith be it unto you."

Faith is belief in action. Faith is acting like we believe something is true. If we believe we're sick and we act like it, more likely than not, what we believe is what will come to be.

21

What we need to do is to use our faith in a positive way. Act like the positive things we desire is true. Act like we believe what we're expecting is not only possible but *will* come to pass. That's what the woman with the issue of blood for twelve years did when she heard about Jesus. We find this account in Matthew 9:20–21. "And, behold, a woman, which was diseased with an issue of blood twelve years, came behind him, and touched the hem of his garment. For she said within herself, If I may but touch his garment, I shall be whole."

This woman said within herself what she desired to have in her life. She could have merely said she wanted the blood to stop. Instead, she said within herself, "I shall be whole." To be whole is to be saved, to be healed. She didn't limit what she desired to happen. But she could have also said what she wanted and never moved on it. Believing something is not faith. Acting on what you believe, that's faith.

After the woman said within herself what she wanted to take place if she did a certain thing, she pressed her way through the crowd surrounding Jesus and attempted to do just that. What she declared required her to touch his garment as she said. As soon as she touched Jesus' garment, from that hour she was made whole. When Jesus realized He'd encountered a faith touch, He said to her, "Daughter, be of good comfort; thy faith hath made thee whole." In other words: "According to your faith be it unto you."

May I have a "Word" with you? When Jesus was on the cross, He said, "It is finished." Everything that needs to be done has been done. Jesus gave those who have accepted Him, power. That power is connected to "According to your faith." If things aren't happening, then let us check our faith. Good or bad, "according to your faith, be it unto you."

Let's discontinue using our faith in believing the negative and acting like it's true and purposely use our faith for good!

Beauty for Ashes

hings don't always go the way we want them to. There are times we may even shed tears. But be of good cheer. God can turn whatever situation we're dealing with completely around. Isaiah 61:3 says, "To appoint unto them that mourn in Zion, to give unto them beauty for ashes, the oil of joy for mourning, the garment of praise for the spirit of heaviness, that they might be called trees of righteousness, the planting of the Lord, that he might be glorified."

Our dreams may appear to have gone up in smoke and we're left with only ashes. God will give us beauty for our ashes. Whatever has caused us to mourn, hold on; God will give the oil of joy for our mourning. Do you feel like you can't make it? Like there's a spirit of heaviness pressing on you. Start shouting and watch as God strips away the heaviness and replace it with His beautiful garment of praise.

Why praise God when things aren't going right? Why praise God when people seem to disappoint us and let us down? Why praise God when we can't see how we're going to come up with the money for that bill or that thing we so desperately need? So that we can be called trees of righteousness, the planting of the Lord, that God might be glorified.

This is powerful.

Trees' roots grow deep. A tree will stand through all kinds of weather. But there are times when a storm comes through and uproots a tree. But when God plants us, we're able to proclaim, "I shall not be moved."

Many hurricanes hit in places where palm trees are the trees of the area. When the wind is blowing hard and the rain is beating down, a palm tree stands—its fan leaves appearing to lift up hands in praise to God even in a storm. Interestingly, a palm tree is rarely ever uprooted from a storm.

May I have a "Word" with you? Let us be like the palm tree and praise God regardless of what's going on in our lives. Praise releases the blessings of the Lord. Praise can bring down walls. Praise can lift heavy spirits. Praise will take us to another level in the Lord. Praise takes the focus off the problem and places it on the solution. Let us show anyone who may be looking for us to fall that we're like the palm tree: We shall not be moved, and we're going to praise God anyhow.

From Coal to Diamond

I remember one of my grandmothers heating her home with coal when I was a young girl. For anyone unfamiliar with coal, it's a black combustible rock (actually fossil) found in and on the ground. Miners generally mine coal. Someone would haul coal to my grandmother's house where she kept it in a storage place underneath her house. There was a thing called a coal or scuttle bucket that sat in the living room to hold the coal that was to be fed to a fat-belly, coal burning stove.

Coal has a tendency to make your hands black and dirty when you pick it up. But as I said, it was used a lot to heat homes before the convenience of central heating became the norm of what we've grown to know today. Sometimes when people couldn't afford to buy coal, someone would go where coal was being mined and pick up pieces in order to heat their homes. Like rocks, coal could be found lying there, waiting to be picked up.

There are times in our lives when we may feel like coal. People view us as positive in what we can do for them. But they don't view us as precious as God does. There are times when we find ourselves under extreme heat and pressure. But the substance coal is made into, under extreme heat and pressure, becomes diamonds. So when we find ourselves going through things in life, feeling the heat; when we feel things pressing us from every side, let us not become discouraged. We can rest in the confidence that our all-knowing God is allowing us to be changed from common coal into a soon to be cut, multifaceted, newly formed, high-clarity diamond. And even though coal is a wonderful thing, diamonds are rarer and quite valuable.

Let us not despise the pressure and heat of life. No, it doesn't feel great when we're going through. But when we know that God is in control regardless of what's going on; when we know that "come what may," God not only *can* but that He *will* take it and use it for our good, we can go through whatever life holds with the joy of the Lord.

May I have a "Word" with you? When experiencing the pressures of life, let us praise God, knowing that when we come out of this, we're going to sparkle like no diamond ever seen or possessed. When things heat up, let us not hold our heads down. In fact, let us lift up our head; lifting our eyes unto the hills from which comes our help.

Let us praise God as we're going through, knowing that when God brings us through (and He will); we're going to shine like nobody's business. Know that after it's all said and done and the light hits us, we're going to not only shine but beam the brilliance God has given us to the world.

Let us praise God as we're being transformed from coal to diamond, letting our light not just shine, but *so* shine!

The Full Picture

"Beloved, now are we the sons of God, and it doth not yet appear what we shall be: but we know that, when he shall appear we shall be like him; for we shall see him as he is." (1 John 3:2). Man often will try to put God in a box, but when we have a personal relationship with Him, He walks and talks with us, revealing so much more.

Before digital cameras, there were Polaroid and Kodak cameras that allowed us to take pictures and not have to send them off to be developed. In fact, people began watering down the trademarked name of Polaroid by calling any instant photos that developed before our eyes "polaroids." Prior to this groundbreaking technique, one had to give the roll of film to a person who would go into a dark room to develop them, and only then would the pictures be ready for all to see.

Someone is believing God for something right now. You've taken the picture of what it looks like by faith. The problem comes when we look at it or try to show it and a blank white space is all anyone can see. Hold on regardless of what is unseen right now when looking at the blank picture you hold. Just like with the Polaroid pictures of old, it's already done; it's just taking a little time for the photo to fully develop, to show itself.

When a picture is taken, the image is already there. So it is with your faith-picture of whatever God promised. It's already there (done); it just may be taking what is necessary for it to develop. Some of our

27

pictures may have been taken on film and had to go into a dark room to be developed. Some of us may be holding it as we're looking for it to develop right before our eyes without any other process (other than time) to cause it to appear.

Too many Christians today are looking for the "digital photo faith": we want to see it as soon as we snap it. This is not to say God won't do it that way because there are some things that *will* manifest that quickly. But there are times when we find ourselves holding what looks like, to others, only a blank picture, as we believe and wait for it to fully manifest.

Whether we have to wait due to the dark room experience necessary for development, or wait for the picture to slowly show itself (little by little) because of time, know that it's already done. In the spirit world, the picture is clear, even if in the natural world, it still appears to be developing.

God has a picture of each of us. And just like the instant Polaroid pictures of old, He's holding that picture. This picture shows us as fearfully and wonderfully made, the head and not the tail, more than a conqueror, blessed coming in and blessed going out. This picture shows us as righteous through Jesus Christ and God supplying our every need according to His riches in glory.

May I have a "Word" with you? The Bible tells us, "it doth not yet appear what we shall be: but we know that, when he shall appear we shall be like him." When showing people the picture God has taken of us, let us reassure those who may not see the whole picture yet, "Don't worry, it's still developing."

God is causing the picture of us and the promises He's made to us to become clearer and clearer each and every second. And one day, all will be able to see the full picture in its high definition glory. One day, we'll look just like Jesus!

Okay, smile and say, "Jesus!"

Shouting the Walls Down

Man that is born of a woman is of a few days and full of trouble. That's scripture. The fact is: all of us know something about trials and troubles. Whether we've come through it or are going through it now, we know. Some people put up walls to keep things in; some people build walls to keep things out. Regardless, a wall is a wall. I like the idea of a wall of protection, but there are times when it's necessary to bring some walls down.

Joshua was chosen to carry on after Moses died. Joshua 6:2 says, "And the Lord said unto Joshua, See, I have given into thine hand Jericho, and the king thereof, and the mighty men of valor." What I like about this is that God is telling Joshua He's *already* given something to the children of Israel even before they've actually taken possession of it.

So, what has God told you He's given you? The only thing is: There's usually something we must do for the process to be complete— many times specific instructions.

In the case with Joshua and the children of Israel, they were given their specific instructions. They were instructed to walk around the city once for six days. Sometimes, we must learn to be patient. Most of us want what we want, and we want it now, if not yesterday. Imagine what those people must have thought. "Why do we have to do this for six days? Why can't God just do what He's going to do right now without all of this? He can do it, you know." Isn't that just like us? God is moving on our behalf and that's great, but some of us still question why we have to do (fill in the blank).

In the case with Joshua, there came a number seven. It's interesting that in Joshua 6:4, the Bible says, "And seven priests shall bear before the ark seven trumpets of rams' horns: and the seventh day ye shall compass the city seven times, and the priests shall blow with the trumpets."

We've been marching around the wall. It's been a long journey and it didn't make sense to a lot of people who were looking at us while wondering what our problem was. They didn't see us saying much as we marched. They didn't have a clue what we were doing by keeping our silence. Not doing a lot of complaining, not murmuring. Just marching on: one time, two times, three times, four times, five times, six times. Oh, but on the number seven. On the seventh time, we find we can't hold our peace. On the seventh time, we're told to not just shout, but shout with a *great* shout.

Shout before that promotion. Shout before things get right at home. Shout before people treat you right at church, on your job, in your home. Shout before that child or loved one truly gives their heart to the Lord. Shout before the bills are paid. Oh, you know the bills I'm talking about. The ones where we couldn't see a way, but we knew down deep in our soul, somehow God was going to make a way. Shout knowing that by Jesus' stripes we're healed! Shout before the walls come down, whatever that wall is.

May I have a "Word" with you? It's time to shout! Shout with a great shout. Shout with praises to God Who has already caused us to triumph. Shout because it's already done. Yes, we've walked. Yes, we've held our peace. It's time to shout now! Then watch as those walls fall flat. Walk up in there and possess what God has already given.

Yes, it's yours! Don't be shy. Come on now, shout those walls down!

They That Be With Us

*a*nd when the servant of the man of God was risen early, and gone forth, behold a host compassed the city both with horses and chariots. And his servant said unto him, Alas, my master! how shall we do? And he answered, Fear not: for they that be with us are more than they that be with them." (2 Kings 6:15-16)

Let me give some background on this. Elisha, who followed Elijah and saw him as he was taken up by God without seeing death and asked for a double portion of his spirit, is now being pursued by the Syrians.

The king of Syria was warring against Israel and somehow his secret plans were getting back to the Israelites. The king thinks someone in his camp is a spy but is told that Elisha the prophet is telling the king of Israel the words the king of Syria is speaking in his bedchamber. (God will let you know what your enemies are up to.) So the king finds out where Elisha is, sends a great host (army) with horses and chariots during the night, and they circle the city where Elisha is.

Elisha's servant rises early and, when he looks out and around, he sees they are surrounded by this mighty army. The servant knows they are in trouble. He runs to the prophet of God, his master, and says, "How shall we do?" In other words, we're in big trouble here, what are we going to do. Elisha looks and sees and his answer to the servant is, "Fear not." But then he goes a step further to let his servant know why they didn't need to fear. "For they that be with us are more than they that be with them."

Today I say to you who are looking at things compassing you and the world in which you live: fear not. People digging ditches hoping you'll fall, preferably on your face. People talking about you, some who may not even know you. Gas prices like we've never seen before. Food prices rising as they up the price or give you less for the same price you were paying just months ago (or both). Depression or merely feeling a little down because nothing you do seems to be working these days.

You're trying to do the right thing, but you feel like every time you take one step forward something causes you to take two steps back. Even if you're not taking two steps back, you feel for every step forward you take you end up taking one step back, making you feel like you're not getting anywhere.

May I have a "Word" with you? They that be with us are more than they that be with them. We have God the Father, God the Son, and God the Holy Ghost with us. We refer to them as the Trinity, but the fact remains: God is with us.

No matter how many people or things that surround us to try and do us harm, they that be with us are more than they that be with them. In the case with Elisha, in the seventeenth verse it says, "And Elisha prayed, and said, Lord, I pray thee, open his eyes, that he may see. And the Lord opened the eyes of the young man; and he saw: and behold, the mountain was full of horses and chariots of fire round about Elisha."

God will send angels to surround our enemies when they're trying to surround and overtake us. Now *that's* some kind of fighting power on our side. So I pray that the Lord will open our eyes. Let us see that no matter what's going on, when we feel we're in trouble, when we feel like we're not going to make it, when we think the enemy is about to overtake us, may we proclaim, "They that be with us are more than they that be with them!"

Completion

O ver my lifetime, I've seen God move and do things only He could have orchestrated. Many times, God has encouraged me to go on by placing the word *completion* in my spirit.

How many of us have started something and quit, or started something and *wanted* to quit? I've had that test presented to me many times. Do I stay the course or quit? I can recall working on a project once and I'd finished it, but what I understood the person to want turned out not to be what she wanted. She and I talked, and there was an out for me to walk away. To stay meant I'd have to start all over.

Sure, I could rightfully have blamed the other person for not explaining exactly what she desired; but instead, I desired more that the final outcome be right. So I sat and I listened (again), digesting the words exchanged. I didn't walk away. And I heard God say there was a reason this was as it was . . . that there was something we both needed to learn through this, and that He wanted me to finish it. Completion.

So I started over and worked hard to deliver what I believed was pleasing to both God and this person. As I worked on the project, there were so many obstacles that came up in my life, many of them attacking and affecting me personally. But I continued to hear the Lord say, "Completion." He was telling me to complete it no matter what Satan was doing to distract me. And yes, I recognized early on it was

33

spiritual warfare. And it wasn't just happening with me—many saints of God were fighting this same battle.

I remember talking with a woman during this time also battling spiritual warfare. I told her, "To walk on water, we have to keep our eyes on Jesus." It didn't matter *what* the wind and the waves were doing. I realized those things were mere distractions attempting to garner my attention. But I had my eyes fixed on Jesus and He'd said, "Come." And because He'd said it, I was going to do just that.

How many of us have taken our eyes off Jesus when we were actually *doing* what (at the time) seemed impossible, only to be distracted by boisterous winds and waves that were there to cause us to sink? We need to see the game plan for what it is and not allow it to take us out.

Let's not be sucked into becoming a participant of our own demise. Worries, financial distractions, depression, family troubles, and personal attacks are devices the enemy launches to try and defeat us. Satan wants nothing more than to get us talking wrong. He knows (as we should) that life and death is in the power of the tongue.

I told this woman, "I'm like Nehemiah on the wall. I'm doing a good work, and I can't come down!" You see, that's all negative distractions in life are. They're trying to get us to come down off the wall to see what's going on in order to stop us from finishing the work at hand. When God ministered to me with the Word "completion," He was telling me, "Stay the course; Jesus has *already* finished it! You just need to keep going."

On the same day I handed off the completed work I'd begun, God assigned me a greater, even more glorious work to do. Isn't it exciting to see what God is planning next? Anyone can start a thing, but how many of us can complete it? God desires people who will stay the course. The race is not given to the swift nor to the strong, but to the one who endures to the end.

We're all in some kind of a race at any given time. Sometimes it's a sprint; sometimes, it's a marathon. Sometimes, it's a relay where we're merely handing off the baton to someone else for the next leg of the run. But whatever we're doing, we should always do it as heartily as unto the Lord.

Yes, God may have called us to do a work. But can He trust us to complete it? As important as starting a thing might be, it's better to cross the finish line. Completion. Starting—Staying—Praying—Completing. And trust me: We don't have to wait until we get to Heaven to hear the Lord say: "Well done my good and faithful servant." He encourages us while we're down here.

May I have a "Word" with you? "I am confident of this very thing, that He which has begun a good work in you will perform it until the day of Jesus Christ." (Philippians 1:6) Have you been working on or dealing with something that you've thought about giving up on? Well, it's time for completion!

On your mark, get set, go!

Know Your Character

*D*uring a conversation in the book of Job, God asked Satan, "From whence cometh thou?" Satan's answer: "From going to and fro in the earth, and from walking up and down in it." God then said, "Hast thou considered my servant Job?"

When God told Jonah to go to Nineveh and cry against it for their wickedness had come up before Him, Jonah didn't want to, so he fled to Tarshish. After three days in the belly of a great fish, Jonah was told again to go to Nineveh; that time he complied.

When God gave His only begotten Son to die on the cross for our sins—Jesus, born of a woman (Son of God and Son of man), God knew that no matter how difficult the task to come, how bitter the cup, Jesus would finish it.

When Mary Magdalene (and no, she was not a prostitute as has been widely and erroneously circulated throughout the Christian community) went that Sunday morning to the tomb where she'd "had a little talk with Jesus" after He arose, God was not surprised.

God knows all about us. God knows the character of His people.

I am an author of many novels. An author should have some idea—from the beginning—of their characters' character and their *likely* reaction in a given setting or situation of which they've been placed. I said *likely* reaction. There is still, of course, free will.

Many authors, in some way, record pertinent information about their characters: age, height, weight, race, education, jobs held, family, friends, Christian or not, idiosyncrasies, temperament, beliefs, disappointments, victories, etc. One reason is for future reference. What color are the character's eyes? Hair? Any identifying marks? The list goes on; all the things which *can* and *do* affect a character and how they might respond in certain plots and subplots.

Writing down this information will also help a writer keep track later on. You wouldn't want to give your character green eyes in the beginning of a story only with them to end up in the middle of the story sporting brown ones (sans contact lenses).

There are certain things the "creator . . . the author," knows about their created characters. Things the author may like or not like about them. But the author knows them well enough to know what they'll most likely do in certain situations.

Well, God knows what we'll likely do—"Have you tried my servant Job?" And as much as an author might like to make their characters do what they want, the way they want, or as timely as they'd prefer; the author . . . the creator allows them to be themselves and work it out.

Know your character.

May I have a "Word" with you? Those characters who commune with me consistently, I happen to know more intimately. Are you talking with your Creator? Do you spend time with the Lord?

I love when my characters do what they've been assigned to do. Are you doing what God has assigned you to do? Because don't we, as God's creations, each have our own individual assignment? Then let's get to it! A great storyline is waiting to be written—the story of your life.

A Father's Love

"For God so loved the world, that he gave his only begotten Son, that whosoever believeth in him should not perish, but have everlasting life." John 3:16. Most people know this scripture and can even quote it by heart. But what do we *really* see in this scripture?

I see God loving the world (that's you and me and all the rest of the folks that are here, have come through here, and *will* come through here) so much so that He gave His only begotten Son.

Wait a minute. If you're the Son, think about what that says. God had so much loved for us, that He gave His *only* begotten Son. God gave His Son for us? Yes, God loves us *that* much that He gave His best to keep us from perishing and to give us the opportunity for everlasting life. Not eternal life in the lake of fire, but everlasting life in a place called Heaven. Now that's *some* kind of love.

I like to look at it this way. Because of God's love for us, He was willing to *give*, in order to receive. God gave His Son to receive more sons and daughters. And how exactly does this transaction occur since all of us were born to another? It's by the Spirit of Adoption.

We are essentially *Born Again*. We've been chosen to be part of the family. When I say chosen, we still have to confess our sins, confess our desire to be part of this family the way the Word of God states must be done. But unlike family members that are born into the family where we have no say-so about them being in the family, we were wanted so much so that we were *sought* out. God wants us in His family. Jesus wants us to become heirs and joint-heirs with Him in the inheritance the Father God has for us.

The Son wanted us so much to be a part of the family that He volunteered to do whatever was needed to ensure it could be possible. You see, before Jesus gave His life to pay the debt for our committed sins, we didn't have a way to become part of the family. But Jesus said, "I'll go." Jesus gave His life for us because that was what was necessary. Now, that's a special kind of love there! Our Father was willing to give His Son, and not just His Son, but His *only* begotten Son. The only Son God had. We were worth it enough for God and His Son to sacrifice Jesus' life for us. Someone besides me ought to be shouting right here. No greater love!

And if that's how the story had ended, it might be a nice story, but a sad one. You know: Giving one for another almost like you didn't love the Son you sacrificed as much as the children you were sacrificing for. But you see, Jesus said that no man takes His life; that He was laying it down willingly. Jesus let it be known that He could lay it down, and He could pick it back up. And that's exactly what happened.

The Father who loves us also loved Jesus enough that on that third day, early Sunday morning while most folks were still sleeping, God was doing a work. God raised Jesus from the dead! And when Jesus arose, He rose with *all* power in His hands.

But that's how a true father is. A true father will be there through the good and the bad; through thick and thin.

May I have a "Word" with you? Our Heavenly Father loves us! He's listening and knows *each* of our voices when we call. Deadbeat fathers get a lot of attention, a lot of ink in books and such. But to the strong, unsung earthly fathers doing the right thing, continue to follow our Father in Heaven. And know that God loves you with an everlasting love.

Our Father in Heaven loves all of His children!

The Great Faith of a Mother

*I*n Matthew 15:21-28, you'll find these words. "Then Jesus went thence, and departed into the coasts of Tyre and Sidon. And, behold, a woman of Canaan came out of the same coasts, and cried unto him, saying, Have mercy on me, O Lord, thou son of David; my daughter is grievously vexed with a devil. But he answered her not a word. And his disciples came and besought him, saying, Send her away; for she crieth after us. But he answered and said, I am not sent but unto the lost sheep of the house of Israel. Then came she and worshiped him, saying, Lord, help me. But he answered and said, It is not meet to take the children's bread, and to cast it to dogs. And she said, Truth, Lord; yet the dogs eat of the crumbs which fall from their master's table. Then Jesus answered and said unto her, O woman, great is thy faith: be it unto thee even as thou wilt. And her daughter was made whole from that very hour."

The first time we see great faith recorded in the Bible by a mother when it came to Jesus, is in John the second chapter. It was when Mary, the mother of Jesus, came to Jesus regarding the lack of wine at the wedding situation. Mary, who had such great faith in what Jesus could do, told the servants, "Whatsoever He asks of you, do it."

Here we see Jesus outside the country, in the way of the Gentiles. This is contrary to what Jesus told His disciples in Matthew 10:5-6. Jesus had just left from calling out the Pharisees as being hypocrites. Now here comes a woman of Canaan, a Canaanite woman. Mark 7:26

called her a Syrophenician woman. In other words, the woman was a Gentile. But even being a Gentile—a person not of Jewish descent—someone who was not brought up to know about the Lord, this woman came to Jesus and said, "Have mercy on me, O Lord, thou son of David."

In saying "have mercy," this woman was essentially saying, "I know what I deserve, but please, Lord, hold back from me from what I deserve and give me what I don't deserve—grace." She then recognized Jesus as Lord, and went even further than that by essentially calling Him the promised Messiah when she said, "thou son of David." We need to come to Jesus and let Him know Who He is in our lives.

The next thing the woman did was tell Jesus her problem. "My daughter is grievously vexed with a devil." Now, you would think after all of this, Jesus would have immediately responded. But He didn't answer her. Sometimes when we go to the Lord, it looks and feels like He didn't hear us or that He's not paying attention because nothing seems to change in our lives. But God hears us. Sometimes, He's just looking for faith.

The disciples told Jesus to send the woman away. You know, there's always somebody trying to keep you from getting your blessing. After Jesus said something to the disciples, still not saying anything to the woman, the woman came and worshipped Him.

Let me tell you this: Praise and worship puts you in the presence of the Lord. God inhabits the praises of His people. The woman said, "Lord help me." Jesus then said something to her that sounds cruel. He said, "It is not meet" in other words, it's not good "to take the children's bread and cast to dogs." Wait a minute. Did Jesus just call her and her child a dog?

May I have a "Word" with you? There is so much in this message. More than I'm allotted to write here. But let me wrap it up with this. The woman said to Jesus, "Truth, Lord; yet the dogs eat of the crumbs which fall from their master's table." Bread of Heaven, Master, even if I am a dog, I must be a house dog, because I'm in the house near the table. As the children eat, crumbs will inevitable fall from the table. And as the dog in the house, I get to lick up the crumbs that fall from the Master's table. Crumbs from the Master's table are enough for me to get what I need.

Jesus then answered her and said. "O woman" (woman being a term of great respect) "O woman, great is thy faith: be it unto thee even as thou wilt."

My question to you: Do you have the kind of great faith God is looking for?

Read the Manual

*I*t never ceases to amaze me how people can get something new like a car, a phone, or some other neat gadget, and instead of taking time to read the manual, they'll just play around with things trying to figure out how it works. And I'm not going to *even* get into those who attempt to assemble a thing without bothering to read the instructions.

It's great we feel we can figure things out based on trial and error. But wouldn't it be better instead to just take the time to read the manual? Consider all the things we won't know that's available to us because we neglected to read the manual.

That's how many are who have come into the knowledge of God. . . those who have accepted Christ into their lives as their Lord and Savior. There are benefits at our disposal that we may know nothing about because we haven't taken the time to read the manual. Christians . . . Kingdom citizens, our manual is the Holy Bible. Hosea 4:6 tells us, "My people are destroyed for a lack of knowledge."

I remember when I bought a new car. Sure I knew what and where things were (like the steering wheel, gas pedal, brakes). Sure, I could look around and find the light switch and windshield wipers. There were things in my car that made sense without me having to read the manual. But I still took the time to read the manual from cover to cover, and in the process I learned things like how to make my steering wheel fit me personally. Yes, I have windshield wipers, but I learned if I turned the setting a certain way, my wipers would automatically adjust to the conditions occurring outside when it rained. When this feature is activated, my wipers turn on automatically and work, intermittingly, when it sprinkles; speeds up when the rain comes harder; and turns off completely once the rain stops.

Same thing with my heating and air-conditioner: I set it to AUTO and it will sense and take care of the rest, just as I desire. In fact, this reminds me of how the Holy Spirit is, when we allow Him to be. The Holy Spirit knows conditions and guides us appropriately as needed.

There's so much God has for us that we don't know about because we haven't read the manual.

Many people don't know who they are in Christ (like being the head and not the tail; above only and not beneath; blessed coming in and blessed going out) just because they won't take the time to read the manual. We don't know what can be automatically set to cover situations, because we haven't read the manual. We don't have a clue what all we really can do, because we haven't read the manual. We don't know where things are and how to operate them, because we haven't read the manual.

May I have a "Word" with you? The Bible is our manual. Second Timothy 2:15 says, "Study to show thyself approved unto God, a workman that needeth not to be ashamed, rightly dividing the word of truth." If we want to know how to be victorious in this life, we must read the manual. If we want to know how to have a wonderful marriage, we need to read the manual. If we want to know how to have a friend and be a friend, we need to read the manual. Whatever you need or desire, read the manual.

Do you desire peace that surpasses all understanding, true agape love, and unspeakable joy? Then read the manual. Is money (or the lack thereof) a problem, then read the manual. Are you looking to own your own home? Yes, there are instructions in the manual. Everything we need to know is in the Bible. Why not take some time and see what we can do, have, and be by seeing what the manual says we can do, have, and be?

Did you know you can go from zero to one-hundred in less than fifteen seconds? When you read the manual, you see that accepting Jesus into your life as your Savior, you went from zero to one-hundred in the amount of time it took you to confess with your mouth Jesus the Christ.

In other words, being saved, we went from being a sinner to the righteous of God (0 to 100) just that quickly. And that's only the beginning of what God has in store for us. So let's stop fumbling through life and commit to read the manual . . . the Bible.

Okay, it's time to turn on our lights. The Word of God really is a lamp unto our feet and a light unto our path!

Wearing White After Labor Day

You may have heard that you're not supposed to wear white after Labor Day. There are some who don't care to wear white anytime of the year for various reasons. One reason is that they hate trying to keep white clean. For those who want to wear white after Labor Day, there's what's called winter white. Regardless, many still won't wear white after Labor Day because they don't want to be talked about or judged as "fashionably challenged."

But let's look at this from a spiritual perspective. First Corinthians 3:8-9 says, "Now he that planteth and he that watereth are one: and every man shall receive his own reward according to his own labor. For we are laborers together with God." Hebrews 4:9-11 says, "There remaineth therefore a rest to the people of God. For he that is entered into his rest, he also hath ceased from his own works, as God did from his. Let us labor therefore to enter into that rest, lest any man fall after the same example of unbelief."

Personally, I'm encouraged by First Corinthians 15:57-58 which says, "But thanks be to God, which giveth us the victory through our Lord Jesus Christ. Therefore, my beloved brethren, be ye steadfast, unmovable, always abounding in the work of the Lord, forasmuch as ye know that your labor is not in vain in the Lord." Thanks be to God!

Okay, can we be honest? Those who truly labor sometimes, at some point, may get tired—physically, emotionally, and spiritually. Matthew 11:28 Jesus tells us, "Come unto me, all ye that labor and are heavy laden, and I will give you rest." Jesus promises us rest. And this rest is not just when we get to Heaven either; we can know rest in the Lord here on earth.

Revelation 3:4-5 says, "Thou has a few names even in Sardis which have not defiled their garments; and they shall walk with me in white: for they are worthy. He that overcometh, the same shall be clothed in white raiment; and I will not blot out his name out of the book of life, but I will confess his name before my Father, and before his angels."

So, you may ask: what does wearing white after Labor Day have to do with us?

If we labor now, then after "labor" day, we'll be walking with Jesus wearing white. Yes, we'll be wearing white after *Labor* Day! I don't know about you, but I'm excited about wearing white after Labor Day.

Revelation 7:12-14 gives us a glimpse into what will take place after our laboring days here on earth are over. "Saying, Amen: Blessing, and glory, and wisdom, and thanksgiving, and honor, and power, and might, be unto our God for ever and ever. Amen. And one of the elders answered, saying unto me, What are these which are arrayed in white robes? and whence came they? And I said unto him, Sir thou knowest. And he said to me, These are they which came out of great tribulation, and have washed their robes, and made them white in the blood of the Lamb."

Hallelujah, these are they! These are they made righteous by the blood of the Lamb. These are they, the saved through Jesus Christ. We'll be wearing white after Labor Day because of what Jesus did.

May I have a "Word" with you? Be steadfast and unmoveable, always abounding, in the work of the Lord knowing that your *labor* is not in vain. During the times when you wonder why you go through what you go through, just know: Your labor in the Lord is not in vain.

And one day, I look to see you in Heaven wearing white after Labor Day in glorious fashion!

For your *work* in the Lord is not in vain.

Carrying the Word

*N*ow the birth of Jesus Christ was on this wise: When as his mother Mary was espoused to Joseph, before they came together, she was found with child of the Holy Ghost. Then Joseph her husband, being a just man, and not willing to make her a public example, was minded to put her away privily. But while he thought on these things, behold, the angel of the Lord appeared unto him in a dream, saying, Joseph, thou son of David, fear not to take unto thee Mary thy wife: for that which is conceived in her is of the Holy Ghost." Matthew 1:19-20

Okay, let's set the scene. Mary was engaged to marry Joseph. Before they came together, she learned she was expecting a baby. Mary was already bound or another word would be betrothed to Joseph. They weren't actually married yet. Jewish custom was that vows were to be said at a ceremony. The Jewish custom of that day required a one-year interval of betrothal before the bride could actually take residence in her husband's house and consummate their union.

During that one-year interval, Mary was found with child. Normally, a circumstance like this would indicate adultery, punishable in the Jewish law by death.

But Joseph was a just man. He didn't want to publicly call attention to Mary's expectancy. He was going to privately dissolve their union. But then the angel of the Lord shows up in a dream and tells him to fear not to take Mary as his wife, for she was carrying the Word

(Vanessa Davis Griggs's translation). Mary was carrying Jesus, the *Word* being made flesh!

Many people are excited during the time of the year when we approach Christmas, the celebration of Jesus' birth. You may have heard that December 25 was not the actual date or even time period when Jesus was born, but you know what? The exact "when" doesn't matter to me. What *does* matter is that Jesus *was* born.

And as we celebrate, it's important that we realize the meaning of His birth. It meant it was the beginning of our bridge back to a relationship with God. There had to be a birth in order for there to be a death. And there had to be a death in order for Jesus to be raised from the dead.

God is wonderful about choosing the most unlikely to do great things in His name. Here is Mary (a young girl said to have been around the age of fourteen), someone who had a heart for God (reminds me of David, the shepherd boy).

This is one reason we need to stop looking at people as we attempt to judge their importance. *Who* or *what* we think is important is not the same as whom or what *God* thinks is important. God will take someone we least expect and bless them to do great things for the Kingdom.

We need to stop trying to tear folks down because they don't live up to *our* expectations and see people as God sees them. In fact, many of us need to see *ourselves* as God sees us.

May I have a "Word" with you? What are you carrying that has been conceived of the Holy Ghost? Are people looking at you funny? Are people laughing at you? Are they talking about you behind your back? Well, don't fret! Mary was carrying the Word. I pray we can say the same.

Let's check ourselves right now and ask: Am I carrying the Word?

Writing the Vision

The Bible tells us where there is no vision, the people perish.

One year God placed on my heart to create a Heart's Desire card. He instructed me to write down twelve desires I had for the year. I was about to write them on an index card when he further informed me this was not just for me, but to share it.

So I created a Heart's Desire card and used the scripture reference from Psalm 37:4: "*Delight yourself also in the Lord and He will give you the desires of your heart.*" I shared it. Aware that in life we may have goals, dreams, and aspirations. What gives these things a boost in power is writing them down and, as Habakkuk 2:2 states, to make it plain. There's just something about writing our vision out and making it plain that leaves no room for misinterpretation.

We serve such a big God—there's nothing too hard for Him. Our problem is not that God can't handle the big things, but that in many cases, we don't dream big enough. God is looking for willing vessels so that He can show Himself strong. Therefore, when I come with my dreams and visions, I come specific. I don't just say, "I desire a car." I let God know the make, model, color, and any additional options I may desire.

Think about it. Do we really believe God is impressed with our playing-little, trying-to-be-humble-acting requests? Sure, it sounds so spiritual when we say, "God, just give me a car. Anything you want me to have is fine with me. Just as long as it gets me from point A to point B, I'll be happy and content."

Now, I'm not saying there's anything wrong with this prayer. What I *am* saying is: God is asking you, "What do *you* desire?" He likes it when we're crystal-clear. Does He really care whether we ask Him for a VW Beetle as opposed to a Mercedes? Not really. Either of these is doable for God.

When we tell Him specifically what we desire, do we really think God is scratching His head and saying, "Now how am I going to pull *that* one off?" No. Not *my* God.

So I write my true desires down because God has already told me He will give me the desires of *my* heart. Not your heart. Not what anyone else thinks I should have. Not even what others think is acceptable for me. It's what *I* desire: The desires of *my* heart.

Okay, so what do you desire?

When we write things down, it makes it more difficult for us to go back and try to wiggle our way out of what we said. That's why writing it down is important. It puts it out there for all to see (so to speak). Our vision, at that point, becomes manifested in the form of words. It is *now* before us, so as we run our race, we see it.

I wrote my desires. I prayed about it before I wrote anything down. You see, I believe God gives us a desire for something, before He gives us the desire. No, that's not doubletalk. God *puts* the desire in us to desire a thing. Then He *gives* us that desire (causes the desire to become physically visible).

When I write down my desires, I place them where I can be reminded of them. And when a desire is manifested, I write the word VICTORY in big, red letters over it.

Write the vision, make it plain. It's like writing a story. We may see things clearly in our mind. We may find ourselves watching our characters perform certain acts in our imagination. But it only becomes real, more than just to us anyway, when we outwardly record it in some way so that others can also experience what we see in our mind.

May I Have A Word With You?

May I have a "Word" with you? Write the vision, and make it plain. And when my God—who can do anything but lie and fail; my God whom I know there's nothing too hard for Him—when God brings these things to pass and people ask how. We can point to our Father in Heaven, who loves us so much that He cares about *every* area of our lives (physically, spiritually, mentally, emotionally, financially, and socially), and tell them, "God did it!" Nobody *but* God! God gets all the praise and the glory. Ultimately, that's what it's all about anyway.

Now it's time. Stop right now, write your vision, make it plain, delight yourself also in the Lord, and watch Him give *you* the desires of *your* heart!

You Are Not Alone

I have a Facebook account where I write messages on my status. Mostly, I use it to encourage people as they live life. I wrote something I'd like to expand upon here. "Most people don't have a clue what you've gone through or what you're going through right now. *But* God and but for the grace of God, you might have lost your mind. BUT GOD—who wants you to know and to be assured that you are not alone. God is there!

He's there holding you up when you may have wondered how you were going to make it. God is there now. Rest in the Lord. God is able to keep you, and He will!"

Often people try to judge what they see on the outside, but they don't know how you've cried during the midnight hour for that wayward child or for the troubles you may be going through with that spouse. They weren't there when you opened that envelope containing news you didn't know how you were going to handle, or answered that phone call that left you with no other place to turn to *except* God.

That loved one with mental issues and no matter how much you've tried to get them help, they refuse to be helped. That person with Alzheimer's you've had to watch forget even who *you* are. You, possibly being the caregiver, having to deal with all that you must deal with at the time. And all the time you were holding your head up when all you really wanted to do was ball up in a fetal position and cry.

Nobody knows just how far down you've gone but God Almighty. And through all of this, through those times when someone else might have lost their natural mind, God kept you in perfect peace. Yes, He kept you when you might not have had enough food to eat. He kept you when you lost that job; and you weren't sure what you were going to do, whether or not you might end up without even a place to lay your head. *But for the grace of God!*

May I have a "Word" with you? No one may have a clue what you've gone through or even what you're going through right now . . . today, but God has kept you! Yes, it was no one but the Lord on your side. It was God holding you up when you felt you couldn't stand on your own any longer. It was the Lord who pushed you when the hill seemed too high to climb. The Lord took you by your hand and pulled you when you only wanted to sit down and quit; when you said, "Lord, I can't go any further!"

God was whispering in your heart and to your spirit, "Yes, you can, My child. I'm here with you. You are not alone. You're never alone. I'll be your strength in your time of weakness. I'll be your joy in times of sorrow. I'll be your peace in the midst of the storm."

So I say to you: Don't get weary in well-doing. Don't stop. Don't quit. Don't give up. You're going to make it. How do I know? Because you can look back over where God has *already* brought you and you can see just how much God has kept you.

Yes, God is able to keep you from falling! Continue to allow God to show Himself strong in and through you and your life. God can handle what you can't. So cast your cares upon the Lord for He cares so much for you!

You are not alone.

True Freedom

S ome people call the time we celebrate on July 4, Independence Day; some just call it The Fourth of July. But I want to talk about real freedom, a freedom that was purchased by God through Jesus Christ's sacrifice on the cross. A debt none of us could possibly pay, but a debt that had to be paid if we were ever to have the opportunity to become free.

When sin came into the world, we were instantly separated from God in a way that was true death. Imagine Adam and Eve in the Garden of Eden, everything you could possibly want or need right there in that place, having continuous fellowship with God Almighty. To walk and talk with Him in the Garden, talking about major things and talking about nothing in particular: a real relationship.

Yes, man was free. Then came the separation and the bondage that sin brings with it. Just as we're free to choose today, they were free to choose back then. Don't eat from the tree God told you not to touch—eat from all the other trees. Simple right? Listen to God and obey Him—or listen to Satan and follow his lead. Adam and Eve chose to listen to Satan and, in effect, disobeyed God's will.

Whether you know it or not, there are consequences to every choice we make. Sometimes they're good consequences, sometimes not, but consequences nevertheless. Sometimes we have no idea as to how far reaching those consequences will have. In the case with Adam and Eve, it affected their children and their children's children. Their actions affected all of us. Yes, what they did all those years ago affected you and me, to a degree of sort, going forth. A debt of death someone must pay. But who on earth could pay it?

Then came another choice: Jesus choosing to come from Heaven to earth to *legally* pay the price. Why did I use the word legally? Because God had turned this world over to man. Yes, God is still God, but not only did He create us in His image, but He gave man dominion over the earth. God could have taken it back after man messed up, but that's not how God operates.

You see, once God gives His Word, you can count on it. I know this may be foreign to some because we know people (if that person isn't us) who will give their word and end up going back on it, sometimes in a heartbeat. But when God gives His word, you don't have to worry about Him going back on it. That alone should cause you to shout! If God has given you His word, you can trust Him to keep it.

Another way God gave His Word? In the beginning was the Word and the Word was with God and the Word was God. John 3:16, "For God so loved the world that he gave his only begotten Son." God gave us His Word in the form of Jesus. Why? So we could be saved! So we could experience what it is to be free. Free to worship God in spirit and in truth. Free to love like God loves because God is love. Freed from sin's hold. Freed from the curse of the law as Jesus fulfilled the law. Free to now live under grace and mercy!

May I have a "Word" with you? America celebrates her independence on July the fourth. But we who have accepted Jesus, knowing how and that our debt has been paid, knowing that we are now redeemed; we should celebrate our independence every day! Praise God, the Blessed Trinity! We are free. For whom the Son sets free, is free indeed.

A declaration of freedom—let the redeemed of the Lord say so! Yes, I am redeemed.

Now what say you?

I Have a Dream

"**A**nd Joseph dreamed a dream, and he told it his brethren: and they hated him yet the more." That scripture can be found in Genesis 37:5, but how many of us can take Joseph's name out and replace it with our own? Dreams. One of Dr. Martin Luther King, Jr.'s most famous speeches begins with "I have a dream."

I, as many of you, also have a dream. And I'm sure I don't have to tell you, but not everyone will be happy for you and your dreams. So was the case with Joseph. His dream indicated that his brothers would one day bow down to him. "And his brethren said to him, Shalt thou indeed reign over us? or shalt thou indeed have dominion over us? And they hated him yet the more for his dreams, and for his words." (Genesis 37:8)

Joseph was excited about his dream from the Lord. But as you can see, his brothers were not. One would think if Joseph was in a position for this to occur (his brothers bowing down to him) then that would most likely mean others would be bowing down to him also. This would mean that their brother (Joseph) would be a person in high authority, and as his brothers, they should have been excited about that fact. But they weren't. The first lesson we can glean from this story is: Be careful when you share your dreams, realizing that not everyone will be happy for you. But then, that's okay.

Another lesson: When God gives you a dream, He'll always tell you the end at the beginning, but rarely will He tell you all that will happen in the middle on your way to reaching that glorious end. However, don't get discouraged. You need to keep on keeping on regardless of what things look like. Keep your eyes on the prize until you get there.

As encouragement, let's look at all that happened with Joseph. He dreamed a dream, but God didn't tell him he'd be put in a pit by his own brothers who, incidentally, wanted to kill him yet would be persuaded by two of his other brothers not to do it. That instead of killing him, they would sell him into slavery to the Ishmaelites who would bring him to Egypt. God didn't tell Joseph that Potiphar, an officer of Pharaoh (captain of the guard), would buy him and he would become successful there. That he would be made overseer of Potiphar's house (sounds good) and all would be placed under his hand (sounds *really* great).

God didn't tell Joseph that he would indeed be a blessing to that house, but that Potiphar's wife would want to sleep with him. Or that in being a godly person and doing the right thing by his master and refusing her, she would catch him when he happened to be in the house alone, tear his garment as he tried to flee, and later lie on him saying he was the one trying to get with her. God didn't tell him that Potiphar, upon hearing this, would be angry and put Joseph in prison.

God didn't tell him while there; the king's butler and baker would offend the king and end up in prison. That they would dream a dream and he would interpret those dreams for them. That after he interpreted the butler's dream, he would ask him to remember him and make mention of him unto Pharaoh and bring him out of prison because he hadn't done anything to warrant being there in the first place. God didn't tell him that when the chief butler is restored back, he wouldn't remember him (not good).

Joseph wasn't told he would be in that prison for two years, and at the end of that second year, Pharaoh would have a dream. That nobody would be able to interpret the dream, and the chief butler would then remember while he was in prison, the young Hebrew man who had interpreted his dream. That Joseph would then be called before Pharaoh, and he would correctly interpret Pharaoh's dream, letting him know there would be seven plenteous years and seven years of famine and how those years should be handled. Genesis 41:38 says, "And Pharaoh said unto his servants, Can we find such a one as this, a man in whom the spirit of God is?"

God didn't tell Joseph that Pharaoh would then set him over all the land of Egypt, take off his ring and put it on his hand, dress him in fine clothes, and put a gold chain around his neck. But the dream from God did tell him that his brothers would bow down to him. In Genesis 42:6, it says, "And Joseph was the governor over the land, and he it was that sold to all the people of the land: and Joseph's brethren came, and bowed down themselves before him with their faces to the earth." God is faithful in His promises.

God doesn't tell us all we may have to go through in order to receive the manifestation of our dreams, but rest assured, God sees and knows all that's going on in our lives. So don't get discouraged when things don't look like they're going in the direction of your dreams. As with Joseph, know that God is faithful to His Word.

May I have a "Word" with you? If God said it, it will come to pass if you faint not. Do what God tells you to and allow God to take care of the "how" it will be done.

Then when you reach the dream and you look back over all you came through getting there, you can say as Joseph said in Genesis 50:19–20: "And Joseph said unto them, Fear not: for am I in the place of God? But as for you, ye thought evil against me; but God meant it unto good, to bring to pass, as it is this day, to save much people alive." In other words: What Satan meant for bad, God used it for good.

Trust God. He is faithful!

A Prophet in His Own Country

I'm often asked about how people support me with my endeavors in writing, especially in my own hometown. There was a time when I could identify with what Jesus said about a prophet not being known in his own country. People in other cities were excited about me and my books, while I couldn't always get that attention here in my own area of Birmingham.

But I'm pleased to report that people have really started supporting me, reading my books, telling others about me and my many novels.

Jesus was born to Mary, a woman without a lot of credentials or prestige behind her name, and Joseph, a mere carpenter. So when Jesus began the ministry that He was sent to do by His Father in Heaven, people who knew Him didn't give Him much respect or attention. You can just hear people as they said things like, "Isn't that Jesus, the carpenter's boy?" There were times and places where Jesus couldn't even perform miracles because of their unbelief stemming from who they *perceived* Him to be.

See that's the problem with some of us. It's the reason why some of us miss out on some of our blessings. We grew up with people and know them as they were. But God has a purpose for each of our lives, and He sees us as we will be. That means your past is just that when it comes to how God views it—your past. Whatever happened in the past, once you've given your life to God, He gives you brand new mercy. And that brand new mercy is given to us daily. God sees in you your potential and not what you used to be.

May I have a "Word" with you? Don't let anyone tell you that you're nothing or "a nobody" just because they "knew you when." You see, God created you a unique and rare jewel. And as with any jewel, it doesn't always shine or sparkle in the beginning. There are times when that jewel has to go through some cleaning, sanding, and polishing.

But oh, when God gets through using the fire to burn away impurities, sanding, washing, and polishing away all that garbage that tries to attach itself and disguise what God sees as valuable, you talking about some kind of shining! You want to talk about valuable! You want to talk about how the world sees that jewel (I'm talking about you) after God is finished with you! Now *that's* something to shout about.

From this day forward, don't you ever let anyone tell you who you are. God has already declared it, and what people in your own country may or may not think really doesn't matter. All that matters is what God says.

Now go on, meet up with your divine purpose, and let's make our Father in Heaven pleased!

May I Have A "Word" With You?

In talking with some people, it seems many folks are "down" these days. I hate to use the word "depressed" because words have power. The Bible tells us that *life and death are in the power of the tongue. Out of the heart the mouth speaketh.* Yes, thoughts have power, but our words have more power. Therefore, we should be mindful how we use our power.

I often tell people that Satan really doesn't have any power. He knows we have it. Jesus gave it to us when He arose with all of it. But our mouths can get us in trouble if we're not careful. If Satan can get you talking wrong, then guess what? He has used your God-given powers against you to defeat you. If you can only get this in your heart, you'll see a change in your life. Satan will place images before you (some real; some just your overactive imagination).

The problem comes when we begin speaking what we see with our natural eyes or the fear we may have in our heart. Satan tends to focus our attention on "what we don't have" "what's not going right in our life" and any other thing he can think of to bring our spirits down.

What you need to do is focus on what you *do have* and what God says about you. What have you accomplished? Then think on these things. Don't just discount what you've already been able to do—those things serve as markers in order for you to see just how far God has brought you. Looking back to where God has brought you from encourages you to go on and see what other blessings He has waiting for you.

When I talk with and encourage people who are "a little down" (and I hope you know all of us need encouraging, and there are times where you just have to encourage yourself), my goal is to keep the attention on what God has *already* done.

When David was preparing to face and fight Goliath there was a lot he could have focused on. Instead, he focused on what God had already done for him (there was a lion and a bear he faced in his past, and he defeated them both). When you do that, it builds you up and puts you in a place for God to do great things *now*.

As David declared about the giant he faced—Goliath: "Who is this uncircumcised Philistine who dares to come against the almighty God?" That's what you must do when you face the giants in your life.

Today, begin speaking from a victorious perspective and see how your present and future begins to change. What you do and say today truly does affect your tomorrows. Remember this each and every time you open your mouth to speak a word.

So, if you're a little put out because things don't seem to be going the way you thought or had hoped, focus on what you have, what's going right, who God is, what God has already done, and what God says about you. Speak on these things.

And remember: you're made in the image of God. *"And God said . . . and it was so."* Protect your heart; put a watch over your mouth; and speak only those things you desire to manifest. If you don't want it, don't say it. And use present tense ("I am" "I have") then watch God work in your life.

May I have a "Word" with You? *Lift up your head, o ye gates.* Gates can keep things in and gates can keep things out. Start each day with a blessed bang, using all of your gates (ears, eyes, and mouth gates) the Godly way!

All Hands on Deck

*L*uke 5:1-11 tells the account of Jesus and His encounter with two ships. Verses 1-2 reads, "And it came to pass, that as the people pressed upon him to hear the word of God, he stood by the lake of Gennesaret. And saw two ships standing by the lake: but the fishermen were gone out of them, and were washing their nets."

Jesus then entered into one of the ships which happened to belong to Simon Peter. He asked him to thrust out a little from the land so the people would be able to see Him better as He taught them. Verse four tells us, "Now when he had left speaking, he said unto Simon, Launch out into the deep, and let down your nets for a draught." The word draught means a catch. Verse five: "And Simon answering said unto him, Master, we have toiled all the night, and have taken nothing: nevertheless at thy word I will let down the net."

Verse six and seven: "And when they had this done, they enclosed a great multitude of fishes: and their net brake. And they beckoned unto their partners, which were in the other ship, that they should come and help them. And they came, and filled both the ships, so that they began to sink."

At Jesus' word, Simon launched out into the deep. Here they had fished all night which, as experienced fishermen, they knew was the best time to catch fish. They hadn't caught anything. But at the word of Jesus, they did as He told them. And because they were obedient and launched out when He told them (which incidentally was right after Simon had allowed Him to use something of his, his ship), they caught a great multitude of fish. At this point, they needed all hands on deck.

Everybody who could do something was needed because the catch was so great. In fact, they had so much, they had to call for the other ship to come and help them. All hands on deck! And when the other ship came to help with the catch, it was so much still that both ships began to sink from so much fish!

That's how God works. Matthew 9:37 tells us that the harvest is truly plenteous, but the laborers are few. There are lots of fish out there waiting to be pulled in to the Lord, and we really do need all hands on deck. All hands on deck merely means: Everybody on the ship that's a worker, we need you to come and work. We need every hand to come out and up, and we're going to need you to work.

May I have a "Word" with you? Just as when Jesus told of the harvest being plenteous, He also told Simon (Peter), James and John (who were partners with Simon) in Luke 5:10 to "Fear not; from henceforth thou shalt catch men." Whether it's harvesting things planted or harvesting fish, Jesus is calling, "All hands on deck."

If you have a hand in the Kingdom of God, you need to put your hand to the plough if that's what's needed and you know you can do, or put your hand to gathering if that's where you've been assigned, or put your hand to getting out there and catching fish. Whatever God has called you to do for the Kingdom down here on earth, God needs all hands on deck!

Pulling Down Strongholds

S
ome of you may be aware that I wrote a novel called *Strongholds*. Although my book is fictional, strongholds are real.

Second Corinthians 10:3-5 says, "For though we walk in the flesh, we do not war after the flesh: (For the weapons of our warfare are not carnal, but mighty through God to the pulling down of strongholds;) Casting down imaginations, and every high thing that exalteth itself against the knowledge of God, and bringing into captivity every thought to the obedience of Christ."

We are spiritual beings in a human body. All that we are is not merely this body. Think about it. God breathed the breath of life into Adam. God breathed His spirit into Adam and Adam became a living soul. We are a spiritual being, we live in a physical body, and we have a soul. That which is earth is earth; that which is spirit is spirit.

The scripture quoted says that though we walk in the flesh, we don't war after the flesh. To war is to battle, to fight. War is the opposite of peace. But even though we're in warfare our weapons are not carnal, but they are mighty through God. This is spiritual warfare.

Strongholds—something that has a strong hold on you. Yes, all of us know something about strongholds. Strongholds can be thoughts that tell you you're a nobody. Strongholds can be words you've heard over and over again about how you're not going to make it, whether it comes from outside or within. Strongholds can be those thoughts that wrap around your mind, finding a way to get a hold on you, leading you to do things that will hold you back.

Now don't be fooled. Every "thing" begins first with a thought. People don't just fall into or get caught up in strongholds like smoking, fornication, adultery, gambling, lying, deceit, pornography, drugs, overeating, you name it, except there was first a thought. That's why the Word of God in the scriptures on strongholds emphasizes the pulling down of strongholds and casting down imaginations.

Imaginations are thoughts. Imaginations are pictures in the mind. To demonstrate my point, I'd like for you to do something right now. I want you to *NOT* think of a pink elephant. Whatever you do right now, *don't* think of a pink elephant. Don't allow the thought of a pink elephant to enter into your mind or your thoughts. *DON'T* think of a pink elephant.

What happened? You thought of a pink elephant, didn't you? In fact, you probably saw a full pink elephant with its trunk and maybe even tusks. That's the power of words, the power of thought. They cause you to see. When used the way God intends thoughts to be used, it's a good thing. But thoughts can also contribute to manifested strongholds.

May I have a "Word" with you? Those things that are holding you back from having all that God has already appointed to you, those things that are keeping you from doing what God has called you to do, those strongholds need to be pulled down now. Our weapons of warfare are not carnal. Our weapons are not of the flesh, but mighty through God. Think about that. We have mighty weapons through God to pull down strongholds in our lives!

And we need to begin by casting down imaginations, arguments, and every high thing that dares to exalt itself against the knowledge of God. Bring wrong thoughts into captivity and place them under the obedience of Christ. Pull down those strongholds!

All Things Work Together

omans 8:28 says, "And we know that all things work together for good to them that love God, to them who are the called according to his purpose." I understand many saints of God, Kingdom citizens are working to live lives pleasing unto God. I understand many people have been given a Word from God regarding their future and they are standing on that Word right now. I understand you may feel like Job in the sense that before one thing can be dealt with, here comes someone bringing you news about something else.

You may be wondering how God can give you a dream that's so glorious about your future and plans He has to bless you, but where you are right now looks nothing like that blessing—not even close.

But let me tell you this: When God gives you a dream or a Word, you may find you have to go from the pit to the prison before you get to the palace, but you *will* get there. You see: When Joseph the Dreamer received his Word from God regarding his future, he wasn't told about the pit he would be held in or the prison he would be cast into.

Honestly, he wasn't even told specifically about the palace he would eventually rule from. He was only shown the end result (his brothers bowing down to him) after the blessing was manifested. Yet, through it all, no matter how bad things looked at the time, in the end, all things worked together for good.

Some years ago, God gave me a Word regarding my books. He told me the end, but He didn't tell me anything about the "pit" or the "prison" experiences I would have to go through before attaining that promise (metaphorically speaking). God told the children of Israel about the Promised Land, but they weren't told about the Red Sea and the wilderness they would find themselves wandering in for forty years.

There will be times in your life when things won't look like what God promised you, but let me encourage you: Believe God and don't turn away from what He has promised you. God is faithful and you need to stand on that, I don't care what things look like.

Should you find yourself in a pit, praise God, because all things work together for good. Should you find yourself in a prison (and I'm not necessarily talking about a physical prison because all prisons aren't steel bars, some prisons are people trying to keep you down or hold you up) praise God that all things are working together for good.

When you experience times where it looks like you're not getting anywhere because you're on "lock-down" or "solitary confinement," praise God, because all things work together for good. When you find yourself being lied on or talked about, but you know the truth (and more importantly God knows the truth, and He won't forget nor forsake you), then praise God because all things work together for good.

May I have a "Word" with you? If Joseph the Dreamer had not been thrown into the pit, sold into slavery, put in prison, then he might not have been in position to be promoted into a prominent place in that palace. No, you may not like what's going on right now in your life. It may not feel good. But you need to praise God while you go through it (notice I said *through* and not stop or stuck).

Praise God, because even though this is not how you would have chosen to get to the Promised Land, it may not be the way you would have liked being promoted in the kingdom, praise God because you know that all things work together for good.

Yes, God has a plan. And no, He doesn't always disclose to you everything regarding His plan. Sometimes we or others make bad decisions and God has to take what is bad and use it for our good. Regardless of what or why: Trust God, rejoice, and praise your way through.

Rejoice, I say. And again I say, rejoice as God carries you through!

Got Dreams? Got Goals?

I've often heard the question asked, "What would you do if you knew you couldn't fail?" It's a great question. But I'd like to know what you would do if you truly believed Philippians 4:13, "I can do all things through Christ which strengtheneth me."

Paul spoke these words in connection with the verses that immediately preceded this declaration. To sum up those verses: Paul said he knew how to live skillfully when things were going wonderfully (abound), and he knew how to live skillfully when things weren't so wonderful (abase).

There are times in life when you might attempt to do things, yet feel like you're not getting anywhere. There may be times when it seems no one is trying to help or support you in any way. There will be times when people will look for and sometimes it may even feel like they're praying for you fail.

And yet, there will be times when everything you touch seems to work out wonderfully and everything you touch appears to turn to gold. Times when someone comes along and encourages you or lets you know how much they also believe in you and what you're doing. God will place people in your path who will do whatever they can to help you and they may not even understand why they're doing it (that's called favor).

Allow me to encourage you here. Before you even begin desires, dreams, and goals; set yourself with the same mindset of Paul's. Declare from the beginning, "I can do all things through Christ." Notice this scripture says *through* Christ—not with or in but *THROUGH* Christ. And there *is* a difference. John 15:5, Jesus says, "I am the vine, ye are the branches: He that abideth in me, and I in him, the same bringeth forth much fruit: for without me ye can do nothing."

Get it? Jesus is the vine. In the natural, we understand when it comes to a grapevine that you can't have live, productive branches apart from the vine. The vine feeds, sustains, maintains, and causes branches to bear fruit. And when the vine is a good and true vine, it will produce *much* fruit.

Jesus is the True Vine. Therefore, I (a branch) am being fed by, held up, caused to be healthy and bear much fruit *through* Jesus. A branch that desires to be more than merely dry wood must stay connected to the vine because once a branch breaks off, truthfully, it's dead.

Sure, there may have been fruit on it already, but without the vine . . . without Jesus, there's no way life will remain. It's through the vine . . . through Jesus, that the branch (you and I) can do things, and not just things, but *ALL* things.

So when you're working toward your dreams and goals, and you feel like you're not getting anywhere . . . if what you're doing doesn't feel like it's enough to make a difference, I'd like you to consider snowflakes. That's right—snowflakes.

Snowflakes are small and light in weight. But when you add one snowflake after another, the landscape will begin to change until eventually it's totally transformed. As snowflakes continue, they begin to collect enough to garner some real attention . . . in some cases, enough to cause avalanches. Now that's a lot of power to have begun with what might not have appeared to have been much to start with.

So keep your snowflakes coming; stay connected and put your trust in the True Vine—Jesus the Christ. Then watch as this collective force makes a thundering difference.

May I have a "Word" with you? Is there something you've always wanted to do but either you or someone else talked you out of it? I can't speak for you, but as for me: I'm confident in my dreams and goals no matter how things look. Why? Because I *can* do *all* things through Christ who strengthens me.

Got Dreams? Got Goals? Then what are you waiting for? Get up and get going! Walt Disney once said, "All our dreams can come true—if we have the courage to pursue them." So don't be afraid to do something new or different.

God has not given you the spirit of fear, but of love and of power and of a sound mind. And when you or someone else begins to question whether or not you can do what God has given you, remember this: An amateur—called by God—built the ark; it was professionals who built the Titanic. Oh yes, you can do ALL things through Christ!

What's Love Got To Do With It?

Okay, when some of you saw this headline, you may have instantly thought about Tina Turner, whether it was the song she made popular, or the movie of her life played by Angela Bassett. Whenever I write anything or am asked to speak, I go before God and inquire of Him what He would like me to write or speak on. I admit: there are times when He'll direct me one way, and I end up going back just to ensure I heard correctly.

There were several topics God gave me this time around, but the one pressing has to do with love. Matthew 22:36-39 reads, "Master, which is the great commandment in the law? Jesus said unto him, THOU SHALT LOVE THE LORD THY GOD WITH ALL THY HEART, AND WITH ALL THY SOUL, AND WITH ALL THY MIND. This is the first and great commandment. And the second is like unto it, THOU SHALT LOVE THY NEIGHBOR AS THYSELF."

Now, you might be expecting this to be about how important it is for you to love others. Actually, I believe we have an even bigger problem. Many people, including a lot of Christians, apparently don't love themselves too much.

What? You may be thinking. *Don't love myself? Of course, I love myself. It looks to me that the problem is that people only care about themselves. That's the problem!*

All right, you may love yourself. But how much?

How many times do you look in the mirror and only find things to dislike or find fault with? Okay, so you've put on a few pounds. So have I. And truthfully, I've seen pictures of myself and others during younger years, and quite frankly, some of us needed to fill out a bit. Now, I'm not talking about being unhealthy. If you're overweight, and it's messing with your health, then please, by all means: Love yourself enough to take care of you so you'll live a longer and greater quality of life.

I'm talking about having the world tell you what's pretty or perfect that each time you look at yourself in the mirror, you can't find one good or positive thing to say for being too busy criticizing yourself. *My nose, my eyes, my lips, my . . . my . . . my . . .*

So, what's love got to do with it?

A lot! If you can't manage to love YOU right, then how can you possibly manage to love ME right? If you can't say anything nice or positive to the person you wake up with each and every day . . . that person who stares back at you in the mirror whenever you do slow down enough to acknowledge him or her, then what can you possibly say to or about me when you look at me (your neighbor, so to speak)?

The Bible says to love your neighbor *as* yourself. Question: How do you love you?

Do you encourage yourself much? When God is listening in on your public and private conversations, what are you saying *to* and *about* yourself? Do you believe in you at all? Do you believe God loves you in spite of your not being perfect, and that He's willing to work with you as you strive to become better? Would you really like to see yourself succeed . . . obtain your dreams and goals, or are you convinced "You're a nobody", "a loser", or that "You're never going to be anything, so why try?"

To what extent are you using your God-given gifts to become all God created *YOU* to be? Take an inventory right now. How much do you love yourself? Don't hesitate to adjust as needed to love you the way you should be loved.

Here's your homework assignment. Every day for the next 21 days, I'd like you to look in the mirror (looking right into the eyes looking at you) and say something special, positive, and encouraging to that person staring back at you. Get a notebook or a journal and write down the things you love about yourself as well as things you're thankful for.

May I have a "Word" with you? Let's be honest here. Some of you have been so down on yourselves, it's no wonder you can't see anything good in anyone else. How do you really want to be treated? Okay, then love yourself enough and start doing that with and for you (consider it practice to be used later on others). I submit to you: perhaps, we haven't been able to love one another better because we really need to learn to love ourselves better.

And just in case you're one who doesn't care for your skin tone . . . your height, or whatever other physical attributes you have no control over, then allow me to say this: God created you. How dare you insult the Creator about His creation! Learn to love who you are and who God created you to be. Then work it, child of God. Work it. Now, let's all say it together: "I am fearfully and wonderfully made!"

If you can get this "self" love thing down right, then and only then, will I look forward to you loving me (as well as others) *as* you love yourself.

What's love got to do with it? Everything! For God is love.

The Attitude in Gratitude

hank you. Yes, thank you. Thank you for taking the time to read this.

Now think about it: How did those words make you feel? Whether we hear them or see them written out, the words "thank you" can cause special feelings to rise up inside of us. Question: have you told God thank You today?

I'm sure that's an easy one for most of you. You can proudly say that you have, even if it may have been an automatic, unconscious thought. But have you really truly considered all that God *has* done, *is doing,* and *plans to do* for you, and reverently and sincerely told Him thank You? Do you have an attitude of gratitude? Or is life in your way so much with things you can find to complain about that you just haven't gotten around to saying thank You lately?

You see, we can be so busy looking at what's *not* right in our lives, we start focusing on that and miss out on all that we do have to be grateful for. I can remember a few times in my life when things were going really, really bad. You know one of those days that if you're not keeping a watch over your mouth, you could easily find yourself saying, "If it ain't one thing, it's another." I recall praying and telling God I really was trying down here and that I could use a little help. It was at that moment I heard in my spirit, "Just say: thank You."

Thank You? Just say thank You?

"Yes," was the response I received as I was directed to look at what in that moment—as awful as things were—I could still find to be thankful for. The point was not to look at other things outside of the situation I could easily be grateful for, but in the midst of these troubles, what could I be grateful for and to thank God for that. So that's exactly what I did. I began to focus on the good and thanked God.

During that time, it was about a vehicle that had broken down. So I thanked Him that when the vehicle broke down, it did it in the place it had (which was better than other places it could have). I thanked Him that someone came along and offered their assistance to call someone (talking through a cracked window, of course—this was before everyone had cell phones). I thanked God we were able to get the vehicle towed. And even though work had to be done on the vehicle, I thanked God we had the money to pay for it.

You see, we can be so focused on how awful things are that we miss seeing God's workings in the midst of it. Focus on the good and just see what happens. Then learn to say thank You.

I can tell you when someone thanks me—it makes me feel good and causes me to want to do even more for them.

Now—how many people have you thanked lately? Has someone done something for you and you took it for granted that they knew you appreciated them? Then right now, tell them, "Thank you." And if right now is not possible, then do it as soon as possible.

Besides it being good manners, why should you say thank you?

Because saying "thank you" takes you to a higher altitude in life. Think of it like putting helium in a balloon. If you put in a little helium, you may rise but not as high as you can when every inch is filled to capacity. Every time you say "thank you"; it's like putting more helium inside of you and causing yourself to rise to an even higher altitude.

Write down or speak the things you're grateful for and watch how many more things start coming your way. And if you think taking the time to say thank you doesn't matter to God, then consider the story in Luke 17:12-19 of the ten men that were lepers. The ten asked Jesus to have mercy on them and heal them. Jesus told them to go and show themselves to the priest, and *as* they went, they were cleansed.

When one of them saw that he was healed, he turned back, and with a loud voice glorified God, fell on his face at Jesus' feet, and gave thanks. Verses 17-18 says, "And Jesus answering said, 'Were there not ten cleansed? but where are the nine? There are not found that returned to give glory to God, save this stranger.'" Jesus then said to the one who had come back and given thanks, "Arise, go thy way: thy faith had made thee whole." The one who came back and said thanks made his salvation of healing whole . . . complete.

Notice the word "arise." That is: To come up higher from where you are. If someone has blessed you in some way, tell them thank you.

May I have a "Word" with you? If God has brought you through something, tell God thank You. If you're going through something right now, tell God thank You. Thank You, God for believing that, by faith, I can even handle this. Thank You for being with me as I go through this. Thank You . . . for I know I'm already victorious in this through Christ Jesus! You don't have to wait until you see it manifested. By faith, say thank You now.

Were there not ten cleansed? but where are the nine? May I have a "Word" with you? Are you one of the nine, or are you that one? Are you the one Jesus will say, "Arise!"? There *is* altitude in gratitude.

Just say, "Thank You."

The Potter and the Clay

ou may have heard it or said it yourself. "God is the potter; I am the clay." So, where might this have originated from? Jeremiah 18:3-4 states, "Then I went down to the potter's house, and behold, he wrought a work on the wheels. And the vessel that he made of clay was marred in the hand of the potter: so he made it again another vessel, as seemed good to the potter to make it."

When thinking about the potter and the clay, I immediately thought of plates. You see, there are plates you can eat off of and those you just shouldn't. There are your everyday plates, fine china, and decorative plates. I, as possibly many of you, own all three types. But what or who determines what this original clay will turn out to be?

The creator of it has a huge hand in the beginning. Should it be a plate or a cup? If it's a plate, will it be one for service, or merely to be admired? However, after it's created, then the one who possesses it, at that point, has more of the say-so.

If it's one for service, then it was most likely created to withstand the pressures and hardships of life. It can be as plain-looking as you may think when you see it, but in actuality, there's a lot more built into it than meets the eye. If it was created for service, it was made to not break easily. It can withstand being in a dishwasher without requiring a special setting. It can handle being heated in a microwave, put in a hot oven, the coldness of refrigeration, and can even stand the extremes of having to go from cold to hot in seconds, if it must. It was created for service.

Then there is the fine china. Beautiful to look at, but so delicate, it has to be handled with care. Sure, it can be used—it just requires special attention when it is. And using it every day, for most people, is out of the question. It's just too fragile for that. Many people will only use fine china on special occasions. It *can* be placed in the dishwasher (the delicate cycle recommended) although washing by hand is often preferred. Careful attention is needed in order not to break, crack, or chip fine china.

Then there is the decorative plate created purely for show. Beautiful on the outside, yet potentially toxic (even deadly), if used for anything other than to be admired. It wasn't made to be eaten off of like an everyday plate or fine china. Washing is not recommended. And should you need to, then extreme care must be taken. A decorative plate's true function is to be seen . . . to be admired (without much touching or handling). It's about how it looks, not what it can do.

My decorative plates are generally stuck in my curio cabinet, and truthfully, I can go years without even looking at them. Occasionally, I glance their way, even picking them up from their perched, upright positions to admire or possibly dust (clean) them.

If I had to pick the type of plate I am, I would honestly have to admit I'm an everyday plate with fine china qualities. I was created to be used every day, and to be used often. I can stand the rigors of life. I've been dropped and tossed around more times than I care to think about, yet, I refuse to break. On the other hand, my Creator gave me my own special, beautiful design (that's where I get my fine china tendencies).

As long as you don't look too closely, you won't see the thickness He used in order to make me strong enough to survive whatever life might try to put me through (fine china is usually delicate and thin which is why it's so easy to break).

But putting me on a shelf only to take me out on special occasions or my being somewhere merely wanting to look good or to be admired without being used, just doesn't work for me. I'm not knocking the art in decorative plates (my youngest son is an artist), but even art should have a purpose and contribute something special to another's life other than to merely exist.

So what am I saying here?

We should exemplify our Creator's original intent as He made us. Isaiah 29:16 says, "Surely your turning of things upside down shall be esteemed as the potter's clay: for shall the work say of him that made it, He made me not? or shall the thing framed say of him that framed it, He had no understanding?"

May I have a "Word" with you? Are you trying to be fine china (only used on special occasions) or a decorative plate (desiring to sit on a shelf, look pretty, and merely be admired) when you were actually created to be used for everyday service?

Now, if you truly are fine china, then how about being used more on a regular basis to make someone else feel even more special? And if you're a decorative plate, get out there where others can see and appreciate all that you have to offer and stop being "stuck up" and somewhere "off to yourself."

To my fellow everyday plates who *know* you were created to serve: Be proud that you were made for God's great service. You're appreciated more than you'll ever know.

So now: What kind of a plate are you? Are you living up to all God created you to be? Don't look at the other plates around you. This question is totally for you!

An Inside Job

I published a book back in 1999 called *Destiny Unlimited*. In that book, there's a scene many refer to as "the oatmeal scene." To summarize: My character, whose name was Amethyst, was in a city where every word spoken would immediately manifest in the physical realm. One really had to be careful of the words uttered while in the "City of Tomorrow's Yesterday" (think about it; you'll get it). In this city, there were no idle words spoken, or a figure of speech, or a slip of the tongue.

While in this place, Amethyst would awaken to a bowl of oatmeal for breakfast. Not liking oatmeal but also not wanting to be rude, Amethyst would say (as a hint), "Oatmeal, again?" On the next day, there would be oatmeal again, whereby she would again say, "Oatmeal again?" Finally, Amethyst decided to tell her hostess that she really desired sausage, eggs, grits, biscuits, and juice for breakfast, but every morning, to her dismay, there was oatmeal. Amethyst was then advised, "Well, say that then."

Catching on to what she was being told, she then asked, "Well, what if I don't want oatmeal, and I say 'I don't want oatmeal.'" At which point she was told that one of *two* things would happen. Saying the word "don't" before what you want generally is not heard and you'll likely get whatever you spoke after the word "don't", in this case that would be oatmeal. Or what you *don't* want is known but what you *do* want still is not.

Here's the point to all of this. When we say what we don't want, inside we must first create the picture of it in order to know what *it* is that we *don't want*. Let me demonstrate what I mean. Right now, I want you to NOT think of an pig. DO NOT think of a pig. Whatever you do right now, DON'T think of a pig.

Okay, so what happened? You thought of a pig, didn't you? You see, the only way you can *Not* think of something is to think about it so you can try NOT to think about it. Have I made you dizzy yet?

The Bible states, "Out of the heart, the mouth speaketh." "Life and death is in the power of the tongue." The words we think and speak are so important that God won't let me leave this subject.

God has given us much power, but we must learn to use that power to create positive things (life) and not negative things (death) in our own lives. This change becomes an inside job; that's when you'll start seeing things begin to happen on the outside. You see, everything is created twice: inside (thoughts, belief, vision) then outside (manifested for all to experience with one or all of our five senses).

Now, what I'd like to show you is how even well-intentioned words can trip us up. How many of you want to be debt-free? How many of you are confessing there's no lack? "No lack for money, no lack for favor, no lack . . ." Are you confessing you're delivered from poverty, sickness, etc.? Yes. Well, these are a few examples of what sounds like great confessions and intentions, but God showed me recently how these words are holding many of us from where He desires us to be.

You see, in order to be debt-free, your thoughts must be directed to the word debt. You don't want debt, but just like the pig, confessing debt-free first produces a picture of debt. Instead of saying what you don't want (debt) why not just change the words you say to what you *do* want. "I have financial freedom." The same goes for the phrase no lack. It sounds wonderful, but there's the word "lack" jumping all around inside of you before it comes out. Instead of "no lack" say, "I am walking in abundance."

I know this is a lot of work for some. But Jesus came that we might have life (notice Jesus didn't say here He came that we might not die, but He said what He wanted—have life), and life more abundantly. So take out your pen and paper. On one side, write down the things you don't want, then on the opposite side of it, write down what you'll be saying from now on of what you actually *do* want. Instead of debt-free, say financial freedom. Instead of no lack, speak abundance. To be healed from sickness, confess you're walking in health. Would you like no worries, then speak perfect peace. Rather than not being sad or unhappy, start speaking the fullness of joy.

May I have a "Word" with you? Matthew 15:11 tells us, "Not that which goeth into the mouth defileth a man; but that which cometh out of the mouth, this defileth a man." You're going to have to change your mind about some things, and take on the mind of Christ. However, that's an inside job the Holy Spirit is both willing and able to help you with, if only you'll ask.

Where Are You?

*J*f you've ever wanted to reach a destination, no matter who you are or how smart you may be, the first thing you must answer is: *Where am I now?*

When Adam and Eve lived in the Garden of Eden—walking and talking with the Almighty God—they knew where they were. They were experiencing a gloriously anointed, blessed, exceeding, abundant life. In addition, God told them they could eat of the fruit of the trees of the garden, except for the tree in the midst of the garden.

Genesis 3:6-9 shows what ultimately transpired. "And when the woman saw that the tree was good for food, and that it was pleasant to the eyes, and a tree to be desired to make one wise, she took of the fruit thereof, and did eat, and gave also unto her husband with her; and he did eat. And the eyes of them both were opened, and they knew that they were naked; and they sewed fig leaves together, and made themselves aprons. And they heard the voice of the Lord God walking in the garden in the cool of the day: and Adam and his wife hid themselves from the presence of the Lord God amongst the trees of the garden. And the Lord God called unto Adam, and said unto him, Where art thou?"

Since God is omnipresent (everywhere at the same time), He wasn't asking Adam where was he because He didn't know. In fact, God knew exactly where Adam was at that very moment (spiritually and physically). If you read on, you'll see that Adam didn't respond with a physical location as to where he happened to be. Adam's response, in verse ten was, "I heard thy voice in the garden, and I was afraid, because I was naked; and I hid myself." To which God responded, "Who told thee that thou wast naked?"

Adam and Eve knew they were in sin although they likely didn't know that was the word for it. They found themselves looking for something to cover up with. They sewed fig leaves together. But even that wasn't enough (as we all know), so they hid, trying to cover their sin. When God asked Adam where he was, it was a spiritual question not a physical location one. "Where are you, Adam? You're running *from* me now instead of *to* me. You realize a separation has occurred, don't you, Adam? Now this will require a blood sacrifice."

God decreed many things following that. To the serpent that had done this, He cursed him, letting him know that the woman's seed would bruise his head although in the process, the serpent would bruise the seed's heel. Right there in Genesis 3:15, God revealed the messianic prophecy and provided us the first glimpse of the Gospel (the Good News).

Here, we learn three things: Satan (the serpent) is our real enemy; a spiritual barrier was put in place between Satan and his people and us (God's people); and that the seed of Eve (a woman, because legally humans are born of women) would be the one to deliver the deathblow to Satan. But also in doing this, the Seed would be bruised (can somebody thank God for Jesus, and thank Jesus for dying for our sins right about now?).

Years ago when we traveled—desiring to get from one place to another—we'd get a map and map it out. Today, we have access to computer maps as well as GPS (Global Positioning System). The principle in how you use these resources is still the same. If I am somewhere, but I want to be somewhere else, the first thing I must have knowledge of is: *Where am I now?* Once I know where I am (pinpointing my present position), and I see where I want to be; I can map out the route I need in order to reach my destination.

When God asked Adam where art thou, He did that for Adam's benefit. Adam had to recognize where he was, which at the time was out of fellowship with God. From that point, God, who loved the world so much, already had a plan . . . a map, to get us back to Him.

Some people believe their works will get them to Heaven. They say they are good people. They brag about how right they're living. Don't get me wrong: These are all good things. But good and Godly are not the same. They're not good enough to get you into Heaven or where you're trying to be if being in fellowship with God is what you desire.

May I have a "Word" with you? The ultimate GPS is God's Positioning System. And God sent His Son, Jesus, all the way from Heaven to earth to show us the way. And Jesus being sacrificed didn't just cover sin, but blotted sin out. In John 14, Jesus tells us not to be troubled; He's going to prepare a place for us; where He is, there we may be also.

Jesus, the ultimate GPS, declares in John 14:6, "I am the way, the truth, and the life: no man cometh unto the Father, but by me." You ask, "How do I get back to God?" "How do I walk in God's promises?" "How do I have the life Jesus said we can have?"

Romans 10:8-10 tells us how. "But what saith it? The word is nigh thee, even in thy mouth, and in thy heart: that is the word of faith, which we preach; That if thou shalt confess with thy mouth the Lord Jesus, and shalt believe in thine heart that God hath raised him from the dead, thou shalt be saved. For with the heart man believeth unto righteousness; and with the mouth confession is made unto salvation."

Salvation in the Lord covers every area of your life: Spiritually, socially, financially, emotionally, and physically. Where are you? Where do you want to be? Jesus is the way, the truth, and He *is* the life.

Follow Jesus; and you'll never be lost again!

Alone

Have you ever felt like you were all by yourself? I don't mean physically, I mean even though people were around you, you felt like you were alone? Most of us don't like to admit things like this, but I believe at one time or another, we've all experienced and possibly will feel a period again where it feels like we're alone.

That's not to diminish the times when you really may be alone. I'm speaking specifically when you have family and friends at your fingertips to touch whether it's in person; in your address book through various airwaves like the telephone, cellphone, texting, Internet, e-mail, Facebook, Twitter, Instagram, Facetime, or Skype.

I'm talking about those times when we go to God and "have a little talk" with Him . . . the times when we feel like He's listening and hearing our every words. But then, for some reason we can't explain; it feels like we're praying and talking with Him but He's not there or, at least, not talking back.

Oh, we don't want to say anything like this out loud because we don't want anyone to know we've experienced those times. Times when we've prayed and believed, and it didn't feel like anything happened. Or what we didn't want to happen *did* happen anyway as though our prayers were in vain. And our friends who know we're going through then look at us like there has to be something bad going on in our lives because God seems to have turned a deaf ear to our humble cry.

I'm talking right now to someone who knows what it is to have nowhere or no one else to turn to *except* the Lord, and even then, you feel like you're all alone. Yes, we can quote the scripture and proudly proclaim that God said He would never leave nor forsake us. And yet, at a certain time or moment, we feel as though we're all by ourselves.

What do you do during these times? What do you do when you're depressed and it feels like the enemy is working overtime to tighten those mental thought screws that can further press you down? What do you do when that bill is due and you've gone before the Lord with a petition to help, and the date has come and gone with no change in your situation? What do you do when you look around and feel like no one is there to care about you, even though you've given so much of yourself to others? But for whatever reason, at the time when you need someone to put their arms around you, you can't find anyone.

May I have a "Word" with you? Jesus knows and He cares. He knows because He's been there. Hanging on the cross as recorded in Mark 15:34, He cried, "Eloi, Eloi, lama sabachthani?" which is "My God, My God, why has thou forsaken me?" Mark 16:37 says, "And Jesus cried with a loud voice, and gave up the ghost." Jesus gave up the ghost. But I'm so glad to report that this is not the end of the story.

Jesus arose and He arose with all power in His hand. So when you're feeling alone, when you're feeling forsaken, when you find yourself asking God why you feel like you do, please know where you are during your dark time is not the end of the story. You may be down for the count, but you're not out! Trust God and trust that even when you're feeling alone, God is still right there, and Jesus is interceding—with full knowledge of the situation—on your behalf.

Sometimes, during those alone-times, God is merely saying, "Be still and know that I am God." Sometimes He's saying, "Be still and see the salvation of the Lord." No matter what you're going through; no matter if you feel alone, God said He would be there with you—that He would never leave you. And my brothers and sisters, God is not a man that He should lie.

Trust in the Lord as you go through. You are victorious. You are more than a conqueror! Don't let the devil deceive you. God said it, and it doesn't matter what it feels like: God is there! No matter what you're going through, God is there.

Another Level

*D*uring graduation time, there are lot of words of "Congratulations!" For many, it may have been a long hard journey. There were times where it may have been tough. But you know what? You made it! There were times when it may have been overwhelming, but you stuck with it. Time to celebrate what has been accomplished. Then after celebrating, what are you going to do?

Oh, I'm sure many people have plans. Whether it's graduating high school with your eye on college or possibly going out and securing a job. If you've graduated college, maybe your decision is to continue on and attain your masters or doctorate degree or to finally start your career or own business. Whatever the decision, hear these words found in Philippians 2:5-7. "Let this mind be in you, which was also in Christ Jesus. Who, being in the form of God, thought it not robbery to be equal with God: But made himself of no reputation, and took upon him the form of a servant, and was made in the likeness of men."

Yes, it's great to make lots of money, but if you'll have the heart of a servant, thinking of what you're doing in the context of others, having a heart to serve, everything else will follow.

Far too many people chase after the money. Don't get me wrong: money is good. But I've learned that if you will follow your heart, the money will follow you. Not always as quickly or as easily as you'd likely like. But when you love what you're doing, there's something special about how you do that work. In fact, you'll find yourself excited about getting up in the morning. You'll look forward to what the new day has in store for you.

Now is the time for all of us to go to another level—another level in the Kingdom. Another level in what we're here to do—your purpose. And just as people hold graduations to show we've progressed from one level to another, there are other levels in our walk with the Lord.

To many I say, it's time out for the elementary and time to move on up to the middle. For those in the middle, it's time for you to move on up to the higher level. For those in the higher, there is another level in higher. Just as it's a good thing to be promoted from one grade to the next, it's a good thing to be promoted in the work and the knowledge of the Lord.

May I have a "Word" with you? None of us should ever think we've arrived. We need to continue to learn more and more. And this goes for things associated with the natural world and those things that are spiritual. Don't ever think you know all there is to know, because you don't . . . and you won't. Continue to have a thirst and a hunger for knowledge and for righteousness. The more you know, the more you continue to grow. Paul said it best in Philippians 3:13-14. "Brethren, I count not myself to have apprehended: but this one thing I do, forgetting those things which are behind, and reaching forth unto those things which are before, I press toward the mark for the prize of the high calling of God in Christ Jesus."

Whether it's school, college, working, teaching, learning, doing, or working in the service of our Lord—on *this* earth, don't ever get comfortable with the thought that you have arrived. There is always another level.

And for those of us who have accepted Jesus, if we are faithful and faint not, we will reach that pinnacle where we'll one day receive our crown and hear the words, "Well done, my good and faithful servant."

But until then, continue to press. Another day, another week, another month, another year . . . another level. Keep pressing on!

We Are Family

amily is important. When you're going through something in life, it's good to have family there supporting you or at the very least, giving you love and encouragement. Same thing when things are going well. What is it to succeed or to acquire things if there's no one in which to share it with? So many people are hurting right now. And it's usually during these times that we turn to family.

May I have a word with you? When you don't know what to say to someone who's going through, just tell them that you love them. Tell them, and then show them by giving hugs and words of encouragement as needed.

One day Jesus was teaching. In Matthew 12:46-50 it says, "While he yet talked to the people, behold his mother and his brethren stood without, desiring to speak with him. Then one said unto him, Behold, thy mother and thy brethren stand without, desiring to speak with thee. But he (Jesus) answered and said unto him that told him, Who is my mother? and who are my brethren? And he stretched forth his hand toward his disciples, and said, Behold my mother and my brethren! For whosoever shall do the will of my Father which is in heaven, the same is my brother, and sister, and mother."

Okay, is anyone who's reading this shouting yet? I know the qualifier is whosoever shall do the will of my Father which is in heaven, and I know there are some whosoevers out there. That makes us family with Jesus! I am the oldest child in my family. In fact, on 08-08-08, I celebrated my 49th birthday. I had been excited about this date that whole year. I called it triple new beginnings (in Hebrew eight represents new beginnings). The Chinese look at the number eight as the sound for their Chinese word for prosper and wealth. That's why the Olympic Opening Ceremony was on 08-08-08 at 8:08 p.m. (On 08-08-18 I celebrated my 59th birthday, and if you're reading this close to 08-08-28, and I'm still around, it will be my 69th birthday.)

However, I digress here; back to being the oldest. When you're the oldest, you don't necessarily have anyone to take up for you, especially when you're young and people pick on you or want to mess with you. The oldest is normally the one who will stand up for the younger siblings. Yet, I had no older sibling; I was her. But then Jesus made me a "whosoever" who is now officially his little sister. And you know what that means!

It means if you mess with me, my Big Brother is going to take care of you. I don't have to worry about what people try to do; I tell Jesus, and He says He'll take care of it for me. Can't you just see Jesus, our big brother, going to these folks who are trying to hurt us and telling them, "Don't mess with my sister; don't mess with my brother. Because you see: When you mess with them, you're messing with me."

May I have a "Word" with you? "For whosoever shall do the will of my Father which is in heaven, the same is my brother, and sister, and mother." Are you doing the will of God? Are you? Are you? Are you one of the whosoevers Jesus is talking about? Then don't worry about those who don't do you right, those who try to lay a trap for you, those who walk into a place thinking they're better than you as they look down their noses at you (when clearly they're not better). At least they're not better than you in the eyes of our Big Brother. Somebody say JESUS!

From this day forward (if you haven't been doing it already or you haven't been doing it consistently), just tell your brother (Jesus) and don't you worry about it any longer. Jesus has made it abundantly clear. We are family. Trust me: Jesus has you *fully* covered!

Restorer of My Soul

eople are dealing with a lot these days. You don't have to look far to find someone needing something. You'll discover that even the rich aren't always happy with everything going on in their lives, bursting the myth that money makes people happy. The economy is said to be getting better, but for some, it feels like it won't be soon enough.

I must confess: I think a lot. And one thing I've learned is how much I have a heart for God's people. When I say God's people, I'm talking about the ones who have given their lives to Christ. I'm talking about those who are doing as much in their powers to give God all that they have. I'm talking of those who work day in and day out desiring to please God with every moment of their lives. But people are human and people get tired. Yes, our physical bodies tire out; and sometimes, spiritually, we feel wore down, if not out.

I want you to know that God cares about every aspect of your life. He loves you, and He cares. That's why so many people love the twenty-third Psalm. There is a reassurance and a comfort held within that Psalm, penned by a man after God's own heart. Psalm 23 begins by letting us know, "The Lord is my shepherd; I shall not want." God is our protector and our provider. No matter what we're going through, God is able to supply not only our needs, but our wants. The second verse tells us, "He maketh me to lie down in green pastures: he leadeth me beside the still waters."

When you get worn down and worn out, I dare say even prior to that, God will make you lie down, not on rocks, not on pine cones, not on straw, but in green pastures. There's something about pastures, but something really special about green pastures. A green pasture means there is life, but not just life, a newness of life. The second portion of that scripture addresses real peace in saying, "He leads me beside the still waters."

Oh, just imagine the sound of water. There are roaring waters that have great force. There are flowing waters that may not be as loud but can still be heard. Then there are the still waters: the water that causes you to feel at peace. They tell me that still waters also can run deep. God will lead you not in, but beside the still waters because He wants you to be at peace. No matter what you're going through right now, be at peace. Peace, be still.

The first part of verse 3 says, "He restoreth my soul." The prefix *re-* means again, anew, back. To restore means to bring into existence or use, reestablish; to bring back to an original condition. God restores our souls. God will bring you back anew, back to that refreshed condition. Oh, you remember back at the beginning when everything was brand new.

May I have a "Word" with you? You may be tired, you may feel worn out. You might even wonder if you're going to make it. But I want you to know that God restores your soul. "Restores" is present tense meaning continuously doing it. Galatians 6:9 admonishes us not to be weary in well-doing. I want to encourage you as you continue your walk *in* and *of* the service of God.

The Lord is your Shepherd. He knows that you have needs and wants and He cares about you. He cares. When chaos is all around you, God will make you to lie down in pastures of tender green grass. He will lead you beside still waters of rest.

Yes, God is the restorer of your soul!

Your Faithfulness

W e often talk about the faithfulness of God, but what about your faithfulness? Are you faithful? Can God count on you to do your assignment, even and especially during those times when no one knows all that you're doing?

You see, some people will do things if they know others will know or hear about what they're doing. They want credit and praise for anything that they do. They want people to acknowledge what they're up to . . . to make a big to-do about it. And if what they're set to do is a job that won't receive any recognition, they don't even care to perform that job or to perform that part of the job. But the job still needs to be done.

I'm talking about those people who would rather be the hostess rather than the person who cleans up; the person who would prefer to be out front instead of the one in the kitchen doing the cooking; the one who prefers to wear the outfit than to make or clean the outfit. But all of these things are needed. The question we should answer in all that we do is: What is my true motive? Why do I do what I do? Am I doing it with the right heart? How great is *my* faithfulness?

Colossians 3:23 tells us, "And whatsoever ye do, do it heartily, as to the Lord, and not unto men." If I were going to paint a chair, I need to paint that chair as though I was doing it for the Lord. That means: I don't need to half-do the job. I shouldn't beautifully paint only the parts that people can see. I need to paint underneath and the places that may end up covered up—places no one will likely ever look at or see. It's about integrity. Because whatever we do, in word or deed, we should do it heartily as to the Lord. We need to do it with our hearts set on doing our very best . . . for the Lord. We should address the areas no one may look at, realizing that God sees and knows all, and that God sees our hearts.

May I have a "Word" with you? We need to be faithful in what we're doing. We also need to be appreciative of others and their faithfulness to what they've been called to do. Every joint should be a supplying joint. There are truly no little jobs and big jobs, not really.

As Dr. King said, "If you're going to be a street sweeper, be the best street sweeper." Ask yourself: Can people count on me to do what I say I'm going to do? Can God count on me? Where is your heart when you're doing what you do? Do you have a "that'll do" attitude? Or are you approaching everything you say and do as though you're doing it for and unto the Lord?

Not unto men, but unto God. God is so faithful. We all need to step up our game, and note that God does see all. And realize that we will reap, in this life, what we sow!

In Search of Jesus

ow when Jesus was born in Bethlehem of Judea in the days of Herod the king, behold, there came wise men from the east to Jerusalem, Saying, Where is he that is born King of the Jews? for we have seen his star in the east, and are come to worship him." Matthew 2:1-2. I could just say "Amen" and end this right here.

When Jesus was born there came wise men. Wise men, wise women, wise people are wise because they recognize there is something special about Jesus and they want to be in His presence. Furthermore, wise people recognize who Jesus is and they want to come to worship him. You know, it's funny: What I've learned over years of being around and listening to people is just how much so many folks seem to be into themselves. It's amazing the number of people who tell me they have written or are writing a book and desire my help without ever having picked up or read one book I've written.

They don't even know if I can write or not. They don't care that I've gotten out there and worked hard at making this work. They're only interested in letting me know how it will be my great pleasure to be able to help them as they become the bestselling author of all times. In other words: It's all about them. Well, what I do is all about Jesus.

The wise men in these scriptures were respected in their own right. But when they realized a king had been born, they wanted to find him and to be a blessing to him. They weren't trying to find Jesus to see what He could do for them. They weren't trying to find him to show off. They wanted to find Jesus to worship Him, further proof of their wisdom. Well, there are many today who don't know Jesus.

They have lots of problems they're dealing with not knowing which way to turn. We, who know Jesus, know that He's a problem solver; that He is the calm in the midst of a storm; peace in chaos; joy in despair; strength in weakness. We, who know Jesus, know that He is a mind regulator through the craziness in this world. So . . . how many of us are pointing folks to Jesus?

Oh, sure. A lot of folks talk a good game. We can tell folks all these things from our heads. But when trials and troubles hit you, how do you react? You see, people *hear* more of what you do than what you say. You may say what the Lord is to you, but when the rubber meets the road and you have your cross to bear, how do you respond? Are you running around saying you don't know what you're going to do? Do you wring your hands and pace the floor trying to figure out how you're going to work it out? Or do you show, by your actions, that you trust God? That God is both willing *and* able.

May I have a "Word" with you? People are searching. They're in search of love. Are you pointing anyone to Jesus in the way you love? Or are you running folks away, not only from you, but from who you say you represent?

People are in search of peace. Are you showing how you have peace no matter what's going on around you? I'm talking about a peace that surpasses all understanding. The kind of peace that makes folks think you've lost your mind when you're not running around like a chicken with your head cut off. The kind of peace that will cause a person to say, "I don't know what you're on, but whatever it is, I want some of it!" Then you can say, "Oh, it's Jesus! I have Jesus in my life, and what a wonderful gift God gave us when He gave us Him."

Wise folks have Jesus. And wise folks know how great it is to be able to worship Him!

Finding Jesus

I cringe a little whenever I hear people say, "I found Jesus." Mostly because I pay attention to words and when you think about what these words are implying, it sounds like Jesus was lost and someone "found" Him. You know like: I lost my keys. Oh, here they are; I found them! Well, I understand what people mean when they say that. But just like those keys you claimed were lost, those keys were always there. You just didn't know where they were. Jesus has always been there. It's just some folks didn't know where Jesus was even though Jesus knew where He was all the time.

If you're saved now, you were still once lost. Yes, I know. Some folks believe they've always had it together only to learn later they really didn't. But God so loved the world that He knew one day you'd need to establish a connection with Him and His Kingdom. So God made a way for us to do just that through His Son, Jesus. But to make sure everything was done legally, this Son had to come through the earth just like the rest of us. Jesus was born of the Virgin Mary. I'm talking about Jesus—God's only begotten Son.

I can't tell you the exact day and month Jesus was born (although we celebrate His birth on December twenty-fifth). There are some who say it may have been in March; some say it was likely in September (because the shepherds were tending flocks in the field, and they wouldn't be doing that in the month of December). Honestly, as I've said in other writings, the exact date is not as important as the fact that Jesus was born!

Matthew 2:1-2 tells us, "Now when Jesus was born in Bethlehem of Judea in the days of Herod the king, behold, there came wise men from the east to Jerusalem. Saying, Where is he that is born King of the Jews? for we have seen his star in the east, and are come to worship him."

In the past, as still today, wise men seek Jesus. They were looking for Jesus even though Jesus wasn't the one lost. And because Jesus had a star that was "His" star—a star that indicated the birth of a king, the wise men were able to find Him. I have some Good News for you: Jesus came to earth and wise people do well to seek and to accept Him.

Matthew 2:10-11 tells of the wise men, "When they saw the star, they rejoiced with exceeding great joy. And when they were come into the house, they saw the young child with Mary his mother, and fell down, and worshipped him: and when they opened their treasures, they presented unto him gifts; gold, and frankincense, and myrrh."

When the wise men found Jesus, they fell down and worshipped Him. Jesus, the King of kings who wasn't sitting on any throne when they found Him, wasn't wearing a crown, and most likely at the time, living in a little rented house (not a palace). Yet, these men (who weren't religious people) recognized they were in the presence of a king and worshipped Him. Jesus—sent from Heaven to the earth by Almighty God as a gift to the world.

May I have a "Word" with you? For God so loved the world that He gave His only begotten Son, that whosoever believed on Him would not perish, but would have everlasting life. Again, Jesus was never lost. Mankind was the one lost. But in us "finding Jesus," we have found a Savior who is not only King of kings and Lord of lords, but awesome and powerful. Jesus Who, after we receive Him, calls us an heir and a joint-heir with Him. Jesus is waiting.

So tell me: Where exactly are you? No matter what time of the year, I say to you, "Merry *CHRIST*mas!"

As a Little Child

I know lots of people think children are cute, but Jesus put an even greater emphasis on them in Mark 10:13-14. "And they brought young children to him, that he should touch them: and his disciples rebuked those that brought them. But when Jesus saw it, he was much displeased, and said unto them, Suffer the little children to come unto me, and forbid them not: for of such is the kingdom of God."

The disciples thought they were right to rebuke those who brought the children to Jesus, but Jesus wanted to show just how important children are as well as what can be learned from them. Mark 10:15-16, Jesus says, "Verily I say unto you, Whosoever shall not receive the kingdom of God as a little child, he shall not enter therein. And he took them up in his arms, put his hands upon them, and blessed them."

As a little child.

Just reading these scriptures causes my heart to leap for joy. Jesus says we should receive the Kingdom of God as a little child. Then to see how Jesus took the children up in His arms (can't you just feel His arms around you when you need a spiritual hug?), put His hands upon them (Jesus cares what's going on in your life even as He sits on the right hand of the Father as our advocate and makes intercessions on our behalf), and Jesus blessed them.

Come as a little child. One great thing about children is they are eager and open to learn. I watched a four month old baby the other day, and it was more than apparent he had been talked to a lot. I watched this baby as he looked up into the face of the person who held him with excitement and occasional bursts of smiles. He was so loving and content.

But what was really interesting was watching this baby as he paid attention to his caregiver and others, trying to pick up on what he saw being done. At the time, he was learning how to talk by watching others talk. If we would come as a little child, paying attention to what Jesus did, learn to walk like Jesus, learn to talk like Jesus, and live our lives like Jesus and the Holy Spirit directs us, just think of how wonderful and content our lives would be.

May I have a "Word" with you? In these scriptures, someone brought the children to Jesus. People, bring the children and young people to Jesus. Stop putting up barriers in an attempt to keep them out. Then check yourself. Yes, I said CHECK YOURSELF. Have you gotten so grown that even God can't tell you anything anymore?

"Whosoever shall not receive the kingdom of God as a little child, he shall not enter therein." I know some of us think Jesus is talking about Heaven here, but what Jesus is talking about is the Kingdom of God "on earth, as it is in Heaven."

Presently, we are here on earth, and through scriptures, Jesus has repeatedly given us the keys to the Kingdom of God. We need to stop with the "I'm grown" mentality and come as a little child. Come open to receive the Word of God. Be excited. Trust God. That's how little children are: open, excited, teachable, and trusting. Depend on God for what you need.

Yes, God is our Father, and it's great having a Father who loves us and cares. Now trust Him completely. Allow Him to take you in His arms, place His hands on you, and bless you. Yes, just like a little child.

God Knows You

S ometimes when I speak to young people, I tell them that occasionally someone will or have told them negative things about themselves. I advise them when hearing negative comments to say (inside their minds), "You don't know me."

All of us, no matter our age, have had someone to put us down. Some people may have thought they were helping by "giving it to you straight" or by "telling you the real truth." But still, it may have been a putdown (possibly even a backhanded compliment). You know like: "I don't know about that. That's a hard thing to do, especially for you." In other words, I don't know if you have what it takes. Or "Who do you think you are?" Well, I know who I am, and so should you.

I know that people want to keep us from being hurt. I get that. They want us to be realistic in our goals and thinking. That's fine, and I understand that. But how many people have been stopped from even trying because they were told they were the wrong something or another to accomplish a thing? How many people would have succeeded in doing more with their lives had someone told them to go for it, and maybe told them why they *could* be just the one to do it whereas others were not?

Jeremiah 1:4-5 says, "Then the word of the Lord came unto me, saying, Before I formed thee in the belly I knew thee; and before thou camest forth out of the womb I sanctified thee, and I ordained thee a prophet unto the nations." Before you were a thought, God knew you. That should encourage somebody right there.

God has placed inside of you all that you need to do what you need to do. I often tell people, "You just need to work it out." By that I mean, something can be on the inside of you, but you have to work at bringing it out of you. You have to walk it out. Put action behind your talk. No one can pull out of you what God has put in you except you. Now, situations and people can force you to go inside and do what needs to be done. But you still must be the one to do it.

That's why it's important for you to go to the One who created you, and ask Him about you. God knows who you are. He knows you inside and out. God told Jeremiah that before He formed him in his mother's belly, before Jeremiah came out of the womb that He knew him, He sanctified him (which means to set aside), and He ordained Jeremiah a prophet. And not just any old prophet, but a prophet unto the nations.

As you read on, the first thing you'll see is Jeremiah telling God what's wrong with him, and why he can't do what God is saying that He can. "Then said I, Ah, Lord God! behold I cannot speak: for I am a child." My question to you is: When God is telling you who you are, what are you saying to contradict Him? When God tells you that you can do all things through Christ who strengthens you, are you trying to tell God just why you can't? When God is telling you that you are fearfully and wonderfully made, are you telling Him how deficient you really are? Are you arguing with God about whom God and His Word is telling you that you are?

May I have a "Word" with you? Before God formed you in your mother's belly, He knew you. That's powerful! God knows you. So the question is: When you argue for the negative about you when God is speaking the positive, who are you really arguing with?

God knows you. Find out what God says about you. Then hear ye the Lord!

Stir Up the Gift of God

*H*ave you ever prepared something that called for you to stir it? Maybe you've baked a cake . . . made icing for that cake. Possibly you put something on the stove that called for you to stir as it cooked to ensure that it didn't burn or turn out wrong. For sure, you may have made tea or the ever popular and always reliable (at least back in my day) Kool-Aid. You know: You put the content from the package into the pitcher, added sugar, then stirred. If you were to only put the Kool-Aid powder and the sugar in and didn't stir, the sugar would settle to the bottom and wouldn't absorb into the water and the powder would sit in the water but hardly mix well in it. To get the desired outcome from this process, you need to stir it up.

Second Timothy, chapter one, verse six tells us, "Wherefore I put thee in remembrance that thou stir up the gift of God, which is in thee by the putting on of my hands." Here we see the apostle Paul writing to his spiritual beloved son Timothy, a young man whom Paul stated in Second Timothy 1:5, "When I call to remembrance the unfeigned faith that is in thee, which dwelt first in thy grandmother Lois, and thy mother Eunice; and I am also persuaded that in thee also." Paul reminded Timothy to remember to stir up the gift of God. It sounds to me like this an ongoing process and not just a one-time thing.

Paul was telling Timothy to not allow what is needed to be done in order to receive the desired outcome to settle to the bottom or to find itself floating around somehow disconnected, but that he needed to stir up the gift of God. Then Paul went on to write in verse seven, "For God hath not given us the spirit of fear; but of power, and of love, and of a sound mind." Think about the order of this. First, remember to stir up the gift of God, then realize that God has not given you . . . me . . . us the spirit of fear; but of power and of love and of a sound mind.

In other words, don't say what you can't do, don't be afraid of whatever may be around the corner. Because once you stir up the gift of God, once you mix the gift God has placed inside of you with you, once you have stirred up the gift of God and caused that which may not have become an integral part of you the way it should be inside of you . . . the way God intends for it to be; once you have stirred up the ingredients inside that gift of God with you, you can do what needs to be done without any fear and with power and love. And you don't have to worry about losing your mind because your mind is sound.

May I have a "Word" with you? Lay hands on yourself if you have to and begin to minister to yourself, encourage yourself. Talk to yourself and tell yourself that inside of you there is a great gift, and that gift is the gift of God. Starting shouting and praising God, knowing that as you're doing this, you're stirring up the gift of God. Praise God so that what's on the inside of you becomes mixed with you the way God needs for it to be inside of you.

Then realize that you don't have to be afraid. That you *can* do all things through Christ who strengths you. Stir up the gift of God. Do it now and do it often. Keep the gift stirred up, then take care of the business God has commissioned you to do!

The Called with Purpose

I'm excited regarding calling and purpose. You see, we often quote the first half of Romans 8:28, "And we know that all things work together for good to them that love God" but there's more to that verse that states, "who are the called according to his purpose."

As an author, I pay close attention to words. I understand sentence structure and techniques. I know that a mere word as well as the arrangement of words in a sentence can totally change the meaning of a sentence. For instance, in Romans 8:28 (that last part I just emphasized above) there's the word "the" sitting right there. Some people read that scripture as "who are called according to his purpose" when it should be "who are *THE* called according to his purpose." Can you see the difference?

There is absolutely nothing wrong with being called. I believe I've been called to do what I do. In fact, I believe we all come here with a purpose. But there's something divinely special about being THE called. Whether you're walking in it or not, you are *the* called—called to a work in the Lord. My question is: What are you doing about it?

Romans 8:30 says, "Moreover whom he did predestinate, them he also called: and whom he called, them he also justified: and whom he justified, them he also glorified." The calling referred to in Romans 8:28 was before the creation of the world (see Ephesians 1:4). The called in verse 30 has a lot of past tense words in it (called, justified, glorified). So tell me, when it's comes to your purpose in God, what are you afraid of?

From God's point of view: It's already done. That's why we can move on to verse 31, "What shall we then say to these things? If God be for us, who can be against us?" There is so much I want to say here. However, I try hard to keep these writings down to a certain word count. I don't know about you, but God's Word is life to and for me. I love hearing what He has to say about me and to me.

I continue on to Romans 8:32, and I find myself shouting as I'm walking in my purpose—walking in my calling because it says, "He that spared not his own Son, but delivered him up for us all, how shall he not with him also freely give us all things?" Did you see that? It's in the Word. God loves us so much He didn't even spare His own Son, but delivered Him up for *us* and freely gives *us* all things. Somebody hold my computer keys, I'm about to shout right about here!

I am "*The* Called." You are "*The* Called."

May I have a "Word" with you? Don't be afraid to step out on faith. Trust that if God told you something, called you to something: He's more than able to bring it to past. I know you think people may be out to trip you up and keep you from what God has called you to do. But you have to buckle up and say it as it is written in Romans 8:37, "Nay, in ALL things we are more than conquerors through him that loved us."

Now gird up your loins, and move forward as *the called* who has been *called* with purpose.

Sufficient

I've had a few things on my mind these days. That's just being human. We think about things even when we know God is at the helm steering the ship. When I opened my eyes this morning, I heard, just as clear as someone physically whispering in my ear, "My grace is sufficient." Keep in mind now that I, as many of you, likely know this part of the scripture backward and forward. It's found in Second Corinthians 12:9 where it states, "And he said unto me, My grace is sufficient for thee: for my strength is made perfect in weakness. Most gladly therefore will I rather glory in my infirmities, that the power of Christ may rest upon me." Glory!

So when I heard, "My grace is sufficient," I said, "Lord, I know your grace is sufficient." He said, "No, you're not getting what I'm saying." That was when I felt a need to break down the words: My . . . grace . . . is . . . sufficient. These words spoken are those of Jesus. I'm talking about God the Son. "My" is Jesus saying it's His; He owns it. Whatever He's talking about, belongs to Him. My. Then there's the word *grace*.

Now this is what really stopped me. Not because I don't know what grace is (I learned the spiritual definition of grace when I was a young girl). Grace—God's unmerited favor. Unmerited, meaning you didn't earn it. But there's the word merited embedded in there, which means value, superior quality or worth, excellence. And what about this

113

definition of merit: "Spiritual credit granted for good works." I'm talking about favor.

In other words, we didn't earn it—Jesus did. So it belongs to Him. "My grace—My unmerited favor." Belonging to Jesus. And Jesus loves me enough, loves those who are His enough, to say that He knows you may not have enough (fill in the blank), you may be having a difficult time in areas of your life, sometimes it feels like whenever you take one step forward, somehow you're being knocked two steps back, *However,* Jesus says, "My grace is sufficient."

Sufficient. Sufficient: "Being as much as is needed." Glory to God, if you could just get what this scripture is saying to you, you would be shouting right now. Okay, it might look bleak, but Jesus is saying, "My grace is sufficient." Everything you need, God has it, and He's making it available to you. Need peace? God has it. Need joy? God's got it.

Wondering how you're going to pay that bill even though you've been working like crazy? Jesus has you covered. But you have to quit doubting God and what He can do. With our minds, we're always trying to figure things out when God worked it out before it was ever a problem for us. Yes, yes, I know you can quote the scripture about trusting in the Lord. But are you? Are you really? Can you rest in the sufficient grace of Jesus?

May I have a "Word" with you? There's a lot more in this scripture. And that is, "For my strength is made perfect in weakness." Whoa! Somebody hold my mule! Jesus' strength is *made* perfect. Do you know what kind of power we're talking about in Jesus' strength? And for Jesus to tell you that His strength is made perfect in weakness. Weakness is what we deal with. Weakness is what our minds go through when we can't see a way out. But Jesus strength—His power is *made* perfect in weakness.

Latch on to this and watch Jesus' grace. Glory in your infirmities that the power of Christ may rest upon you. Walk in peace knowing that, no matter what: Jesus' grace is sufficient!

Blessings in the Mouth

atthew 17:27 says, "Notwithstanding, lest we should offend them, go thou to the sea, and cast a hook, and take up the fish that first cometh up; and when thou hast opened his mouth, thou shalt find a piece of money: that take, and give unto them for me and thee." Matthew 4: 4 tells us, "But he answered and said, It is written, Man shall not live by bread alone, but by every word that proceedeth out of the mouth of God."

For all of you who have been searching for "The Secret," here's a secret for you: There are blessings in the mouth. Romans 10:8 clearly tell us, "But what saith it? The word is nigh thee, even in thy mouth, and in thy heart: that is, the word of faith, which we preach."

The word of faith: There are blessings in the mouth. The Word of God should forever be in your mouth, and you need to be speaking those things.

Many scriptures address the power the mouth can possess. One I've quoted before is, "Life and death is in the power of the tongue." And the tongue—it's in your mouth.

Matthew 17:24-27 speaks about tribute money or as most of us are familiar with: taxes. Every Jew over 20 years old was expected to contribute to the upkeep of the temple. Jesus told Peter where he could find a piece of money. A piece of money (the silver tetradrachma) was equivalent to the shekel, in other words, the exact amount of taxes for two persons. How awesome! Of all Jesus could have commanded done

115

to get this, he instructed Peter to cast a hook and catch a fish. Then when he caught the fish, he was told to open the mouth of the fish (not gut it), and he would find a piece of money.

The money was in the mouth. The blessing was in the mouth. Your money, your joy, your peace, abundance, blessings of life is in your mouth. But first, we must check our hearts. For Matthew 12:34-37 declares, "O generation of vipers, how can ye, being evil, speak good things? for out of the abundance of the heart the mouth speaketh. A good man out of the good treasure of the heart bringeth forth good things: and an evil man out of the evil treasure bringeth forth evil things. But I say unto you, That every idle word that men shall speak, they shall give account thereof in the day of judgment. For by thy words thou shalt be justified, and by thy words thou shalt be condemned."

People, be careful what you allow into your heart. Whatever is in your heart, when it comes out of your mouth—that's what will manifest in your life.

May I have a "Word" with you? Don't ever let it be said about you as James 3:10. "Out of the same mouth proceedeth blessing and cursing. My brethren, these things ought not so to be." Don't allow people and circumstances to cause you to use your mouth for anything except to bless God, bless others, and bless yourself.

The Bible tells us in Genesis when God created the world, "And God said . . . And it was so." Let this be your motivation and your assurance. HuMan was created in the image and likeness of God. Realize today there are blessings in the mouth.

Now open your mouth, and let's get those blessings out and into the world.

The Power of Now

ebrews 10:38 says, "Now the just shall live by faith: but if any man draw back, my soul shall have no pleasure in him." Hebrews 11:1 tells us, "Now faith is the substance of things hoped for, the evidence of things not seen." Hebrews 8:6, "But now hath he obtained a more excellent ministry, by how much also he is the mediator of a better covenant, which was established upon better promises." First Timothy 4:8 says, "For bodily exercise profiteth little: but godliness is profitable unto all things, having promise of the life that now is, and of that which is to come."

First John 3:2, "Beloved, now are we the sons of God, and it doth not yet appear what we shall be: but we know that, when he shall appear, we shall be like him; for we shall see him as he is." And Jude 1:24-25, "Now unto him that is able to keep you from falling, and to present you faultless before the presence of his glory with exceeding joy, To the only wise God our Saviour, be glory and majesty, dominion and power, both now and ever. Amen." Oh, the power of now.

So when is now?

Now is now. Not yesterday. Not the next second, minute, or hour. Not tomorrow. Now is truly the only time you ever really experience anything. Now is always . . . now.

I love Mark 11:24 because it tells us, "Therefore I say unto you, What things soever ye desire, when ye pray, believe that ye receive them, and ye shall have them." When? Now! This verse doesn't say after you pray. It didn't say when you see it show up then believe. It says, when you pray, believe that you receive them. When is right now, at that very moment. Faith is now. And *now*, the just shall live by faith.

Please know that there will be times in life when it may look like you prayed and nothing happened right then. But don't get discouraged. Believe that you have received it no matter what your reality may be showing you differently. Don't doubt. You see, doubt will kill a prayer or a request to God faster than any devil ever can.

That's how the devil defeats you—he causes you to doubt. Do you want to please God? Well, God's Word says, "Without faith it's impossible to please Him." Now faith is, and *IS* is present tense, meaning it's already done. When it comes to faith in God, know that when you ask God for whatsoever things you desire, it's done now. Not He's doing it or going to do it. It's done *now*.

Oh, I just love how God operates! He assures us that when we ask Him for something that's in His will (check the Bible to know His will; it's in there), it's done right then. Some people may say that what they prayed for is coming. But our God is a right now God. Just because you don't see it, doesn't mean He didn't do it.

May I have a "Word" with you? "Now faith is the substance of things hoped for, the evidence of things not seen." When you don't see it manifested yet, realize your faith is your evidence that it's already done. "Beloved, now are we the sons of God, and it doth not yet appear what we shall be: but we know that, when he shall appear, we shall be like him; for we shall see him as he is." Now *that's* the power of God's now.

And just in case you've never noticed this, the word "now" spelled backwards is "won." When you believe in God's now, then you've already won.

Blow the Trumpet; Crack the Clay (Part 1)

"hen I blow with a trumpet, I and all that are with me, then blow ye the trumpets also on every side of all the camp, and say, *The sword* of the Lord, and of Gideon." (Judges 7:18) Let me give you a little background leading to this verse. Gideon was a military and spiritual leader who destroyed his father's altar to Baal and erected an altar to the one true God. With 135,000 in their military, the Midianites (the descendants of one of the several children born to Abraham and Keturah) were oppressing the children of Israel. Gideon was an Israelite and the children of Israel were greatly outnumbered.

Impoverished because of the Midianites, the children of Israel cried out unto the Lord. Judges 6:8-10 explains, "That the Lord sent a prophet unto the children of Israel, which said unto them, Thus saith the Lord God of Israel, I brought you forth out of the house of bondage; And I delivered you out of the hand of the Egyptians, and out of the hand of all that oppressed you, and drove them out from before you, and gave you their land; And I said unto you, I am the Lord your God; fear not the gods of the Amorites, in whose land ye dwell: but ye have not obeyed my voice." An angel of the Lord appeared unto Gideon and Judges 6:14 relays how the angel told him to, "Go in this thy might, and thou shalt save Israel from the hand of the Midianites: have not I sent thee?"

Gideon was being sent into battle, but he was told by God (with a mere 32,000 men against the Midianites) that he had too many. Keep in mind this was after Gideon had asked God for several signs just to ensure God really was with them. Gideon did the fleece test. He specifically asked God to make the fleece of wool dry and the ground around it wet, then switched it around just to be sure this was really God (sound familiar?).

After God, who showed His patience with Gideon during this fleece-testing time, convinced Gideon that what He was saying was true; Gideon gathered the men and they pitched beside the well of Harod on the mount of Gilead. That was when God told Gideon, with 32,000, he had too many men. Gideon was instructed to let all who were fearful and afraid, go home. Twenty-two-thousand of the thirty-two-thousand men left! This lets us know God doesn't need fearful people fighting in His army or hanging around those who will be fighting.

So now it's 10,000 men against 132,000. God tells Gideon again he still has too many. Can't you just see Gideon saying, "What?" But when God instructed Him to bring them down to the water where he was to set aside those who lapped the water with their tongues from those who bowed down upon his knees to drink, God told Gideon to keep those who lapped (300), putting their hands to their mouths. You see, God is looking for people who will trust Him totally and without fear when hearing His Word.

I find it interesting how God chose those who put their hands to their mouths. Judges 7:8 (a) says, "So the people took victuals in their hand, and their trumpets." The mouth is a powerful instrument, much like a trumpet which can make a pretty loud noise itself.

May I have a "Word" with you? God is looking for people who will trust Him without a spirit of fear. Fear can be contagious which is why God was not interested in those who were fearful hanging around to fight a battle that wouldn't require physical strength to win. When in warfare, we must trust (without question) God and trust that He will do what He says He'll do.

There is a time to speak, a time to put your hand over your mouth, and a time to blow the trumpet. In part two, we'll see what God has to say about blowing the trumpet. But first, let's be certain we've gotten rid of any fear that may be hanging around to hinder us in our victory.

Blow the Trumpet; Crack the Clay (Part 2)

*P*reviously, we were looking at Gideon with 300 men set to go up against an army of 135,000. One thing I've learned is that we must put a watch over our mouths as we fight various battles. As Ecclesiastes 3:1 tells us that there is a time to every purpose under the heavens. And yes, there is a time when we should keep quiet and there's a time when we should blow the trumpet.

In Judges 7:16-18, regarding Gideon, it states, "And he divided the three hundred men into three companies, and he put a trumpet in every man's hand, with empty pitchers, and lamps within the pitchers. And he said unto them, Look on me, and do likewise: and, behold, when I come to the outside of the camp, it shall be that, as I do, so shall ye do. When I blow with a trumpet, I and all that are with me, then blow ye the trumpets also on every side of all the camp, and say, *The sword* of the Lord, and of Gideon."

I'd like to focus on the trumpet and the pitcher. Let's look at the trumpet as being our mouths and the pitcher (made out of clay) as being our bodies. Gideon told the men when he blew his trumpet for them to blow their trumpets. Through this whole process, Gideon was being directed by God. This is so important. We need to be certain if we're following anyone, that they're hearing and getting their directions from God.

As the story goes, Gideon and his men gathered outside of the camp of their enemies. They blew their trumpets then broke the pitchers they were holding in their hands. Judges 7:20 says, "And the three companies blew the trumpets, and brake the pitchers, and held the lamps in their left hands, and the trumpets in their right hands to blow withal: and they cried, The sword of the Lord, and of Gideon."

Remember when I said the pitcher represents us (our bodies as clay)? Well, in this telling of Gideon and his men, inside their individual pitchers were light. When we accept Jesus into our lives, inside our individual clay pitchers (us), Light resides. Gideon and his men broke their pitchers and the light was then revealed. There may be times in our life-walk where we find ourselves broken.

At the time, being broken may seem and feel like a bad thing. But what I've learned about God is: He will always take what was meant for our bad and use it for our good. Sometimes God needs our pitchers to become broken. So whether we break our own pitchers (deny the clay called our bodies) or find ourselves broken at the hands of another, it's a perfect opportunity for God's Light to shine.

May I have a "Word" with you? There are times when we need to be quiet. There are times when we need to blow our trumpet, and times when we need to shout "The Sword of the Lord" (God's Word). And yes, there are times when we may need to break the pitcher that contains the Light of the Lord, hold up that Light, and let God's Light shine brightly. As in the case with Gideon and his men, this type of action can confuse the enemy and cause the enemy to turn on themselves and/or to flee. So take a page from Gideon's fight.

Blow your trumpet at the appropriate time, crack the clay pitcher, let your light so shine, then watch God as He continues to demonstrate that the battle is not ours, but truly His.

This Little Light of Mine

"No man, when he hath lighted a candle, covereth it with a vessel, or putteth it under a bed; but setteth it on a candlestick, that they which enter in may see the light." Luke 8:16. Just the other night, there was a big storm that came through and totally knocked out the power. Unfortunately, this has happened quite a lot lately, even times where we've been without power for as long as three days.

When the lights go out at our house at night, I immediately light a candle. I notice that no matter how large the room is and how small the candle may be, that little light always, always makes a difference. I've heard from a few people who were reading one of my novels when their lights went out, and they've admitted to using their candle to continue reading because they couldn't put my book down. I confess to having done this myself when I was trying to finish edits on one of my books.

But what happens when a lit candle is covered up with an object or placed under the bed (not even counting how dangerous putting a candle under a bed could be)? When a candle is hidden, the light doesn't make the difference it makes when it's out in the open; and even better, lifted up on a candlestick.

This is how light works: it dispels the darkness only when given the chance. This is how our light must be. But it's not necessarily our personal lights we want to shine, but the Light of Jesus that shines in us. Our goal should be to lift up Jesus and let His Light *so* shine.

Getting back to my analogy of when the light is out in our homes. We find that one light can be carried with us as we move. If available, most of us will light various candles throughout other areas of the house where needed. But if you only have the one light, you take that one with you from room to room, from place to place.

This is how we should carry the Light of Jesus that resides in us. Leaving your Light at home when you're out and about, whether you're at work, school, fellowshipping or just hanging out with others, doesn't help dispel the darkness. From this day forward, consider yourself the candlestick that holds up the Light. The Bible tells us that if we will lift Jesus up, He will draw all men unto Him. We need to hold up the Light of Jesus and let His Light shine.

May I have a "Word" with you? At times, this world can be so dark. But we have the solution. Jesus is the Light of the World, and we must stop being shy, embarrassed, timid, or simply complacent when it comes to sharing this Light with the world. The world desperately needs this Light. Are you letting your Light shine or are you hiding your Light under a vessel or under the bed?

And if life for you continues to be dark, then I would encourage you to ensure, first of all, that your Light is lit. Then and only then, can you let your little Light shine. You'll be surprise at what a little light can do to the darkness.

Darkness cannot contend with the Light. And that's a scientific and spiritual fact!

The Power of God

nd when the sabbath was past, Mary Magdalene, and Mary the mother of James, and Salome, had bought sweet spices, that they might come and anoint him. And very early in the morning the first day of the week, they came unto the sepulcher at the rising of the sun. And they said among themselves, Who shall roll us away the stone from the door of the sepulcher? And when they looked, they saw that the stone was rolled away: for it was very great." Mark 16:1-3

Jesus had been crucified. He was buried in a sepulcher which was a cave hewn out of a rock with a huge stone covering the entrance. Rolling the stone into its slot had been relatively easy as reported in Mark 15:46. But moving it away would have required the power, the strength of several men. Jesus was crucified on a Friday.

When the evening was come that Friday, preparation for the Sabbath (Saturday) was to begin. Because of this timing, Jesus' body could not be properly taken care of for burial. Jesus' body had been given to Joseph of Arimathea (an honorable counselor) who had come boldly to Pilate and asked for Jesus' body to bury Him. Joseph had bought fine linen, took Jesus down, and wrapped him in this linen, laying him in the sepulcher. This is the same Jesus who was born in a stable (a cave), wrapped in swaddling clothes, and laid in a manger.

Sunday morning, the women were on their way to properly prepare Jesus' body with sweet spices, and they were discussing among themselves how they would move the stone. Yes, I dare say we all know a little something about huge stones blocking our way. Our thoughts begin to concentrate on how to move our stone out of the way. Mark 16:4 says, "And when they looked, they saw that the stone was rolled away: for it was very great."

Okay, they were on a mission. Here's the difference in these women and some of us. They knew there was an obstacle in their way that they couldn't handle in their own strength, their own power. But they didn't let that deter them from taking steps toward their goal. Why didn't they ask a few men to come along with them? I can't say for sure, but I suspect it's because many of the men who should have been listening to Jesus and what He'd been saying about rising from the dead, were MIA (Missing in Action).

Jesus told them He would rise on the third day. Even the women on their way to the gravesite didn't really seem to have believed that, since they were preparing to take care of the dead. Still, they went, and upon arriving, found the stone was moved! Already done!

By faith, you need to take the necessary steps toward your goal and trust in the power of God and not your own power. Trust that the stone you're concerned about, God will cause to be rolled away. But the true power of God is that when the women reached the sepulcher and stepped inside, Jesus was not there. Yes, the stone was moved, but God had raised Jesus from the dead! Now, that's power. The power of God!

May I have a "Word" with you? Is there anything too hard for God? Is there anything too hard for the power of God? Know this: God is able to do exceeding, abundantly above all you can ask or think. If God raised Jesus from the dead, then what is your problem to Him? What is your problem when it comes to the power of the Almighty God?

Stop worrying. Turn it over to God. There's nothing too hard for the power of God!

Unbelief

"And he went out from thence, and came into his own country; and his disciples follow him. And when the sabbath day was come, he began to teach in the synagogue: and many hearing him were astonished, saying, From whence hath this man these things? and what wisdom is this which is given unto him, that even such mighty works are wrought by his hands? Is not this the carpenter, the son of Mary, the brother of James, and Joses, and of Judah, and Simon? and are not his sisters here with us? And they were offended at him. But Jesus said unto them, A prophet is not without honor, but in his own country, and among his own kin, and in his own house. And he could there do no mighty work, save that he laid his hands upon a few sick folk, and healed them." Mark 6:1-5

I'm sure you've heard the saying about a prophet not being known or a prophet being without honor in his own country. I hear a lot from people who live in a place or lived in a place and find that they don't receive the kind of support that they do when the visit other places. Places where people have never heard of them before. But Jesus knows; He understands. Jesus was the one who made this statement recorded here in Mark.

People who know you or grew up around you sometimes don't appreciate what God has placed inside of you. Here was Jesus who was causing the lame to walk, the deaf to hear, raised one from the dead, being a blessing to those who had lost hope. And those who knew Him "when" were essentially questioning who did He think He was.

They were questioning who Jesus thought He was. But note, and you'll see, that it wasn't Jesus Who was losing out because of their unbelief. It was the people who needed what Jesus had to give that were missing the blessings they could have experienced. Mark 6:6, "And he marveled because of their unbelief. And he went round about the villages, teaching." Because of the people's unbelief, no mighty work could be done. Jesus healed a few sick folk, but imagine what could have been done had more believed.

I want to encourage someone. God has called you to do something extraordinary, but you're afraid of what people will say. You may even be thinking about your past and feel people won't be able to get past your past. Unbelief robs everyone concerned. It robs people from the blessing God has for them. Why? Because faith works.

You have to believe what God has spoken into your life. Believe that God can and will do what He said He would. Believe God will never leave you nor forsake you. Don't let unbelief keep you from God's best. Don't let unbelief rob you of the blessings God has for you.

May I have a "Word" with you? When God sends someone with a Word for you, a blessing for you, don't miss it because of unbelief. Don't let the messenger who's bringing it keep you from receiving the message being brought.

And if you're the one whom God has given a Word to do something, don't get bogged down in those who refuse to receive you. If they don't want to hear you, if they don't want what God has given you to bless them with, it's their loss. Shake the dust from your feet and keep going. I don't see Jesus sticking around trying to make these people receive what He had to give. There are people out there who *will* appreciate what God has given you. There's too much work to be done!

Shake off the dust, smile, and keep on pressing! Whether you're the giver or the possible receiver, don't allow unbelief to rob you of blessings!

Do You Really Believe?

*H*ave you ever heard: Seeing is believing? There are some people who won't believe a thing unless they see it with their own eyes. Jesus was crucified and it was told to Thomas that Jesus had risen from the dead. John 20:24-25 says, "But Thomas, one of the twelve, called Didymus, was not with them when Jesus came. The other disciples therefore said unto him, We have seen the Lord. But he said unto them, Except I shall see in his hands the print of the nails, and put my finger into the print of the nails, and thrust my hand into his side, I will not believe."

Imagine Thomas being close to the Lord and hearing that He was not dead but had risen. Then you hear others saying they'd seen Him, but you think this must be some trick.

Thomas wanted to do more than just see, he wanted to put his finger into the print of Jesus' hand where He was nailed to the cross. He wanted to check out Jesus' side where He was speared in the side. Just writing this brings tears to my eyes and a joy to my heart as I think on all that Jesus did for not just me, but for you to pay a debt we owed that we could never pay. Excuse me for a minute while I thank and praise God right now!

John 20:26-27 goes on to state, "And after eight days again his disciples were within, and Thomas with them: then came Jesus, the doors being shut, and stood in the midst, and said, Peace be unto you. Then saith he to Thomas, Reach hither thy finger, and behold my hand,

and thrust it into my side: and be not faithless, but believing." After seeing Jesus and being able to touch Him, Thomas then believed. But the question now is: Do you believe? I mean do you *really* believe?

You see, there are some people who say they believe just to "hedge their bets" if I might put it this way. They have decided to accept that Jesus died and arose "just in case" what the Bible says turns out to be true. To elaborate: Just in case at the end of this life there really is a Judgment Day; and the question comes down to a person having accepted Jesus, believing in His death, burial, and resurrection. They want to make sure they're covered.

But my question to you today is: Do you really believe that Jesus died, but more importantly, that He rose on that third Jewish Day? Do you believe Jesus ascended to His Father in Heaven, and do you believe that the same way He left, He's coming back again? Or are you the least bit like Thomas, and you have to see it to really believe it?

May I have a "Word" with you? Do you believe? Do you have faith? Hebrews 11:1 says, "Now faith is the substance of things hoped for, the evidence of things not seen." Hebrews 11:6 says, "But without faith it is impossible to please him: for he that cometh to God must believe that he is, and that he is a rewarder of them that diligently seek him."

You see: I can't physically see Jesus sitting on the right hand of God, but I believe this. I didn't physically see Jesus being crucified, buried, then rise from the dead; but I believe this. I haven't physically put my hand in the print where He was nailed to the cross and pierced in the side; and yet, I believe. But I don't physically see air either, yet I know it's there.

When it comes to salvation, I draw much comfort from the words of Jesus to Thomas from John 20:29, "Jesus saith unto him, Thomas because thou hast seen me, thou hast believed: blessed are they that have not seen, and yet have believed." I believe and, by the words of Jesus Himself, I am blessed.

What say you?

Been Through It

Sometimes I'll write something on Facebook, and it will strike a chord. I went to visit my daddy one Father's Day as I do every Father's Day (since writing this, my father passed away April 30, 2018). While there, my sister, Danette, and I started one of our running discussions on cell phones. You see, I had a pretty inexpensive cell phone (okay, it was cheap) while she generally always has the top of the line. It has become a recurring joke in our family because everyone knows that if I wanted to, I could get a more up-to-date phone, expensive phone. I just don't seem to want to.

While discussing our cell phones, my daddy picked up his cordless phone. "This little phone is a good little phone," he said. Now see, my daddy says that a lot about that same little phone. We've heard him talk about it before, not because he forgets he's said it. In his seventies (at the time), my daddy's mind is sharper than most people in their teens. Daddy just happened to love that one particular phone. The thing about the phone is: it's been dropped in a bucket of water when he was working outside in his vegetable garden on the patio; it's been run over by his mobile scooter; and even struck by lightning.

Daddy has glued it back together with gorilla glue, taped it, and regardless of the fact that he's been given lots of newer and better cordless phones (in all of our opinions); he still loves that old beat-up phone.

So, as he sat there on Father's Day with a newer phone clipped to his shirt, he held up the phone he lovingly cradled in his hand. "This is a good phone here," he said. "It's been through a lot, but it's still the best phone I have." My daddy was bragging about a phone that wasn't pretty by any means at this point, had been through a lot for sure. But it was still here, still doing what it was put on this earth to do—no matter what it's been through, no matter how beat up it appeared on the outside.

I couldn't help but to think about us. How many of us have been through a lot? Been dropped in the water, run over by the things of life, struck by lightning when the storms have rolled through our lives? But God, in His loving mercy, picked us up and dusted us off. God looked us over, and where we needed it, he glued us back together again. If it called for it, He taped us to hold us together.

And when others would have strongly advocated it was time we be put away, that our usefulness was over, God has held us up, and declared our benefits to the world—declared how great we really are in His sight. What a wonderful God we serve!

May I have a "Word" with you? God loves you. God is the potter and we are the clay. When we find ourselves broken, God has put us back together again and used us as He has told the world just how much He truly loves us. When others would put you down, God brags on how fearfully and wonderfully made you are.

That's why you have to keep going; because God believes in you. He believes in what you still have in you, to do what He has called you to do. And one of these days, when it's time; I don't know about you, but I want to hear the Lord say, "Well done, my good and faithful servant. You have been faithful over a few things. Come on up higher. I'm going to make you ruler over many."

Yes, you may have been through it, but God will continue to raise up a standard. And God will continue to lift you up, as long as you lift up the name of Jesus!

Encouraging Yourself

Who are you waiting on to tell you that you have a gift, that you have a purpose on this earth? Who are you waiting on to encourage you? In Deuteronomy chapter 3, verses 26-27, Moses speaks of how the Lord was angry with him on the people's account and would not hear him. The Lord said to Moses, "Let it suffice thee; speak no more unto me of this matter."

God told Moses he could go to the top of Pisgah which was a mountain, to look in all direction with his eyes, but Moses would not go over this Jordan. In verse 28, God tells Moses, "But charge Joshua, and encourage him, and strengthen him; for he shall go over before this people, and he shall cause them to inherit the land which thou shalt see."

God told Moses to encourage Joshua.

But in First Samuel 30:6, David, a man after God's own heart was greatly distressed. You see the people were talking about stoning him, because the soul of all the people was grieved, every man for his sons and for his daughters. But the end of verse six says, "but David encouraged himself in the Lord his God."

Just as David discovered, there will be times when no one is either there to encourage you or if they're there, they won't encourage you. You'll have to encourage yourself. But not just encourage yourself, encourage yourself in the Lord your God. That means you need to know what God has to say about you and about the situation.

The problem with many of us is that we don't know what God says about us. We don't know who God says we are in Him. It's in our darkest hours when we recall what God says that God's Word will see us through. But how can you recall what you don't know?

There's merit in knowing that it's okay to encourage yourself. Often when we meet people who seem confident in who they are, we call them arrogant. Trust me, I know and have met more than my share of arrogant people. The difference in arrogance and confidence can often be found in people who think it's all about them and what they can do (the arrogant folks) and those who will let you know it's all about God and what He can do.

It's about Christ who saved us in His dying and being raised up. It's about what we can do through Christ, whose mind we have, and whose strength we use. It's about Jesus in Whom we live, move, and have our being. My confidence is in the Word. Yes, the Word found written in the Holy Bible. But even more so in that Word that became flesh!

May I have a "Word" with you? Stop letting the things of life get you down. Stop allowing people who would like nothing more than for you to go somewhere and sit down to discourage you from either trying or continuing on. Press toward the mark in Christ Jesus. And as you put one foot in front of the other, encourage yourself. Say what God says about you. Yes, yes! You *are* fearfully and wonderfully made. Yes, you can do all things through Christ Jesus. Yes, God did call you and He has equipped you for the journey you're on.

Learn to do your part, encourage yourself when others don't or won't, and let's run on and see what the end is going to be. Oh, that's right! Jesus has already gone to take care of that. He's preparing a place for us right now. We just need to do what He's called us to do.

Ready, set, go! Encourage yourself!

Only Believe

*L*et me set the stage. Having spoken, Jesus has just come from one side on a ship, and there were many who gathered around him when he reached the other side. Mark 5:22-23 tells us, "And behold, there cometh one of the rulers of the synagogue, Jairus by name; and when he saw him, he fell at his feet, and besought him greatly, saying, My little daughter lieth at the point of death: I pray thee, come and lay thy hands on her, that she may be healed; and she shall live." What powerful jewels we find in these verses.

Here's a father who loves his child very much. She's sick, and according to him, at the point of death. This man didn't care what it looked like to anyone else. He found Jesus and, recognizing there was no other hope except in Jesus; he fell down at Jesus' feet (a sign of worship). Jairus told Jesus what was going on, then asked specifically what he wanted. Is anyone getting this already?

Look: Jairus quickly found Jesus, fell down at His feet, told Him the problem, then specifically asked for what he wanted, which was to "Come and lay your hands on her that she may be healed and she shall live." What faith!

I know some of you have asked for things in Jesus' name, and it may not have or be looking like it's working out for you. Someone may have told you later that it didn't happen because you didn't have enough faith. But let's look at what occurred with Jairus; and see if we can't mine deeper things at work, find encouragement for our own situations.

As Jesus was on His way to help this man with his problem, there were others pushing, also trying to get their needs met. Now, I know you're probably more than familiar with the story of the woman who had the issue of blood for twelve years. You've been encouraged by the miracle that occurred. There she was trying to get to Jesus, pressing her way through, having to fight through the crowd of people. But she was determined and even said to herself that if she could just touch his garment (in another recanting of this story it says the hem of His garment), she believed she would be whole.

On the flipside, can't you feel the desperation this father seeing how long it's taking Jesus to move, the realization that every second loss is detrimental to the possible saving of his daughter. Just imagine what he was likely thinking every time Jesus stopped when they were so close. Seeing Jesus stop to inquire who touched Him with all these people surrounding Him, this father knowing if they don't hurry it could be too late for his child. Then the news he was dreading: "Thy daughter is dead. Why trouble the Master any further?"

But they didn't understand at the time just how the Kingdom of Heaven principle works. You see with Jesus it's never too late. Oh, you may give up because you see things as it is. You may start speaking negative things because in your way of viewing things, it's over. You say you're just "keeping it real." You may even become afraid. But look at what Jesus did when the negative talk began to rear its ugly head. He immediately stepped in as soon as He heard the word spoken that was contrary to what Jairus had spoken with such clarity and faith and simply said, "Be not afraid, only believe."

Powerful! Only believe. This is what Jesus had to say in the face of what appeared to all around Him to be hopeless. Only believe. This is the Word that's being spoken to you right now as you're getting that negative report about your situation. Only believe.

May I have a "Word" with you? God knows you get discouraged. He knows you're up against thoughts that may tell you you're not going to win, that you can't do this, or that God is able to do all things; leaving you to ask, "But will He do it for me?"

Let me say this: Choose to hear and believe the Word of the Lord. What Jesus said to Jairus and what I believe we can stand on can be found in Mark 5:36, "Be not afraid, only believe." Only is a powerful word. Only believe. Don't worry about the chatter you may hear in and around you. Don't worry about who supports you or who doesn't. Don't worry about what others may think you can or cannot do. Only believe.

Pregnant With Purpose

*I*saiah 61:1 states, "The Spirit of the Lord God is upon me; because the Lord hath anointed me to preach good tidings unto the meek; he hath sent me to bind up the brokenhearted, to proclaim liberty to the captives, and the opening of the prison to them that are bound." Verses 2-3 continues letting you know the good tidings of salvation of which Jesus read from this scroll of Isaiah in the New Testament when He was in the temple.

All of us here have something placed inside of us that we brought with us to this earth. Now, not all of us are doing what we're here to do. But you do have something placed inside of you to do for the Kingdom of God. I spoke on this subject at a church in Oneonta, Alabama, and God gave me a powerful Word (too much to write it all here).

Let me say this: Some of you are pregnant with gifts, talents, ministry, peace, joy, healing, praise, dreams, goals, purpose, and the Word of God. You know God has placed "this" inside of you. And you know that God is the Father of this wonderful gift. To be pregnant means to "be expecting." So my first question to you is: Are you expecting? Since your encounter with the Lord, are you expecting?

In today's high technology world, we have all kinds of wonderful equipment that help during our time of expectancy. One technology that's quite popular during pregnancy is the ultrasound machine. Ultrasound produces a picture of what you can't see with the use of sound. The baby (or thing in the case of tumors) inside of you is able to be seen by use of sound that produces a picture. Well, in the spiritual realm, we have spiritual ultrasounds. The Bible tells us that faith comes by hearing and hearing by the Word of God.

Okay, let me do this again.

Faith comes by hearing (sound) and hearing produces the picture of that which you can't physically see . . . yet! We get our spiritual ultrasounds based on the sound of the Word of God. No one can see what we are carrying inside of us, but we're pregnant with what God has given us. And when we want to show others our evidence of our pregnancy, of what we are carrying inside, our ultrasound photo is produced by our faith. By faith, we're able to see what can't be seen as yet by the natural eye.

May I have a "Word" with you? What are you hearing? What is your "hearing" producing? Are you pregnant with purpose? Are you expecting from the Lord? If so, what does your spiritual ultrasound show?

People of God, faith comes by hearing and hearing by the Word of God. That good and that perfect gift inside of you, God placed that gift inside of you. That talent, that ministry, that dream, that goal, that purpose, that Word, if God is the Father; He says He'll be there with you as you prepare and deliver and even after that.

So what are you doing to prepare for a healthy delivery of this gift? What picture shows up on your ultrasound?

What Are You Here To Do?

I f any man serve me, let him follow me; and where I am, there shall also my servant be: if any man serve me, him will my Father honor. Now is my soul troubled; and what shall I say? Father, save me from this hour: but for this cause came I unto this hour." John 12:26-27.

Whether you know it or not, we all have a purpose on this earth. It matters not the circumstance or situation into which you were born. If you're here right now, you came here with a purpose. The problem is many people may not think about what their purpose is. Let me ask you: Why are you here? What are you here to do?

Jesus knew His purpose and the reason He was born. He was born to give His life for our sins. He was born to bridge the gap back to us and our Father in Heaven. Just know that what you are called to do may not always be easy. We can see where even Jesus struggled knowing what His purpose would entail. Still, Jesus said, "For this cause came I unto this hour." Then Jesus fulfilled His purpose. God was with Him, and Jesus accomplished all that He came here to do.

God is with you, and you'll be able to accomplish what He has purposed you to do. But we have to do our part. We must trust that even when it looks like we're losing, God has already fixed it, if we'll but trust in Him as we do it.

All of us get discouraged along this earthly journey. I know this for myself. Jesus knows because when He walked on this earth, He experienced the things we experience even today. He knows what it is to be opposed by people who don't want you to succeed. He knows what it is to not be accepted by those who knew you as they look back and bring up your history and don't see your God-ordained purpose. Jesus knows what it is to be mocked, to be mistreated, to be betrayed, to be abandoned. Still, Jesus did what He was here to do, and He allowed God to take care of the rest.

May I have a "Word" with you? You are here for a purpose. Don't allow anyone to tell you anything different from this. Like the seeds we plant in the earth, God has placed inside of you all that you need to do all that you need to do. Trust in God's ability. Trust that God has your back. What are you here to do? If you don't know, go to the one who created you and ask Him. Then walk toward that purpose without fear, without hesitation, and trusting God all the way. God is faithful.

And it's okay to let God know those times you get discouraged or when you're having challenges as you move in your purpose. God understands, and He's right there listening. Then you need to gird yourself up, and keep moving toward your purpose.

Someone is waiting on your gift. Someone is praying for what you have to offer. God is with you. In the end, you'll be victorious!

Proverbs – ProVerbs

My mind tends to look at things from a different angle than is normally done. I love words. I love the power of words. I suppose you can say I get that from my Father in Heaven. After all, in Genesis one, there is the account of the creation. Several times we see: "And God said" as things were being created. The flipside was after those things were said, the Bible tells us, "And it was so."

When I looked at the word "Proverbs" my mind started working. Pro verbs is what I saw. Now, the basic meaning of the Hebrew word for proverb (mashal) is comparison. In the book of Proverbs, the word proverbs is used to refer to a concise statement of principle. What I'd like to do is look at proverbs as verbs or words that are *for* you, which is what the prefix *pro* can mean. Pro verbs: verbs for you.

People have a tendency to focus on the negative much too much. They say, "I can't do this" or "I can't do that." Can't is a negative verb. I'd like to call this type negative: converbs. The prefix "con" means against. Also when I think of con, I think of a scam to deceitfully take away something from another. Words that speak against what God says we can do, be, and have is a con attempting to take away or scam those who are entitled to a Godly inheritance out of their inheritance. Proverbs 18:21 tells us, "Death and life are in the power of the tongue: and they that love it shall eat the fruit thereof."

Satan knows the power God has given you whether you know it or not, the power of the tongue. I've said this before and I'll say it again: Satan really doesn't have any power. He's an imitator and a deceiver stripped of power. That's why he needs you to speak negative things in your life. He'll put thoughts in your mind, but he needs your voice (the power of the tongue) to set things in motion.

Satan knows Jesus took back and arose with all power in His hand. He knows that Jesus gave that power to us. If Satan is to wreak havoc, cause problems, distress, trouble, discouragement, or stop you, then he needs your help. Satan needs your assistance in order to turn "pro verbs" into "con verbs." He needs you to speak those things that don't line up with what God says in order to take you down or, if possible, take you out of here so at least you can't influence others in a Godly way.

May I have a "Word" with you? When the Bible says, "I can do all things through Christ who strengthens me," then I believe that. I step into the pro verbs of "can." When the Bible says "I am blessed coming in and blessed going out, that I am the head, that I am above only, that I am more than a conqueror" then I believe I am that. When the Bible says to speak those things that be not as though they were, then I'm going to "speak" as though they have already happened.

In the Bible, the book of Proverbs is a great place to visit. In fact, there are thirty-one chapters in Proverbs. Why not read one chapter a day and see just how *pro* verbs can impact your life.

There's a lot of wisdom in Proverbs, and there's lots of power in pro verbs! "A merry heart doeth good like a medicine: but a broken spirit drieth the bones." That's Proverbs 17:22.

Get into the Word of God and find out what God has to say about you. Then live life like what God says is really true.

Seasons (Part 1 of 3)

I have spoken at a few churches recently where they used scriptures taken from Ecclesiastes chapter three for their theme. I always pray about what God would have me to speak on before I step one foot in anyone's door. There have been times where God has turned things a totally different way from the normal way you might expect it to be brought. This is the case with Ecclesiastes 3:1 which states, "To every thing there is a season, and a time to every purpose under the heaven."

Most of us have heard this scripture. You may even be able to quote it by heart. For the most part, people generally approach this scripture with the four seasons in mind: fall, winter, spring, and summer. The first time I spoke on this, God gave me a different way to come at seasons.

The word season can be defined as: a time characterized by a particular circumstance. It can also be one of the four quarters of which a year is divided. In addition, season can be something to give food more flavor or zest. Or it can mean to treat (as wood or a skillet) so as to prepare it for use, to make fit by experience. I plan to address all of these before I'm done. But in the space I'm allowed at this time, I'll break it down into separate pieces.

The first time I spoke on this, God had me to address the word season from the standpoint of giving flavor to by adding season. You know what I'm talking about: what we do to make something taste better. If you're cooking collard greens, some of you may add a little ham hock along with salt and pepper to your mix. Those who are health-conscious and trying to eat right may add olive oil in place of grease-laden additives like bacon and ham-type products as well as salt, sea salt, or a salt substitute. We add flavor to things to make it better to our taste buds.

In the spiritual realm, sometimes we're presented with things that don't taste all that great by themselves. But we can add a little spiritual season to it. Like when you're dealing with lack, you might find the need to sprinkle a little "But my God shall supply all my need according to His riches in glory" season.

When people are trying to feed you negative thoughts and negative words about your situation and you find yourself nibbling on a little bit of depression, shake a dash of "The peace of God that surpasses all understanding" season on it. When that bowl of defeat is set before you, why don't you just add some "Thanks be to God who always causes me to triumph" season! In other words, it's time for you to "O taste and see how good the Lord is!"

May I have a "Word" with you? It's time for you to take out the season that you need to make whatever you're dealing with better. God has given you everything that you need. As you deal with whatever you're dealing with, today, at this very moment, God has a season of Word that works with whatever has been set before you.

You see, I'm not depressed because the joy of the Lord is my strength! When in need, just reach for a little Jehovah-Jireh, my Provider. Jehovah-Jireh is so powerful that a little dash will do you. There's a Word that applies to every area in your life, and you can find it in the B-i-b-l-e. Whatever you need to make whatever is before you better, God's got it. You just need to start using what God has placed in your hand.

Until next time—what season are you using? Choose and use it, then taste the goodness of our Lord.

Seasons (Part 2 of 3)

*L*ast article I addressed season from the standpoint of adding flavor to what's cooking in life. Now I'd like to focus attention on season as meaning to treat (as wood or a skillet) so as to prepare for use, to make fit by experience. Back in the day when iron skillets were popular, before you used it, you had to do what is called "season it." I've seen this process still being encouraged with the new cookware type products. When something is seasoned, it means to apply oil to it in order to treat it. This is done prior to the item being used or to ensure it maintains its usability, especially should rust desire to manifest.

In Psalm 23, verses 5-6, we find scriptures many of us have committed to heart. "Thou anointest my head with oil; my cup runneth over. Surely goodness and mercy shall follow me all the days of my life." Think about that. God anoints my head with oil. In other words, David was saying that God was preparing him to be used. I love thinking about God anointing us for His use. There's something God desires each one of us to do. God created us to be used in His Kingdom while we're down here on earth. And to prepare us for use, He not only fashions us and appoints us, but He anoints us.

I can't speak for anyone else, but I can say that my cup has run over quite often. Admittedly, running over can sometimes be bad. Like when we reach boiling points in our lives, and what's on the inside rises up and bubbles over, making a mess of things. But I prefer focusing on the positives and letting the negatives go—the good "run over."

Have you ever started out with a small amount and before you know it, it has doubled, even tripled in size, so much so that there's not enough room to contain it all? Well, I've been there! A place where you started out with what others might laugh at and say is not enough to do anything. But when God got through adding His special touches here and extra ingredients there, you had to get more containers to hold it all.

Then there are times when I'm worshiping God for all of His goodness and mercy (you know, the goodness and mercy that follows you all the days of your life) that my cup completely runs over. I love God so much that I can't contain myself. I'm standing, kneeling, or bowing before Him and His awesome presence—loving on Him while He's loving right back on me. I become so full that what's inside of me begins to bubble up and spill over, touching all that's around me.

Then there are the times when He's filling me up with more and more that my cup just runs over. It just runs over. But it's okay—what I can't hold, I can share with someone else. Because I know that God is my source. And whenever I need more, He will pour more into me again.

May I have a "Word" with you? God created you *on* purpose *with* a purpose *for* a purpose. He created you to be used in His Kingdom. What an honor! To be used in the service of the Lord. But in order to be used, we must go through preparation phases.

In the case with a skillet or wood in need of being treated, oil is wiped on it to get it to a place of optimum service. Sure, it can be used without the preparation process; but it won't perform to the ability and effectiveness of the creator nor possibly perform for the time it was made to be used. So when you're going through your preparation process, rejoice as you realize your Creator is merely ensuring that you're ready for optimum use! It may not feel good at the time, but wait until you're doing your thing—all to the glory of God!

Seasons (Part 3 of 3)

*E*cclesiastes 3:1. "To every thing there is a season, and a time to every purpose under the heaven." For the last installment on seasons, I want to talk about times in our lives characterized by particular circumstances as well as what's classified as one of the four quarters a year is divided into. We know the four seasons as fall or some call it autumn, winter, spring, and summer. We also refer to times as the Thanksgiving season, Christmas season, holiday season, etc.

When it comes to the way the year is divided, we know generally what season it is based on what's happening around us. In the spring, there are times of budding and new growth. The weather is pleasant—not too hot, not too cold. Flowers begin to break through and spring up. It's a time for planting and growing. Of course, there are people who fuss about the pollen because it messes with us, whether physically causing some to sneeze or covering vehicles and things yellowish-green. But the bees love the pollen as do plants that need it in order to produce.

Then there's summer. Everything is pretty much in full bloom. It's a time of harvesting that which was planted. The weather is mostly hot. Even in the north and the west where they might not normally need air-conditioners, summer is hotter than any other time of the year. But then again, there are people who don't care for the heat, so summer might not be their favorite season of the year.

Fall/autumn brings us cooler, more pleasant temperatures. And it's also the time when the leaves become a beautiful canvas of color. Leaves on trees change to some of the most vibrant, deep hues you can image. I can look out of one of my bay windows in my bedroom and see one tree that's full of gold leaves. It appears to have gold coins dangling, then falling from it. Nobody but God could care so much to give us such a gorgeous, living painting. In the fall, the leaves soon fall from the tree, which a lot of folks aren't so crazy about since someone now has to clean up those fallen leaves.

When winter arrives, the temperature drops sometimes to freezing and below. In the dead of winter, the trees have shed all their leaves and everything appears to be barren—merely sticks with brown grass that is now considered dead.

Winter can be a dead time for many. However, in the winter, there are holiday seasons to enjoy such as Thanksgiving, Christmas, New Year's, and Valentine's Day. Some don't like the winter because it's cold and nothing much seems to be happening outside.

But wintertime has many advantages. It kills a lot of bugs and pests that could overrun us were it not for this time of the season. And did you know that winter is the perfect time to plant things, especially fruit and nut trees as well as bulbs like tulips and camellias.

You see, if you plant bulbs in the spring, they can tell the weather is favorable for them to spring up, and they'll begin to bloom. But in the winter, they know it's not a good time to bloom. During the wintertime, below the surface, the roots can still develop. That means all the energy can be devoted to developing strong roots instead of divided between the roots and the rest of the plant. Getting the root system established means you'll have bigger and better blooms and stronger stems.

May I have a "Word" with you? Don't despise the winter season in your life. Think of it as a time to rid yourself of bugs and pests in your life. Concentrate on planting things where you can have more established roots, realizing that spring is coming. And when spring comes, what you planted will be stronger and produce even more and greater fruit. And because the roots are now deeper and more established, they'll be able to handle the larger blessings of blossoms and fruit.

We can be thankful for spring because it's a time of growth. We thank God for the summer as it is a time of full manifestation of what was planted. We thank God for the fall, as there are things and people in our lives we may need to release. And we thank God for the winter because it's a season of rest and renewal, a time of preparation for the other glorious seasons to come.

Thank God for all the seasons in your life. They all have their own specific purpose.

The Seeds We Harvest Later

Sometimes our greatest challenge is watching people who seem to do all sorts of evil things and never seem to get their just due. They use people and seem to only think of themselves. And you may have found yourself shaking your head, wondering why God appears to let them get away with such awful deeds. Then there are people who have given so much, those who have given their last . . . people who will put others above their own needs, people who have done for others when it was so easy for them not to, and it seems as though they just can't get a break.

Today I want to encourage you. The Bible tells us, "Be not deceived; God is not mocked: for whatsoever a man soweth, that shall he also reap." Galatians 6:7.

If you understand the principles behind seeds and planting, you'll understand why you can be of good courage. A seed may be a tiny thing, and you can't always see the potential inside just by looking at it. But put the seed in the ground, and not long you'll see what was truly inside of it.

The thing about seeds is: Whatever type seed you plant, that's the harvest you're going to get in return, most times, multiplied. If you plant squash seeds, you're not going to get green beans. I don't care how much you pray or believe differently: Whatsoever you sow, that shall you also reap. So if you desire tomatoes, then you need to plant tomato seeds. If you don't want rutabagas, then don't plant them.

When people plant evil seeds, they will reap and have to deal with evil when harvest time comes. So take heart while you're planting good things. Don't get discourage because of the person who may not be doing right, yet appears to prosper. Smile and just keep planting those good things in life, knowing that whatever we sow, we're going to reap.

With this principle, you need to understand that it doesn't matter whether or not you didn't know any better. If you plant it, you will reap it. That's why Hosea 4:6 tells us, "My people are destroyed for lack of knowledge:"

If you don't know what you're planting, then the question becomes: Why don't you know? Intentions are not considered when you plant a thing. If you plant it, you will reap it. You *will* reap it.

Many of you may be hurting these days because of things people have done to you or to those you love. But if I may encourage you right here to continue on in the Lord by planting that which is good. Realize that God has a principle set in place, and that principle is our assurance: We will reap what we sow.

May I have a "Word" with you? "Let us not be weary in well doing: for in due season we shall reap, if we faint not." (Galatians 6:9). Psalm 37:1-4 clearly tells us, "Fret not thyself because of evildoers, neither be thou envious against the workers of iniquity. For they shall soon be cut down like the grass, and wither as the green herb. Trust in the Lord, and do good; so shalt thou dwell in the land, and verily thou shalt be fed. Delight thyself also in the Lord; and he shall give thee the desires of thine heart."

The Word for you, whomever this message is for, is to continue planting good seeds regardless of the evil that others may plant around you. God is not mocked: Whatsoever a person sows that shall he also reap.

I plan to sow my seeds joyfully in the Lord. What about you?

Seedless May Be Great, But...

O kay, I've been buying these fruit called "Cuties" and I must say I love them. Some packages say they are Clementines while others say Mandarin oranges. Besides being easy to peel (something the package also advertises), they are seedless. I enjoy being able to eat these wonderful tangerine-looking fruit and not having to deal with pesky seeds.

But I was thinking as I popped a juicy slice in my mouth, how are these fruit able to reproduce more if there are no seeds? You see: We need seeds in order to grow more plants. Yes, I understand cloning and graphing, but I also understand nature. You plant a seed you get more plants with more seeds in return along with fruit of what was planted.

So, if I want tomatoes, I need to plant tomato seeds. If I want watermelons, I need to plant watermelon seeds. If I want peaches, I plant a peach seed.

In some cases, you have to continuously plant seeds in order to gather a harvest. In other cases, after you plant one seed and produce a viable plant, that plant continues to produce. For instance, after you have a plum tree that produces, you can go to that tree the next year and expect plums to be there. The fruit would also contain a seed that can be planted which, ironically, will give you even more seeds to plant.

But what do you do when you're just getting started and you don't have any seed to sow?

Isaiah 55:10 tells us, "For as the rain cometh down, and the snow from heaven, and returneth not thither, but watereth the earth, and maketh it bring forth and bud, that it may give seed to the sower, and bread to the eater." If you don't have seed to sow, then ask God for seed. And I'm not just talking about money (what many use this for).

There is the seed of joy, the seed of peace, the seed of favor. I like to think of a seed as that which is planted (sown) in the earth that you desire to reap from. Because we know that as long as the earth remains, there will be seedtime and harvest time. When you plant a seed, you don't instantly see anything happening. But know that although you may not see anything, something *is* happening. So when you're in need of smiles, try planting smiles.

If you don't believe this principle works, smile at someone and see if you don't get a smile back. Even if the person you happen to give the smile to doesn't give it back to you, someone else will. And that's the beauty of God's seed. You don't have to always receive your blessing from the one you gave it to.

May I have a "Word" with you? Isaiah 55:11 goes on to tell us, "So shall my word be that goeth forth out of my mouth: it shall not return unto me void, but it shall accomplish that which I please, and it shall prosper in the thing whereto I sent it." God's Word is a seed. It goes out (is planted), but His Word will not return back to Him void (empty).

Plant the seed of the Word of God and see what grows. Isaiah 55:12 says, "For ye shall go out with joy, and be led forth with peace: the mountains and the hills shall break forth before you into singing, and all the trees of the field shall clap their hands." With the fruit we eat, seedless may be wonderfully convenient. And as much as I enjoy eating something void of seeds, I want all the blessings God has for me!

I don't mind planting seeds and sharing the harvest. After all, God is a God of more than enough. And when God blesses us with abundance, there's sure to be an overflow.

Don't Let the Container Fool You

hen people look at you, what do they see? Do you even care? I mean really? Should you care? You see, when folks look at you technically they can only see the outside. They see what you show them. But inside of you is a gift or gifts. It's like when you're given a gift in a box. The box is not the gift. The gift is on the inside of the box. From looking at the outside, you aren't likely to know—with assurance—what's on the inside. You'll have to open up the box to make visible the gift that is housed inside.

God has placed gifts inside each of us. He intended for us to give and use our gift(s) for the edification of the body of Christ. First Timothy 4:14 says, "Neglect not the gift that is in thee." Second Timothy 1:6 says, "Wherefore I put thee in remembrance that thou stir up the gift of God, which is in thee by the putting on of my hands."

Has your gift been merely lying on the inside of you waiting on you to move? Has your gift just settled to the bottom? You know how things sometimes settle at the bottom, especially the heaviest things? Well, it's time you allow the Holy Spirit to stir up the gift within you. Activate your gift and get it swirling around so others may see it in operation.

If you say you have a gift to teach, then teach. If your gift is singing and you're hoping to minister with a CD or recording someday, then what are you waiting on? Do you have a book you believe God placed inside of you, a business, a ministry to bless others? Then don't let anyone stop you. Whatever your gift is, it's time out for playing yourself and our God small. It's time for you to give God something to work with. He's placed the gift(s) inside of you, but you need to use your faith. Get up and act like you truly believe.

I know, I know. Somebody told you a long time ago that you weren't anything. Whenever you've tried to step out, somebody whispers (if not saying it loud enough for you to hear them), "Who does she think she is? Who does he think he is?" First off, if you're saved, you can tell them you're a child of God. And secondly, tell people that you were created by the best (yes, God created you) so *that* in itself makes you something special. So why think you can be something when it's obvious to others that you're nothing?

Well, how about because you can do all things through Christ who strengthens you. How about: God is looking for someone so that He can show Himself strong. Tell people when they question you or your gift: "Don't let the container fool you. You don't have a clue what's inside this vessel. But glory to God, God knows."

May I have a "Word" with you? I was finishing up a book that was due to hit the bookshelves in the fall of 2009 called *Goodness and Mercy*. The week before, I had to stop what I was doing to read the proofs from another novel releasing in May 2009, entitled *Practicing What You Preach* so I could get the corrections to my publisher by its Wednesday deadline. That past Saturday I had spoken at a women's conference where their theme was "Gifts Galore!" On this day when I was writing this, I was editing my fall release to turn it over to my editor at Kensington. But right now, right this moment, I'm using my gift of exhortation to tell you to stir up your gift and to let go of the excuses.

And when people look at you like you're nothing, you just tell them: Don't let the container fool you! God has placed a gift inside of me, and I'm going to use my gift to the glory of God. And nobody or nothing is going to stop me!

Do You Know Who I Am?

*D*o you know who I am? I know most of us may not say it out loud, but I would venture you've likely thought this at some point in your life. When someone comes up to you and says something or treats you like you're unimportant. And no, you don't have to be famous to want to say to someone who disrespects you, "Do you know who I am?"

Jesus encountered a lot of people who didn't know who He was. John the fourth chapter tells the story of the Samaritan woman at the well. The woman came to draw water and Jesus said to her, "Give me to drink." First of all, the Samaritans and the Jews didn't have much dealing with each other so this woman let Jesus know right off the bat how she felt about Him saying anything to her. But Jesus went on to tell her, "If thou knewest the gift of God, and who it is that saith to thee, Give me to drink; thou wouldest have asked of him, and he would have given thee living water." Ain't the Lord good?!

The woman was sort of like some folks we probably know (or you if you're the one) who decided to put Jesus in His place by pointing out what He didn't have and why He wasn't about anything, in her opinion. "Sir," she said, "thou has nothing to draw with." How many times has someone looked down their nose at you because of what they perceived about you? How many people have you looked down your nose at because of what you thought or had decided about them?

Jesus continued the conversation with this woman which included Him telling her that the water He could provide would mean she would never thirst again. The water He was offering "shall be a well of water springing up into everlasting life." Jesus eventually told her to go call her husband. The woman informed Jesus that she had no husband to which Jesus said, "Thou hast well said, I have no husband. For thou hast had five husbands; and he whom thou now hast is not thy husband."

You can't fool Jesus. God knows even if we hide things from others. He knows our hurts, He knows of our disappointments, and He knows of those things we've done in the dark. God knows. The woman decided Jesus must be a prophet for Him to know all about her.

The conversation then began to focus on worship. Here are some powerful words we need to hear. John 4:23-24 says, "But the hour cometh, and now is, when the true worshippers shall worship the Father in spirit and in truth: for the Father seeketh such to worship him. God is a Spirit: and they that worship him must worship him in spirit and in truth." Worship God in spirit *and* in truth.

As you read John 4:25 you'll find, "The woman saith unto him, I know that Messiah cometh, which is called Christ: when he is come, he will tell us all things." This woman didn't have a clue who she was talking to. John 4:26, "Jesus saith unto her, I that speak unto thee am he." Here's where I saw Jesus saying, "Do you know who I am?"

May I Have a "Word" with you? When you're thinking about the troubles in your life, I want you to hear Jesus saying, "Do you know who I am? I have overcome the world. I told you to cast your cares on me. There's nothing too hard for Me. You can do all things through Me because I make you strong through your weakness." The woman at the well didn't know who she was talking to.

If you've accepted Jesus, then you have Jesus in your life. Don't worry. Take *all* things to Jesus and *know* Who He is?

Get Out of the Boat!

or the purposes of this message, when you see the word "ship," let's agree that here, we're talking about a large boat. Matthew 14:22-29 states, "And straightway Jesus constrained his disciples to get into a ship, and to go before him unto the other side, while he sent the multitudes away. And when he had sent the multitudes away, he went up into a mountain apart to pray: and when the evening was come, he was there alone. But the ship was now in the midst of the sea, tossed with waves: for the wind was contrary. And in the fourth watch of the night Jesus went unto them, walking on the sea. And when the disciples saw him walking on the sea, they were troubled, saying, It is a spirit; and they cried out for fear. But straightway Jesus spake unto them, saying, Be of good cheer; it is I; be not afraid. And Peter answered him and said, Lord, if it be thou, bid me come unto thee on the water. And he said, Come. And when Peter was come down out of the ship, he walked on the water, to go to Jesus."

When God tells us to do something, that's the very time it seems that obstacles rear their ugly heads. Allow me to set the stage. Jesus had just finished feeding five thousand men plus women and children blessing five loaves and two fishes. Jesus told the disciples to get *into* a ship (boat) and to go before him to the other side. This is very important. Goal: the other side.

During this time, Jesus went up into a mountain and prayed. Evening came, which means some time had passed. Enough time, if you ask me, for the disciples to have been on the other side. But the ship (boat) was in the middle of the sea being tossed by the waves, and the Bible explains that the wind was contrary.

Can't you see this happening in your own life? Jesus tells you to do something, you set out to do it, and you meet up with things that make it hard, seemingly impossible to overcome. You're trying to stay the course, but you can't understand why the "wind is being contrary" (don't you love that imagery . . . the wind being contrary) to the point that it appears to be fighting against you.

But hold on . . . the fourth watch is coming! The fourth watch referred to in verse 25 was between 3 and 6 a.m. People say the darkest hour is just before day. Jesus came to them not by boat, but walking *on* the sea. Can't you imagine when you're out there struggling, trying to stay afloat, attempting to make it to the other side to do what God told you to do, and you start feeling like all hope is gone.

Then on the fourth watch, you look up and here comes Jesus. Sure the disciples were afraid, but Jesus let them know there was nothing to fear. And on top of that, Jesus told them to "be of good cheer."

I know this is a Word for someone today. You're tired from the rowing and you've had to fight countless whispers telling you to just give up—quit. But you know God told you to do this. People watch you being tossed and driven. They may have even told you that God didn't tell you to do what you're doing and that's why it's not working for you.

But I'm here to bring you a Word from the Lord: "Be of good cheer!" You'll see Jesus standing before you saying, "Come." Why come? Because as some of you may have heard it said, "If you want to walk on water, you have to get out of the boat." If you're planning to do the extraordinary, you're going to have to step out of the ordinary and totally trust God.

Matthew 14:30 said, "But when he (Peter) saw the wind boisterous, he was afraid; and beginning to sink, he cried, saying, Lord, save me." You see, you might step out and begin to do what others thought was impossible. Don't take your eyes off Jesus. When you take your eyes off Jesus and begin to look at the circumstances (the boisterous wind making the waves behave unseemly), that's when you'll find yourself starting to sink.

But even if that happens, you don't have to pray a long prayer. You can do like Peter, and just say, "Lord, save me." Matthew 14:31 says, "And immediately Jesus stretched forth his hand, and caught him, and said unto him, O thou of little faith, wherefore didst thou doubt?" Don't doubt. When God tells you something, believe that it's already done.

May I have a "Word" with you? Have faith in God. Have the God kind of faith that will allow you to get out of the boat. I don't know your boat's name, but whatever it is; when Jesus calls you to come, believe that if He called you to walk on water, then you *can* walk on water.

And for those of you who don't believe you can handle this water-walking thing, then Matthew 14:32 further says, "And when they (Jesus and Peter) were come into the ship, the wind ceased." Jesus will get in the boat with you if He has to. And when He's onboard, even the wind understands "Peace be still."

Nevertheless, if you want to walk on water, you have *got* to get out of the boat. Trust Jesus saints of God: Get out of the boat!

Excuse Me, Please

hat is your gift? What is your gift doing?

"Excuse me. Excuse me, please. I'm sorry; I'm just trying to get by here. Can you let me get past here? I'm trying to make it to the front. Excuse me, if you'll just let me squeeze through here. Thank you so much, I'm just trying to make some room here." This is your gift talking. Can't you just see this?

You're wondering how on earth God is going to do what He's promised you when it comes to your gift. He's given you a wonderful gift, and somehow your gift is going about its business, making room for you. That's why I love Proverbs 18:16: "A man's gift maketh room for him, and bringeth him before great men."

God gave me this revelation some time ago. I started laughing as I envisioned my gift making room for me. "Excuse me, excuse me, please. I'm just trying to squeeze through here. We're just trying to make it over there, so we can do what we need to do."

For whatever reason, many folks aren't walking in their purpose, not walking in their gift. With some, it's because they're shy. Some don't know how to go about it. Some don't want to come off as being showy. And some of you have been knocked down and knocked back so many times that you've decided to just sit down and not bother trying anymore.

But this scripture states, "A man's gift maketh room for him, and bringeth him before great men." Maketh is present tense. Your gift makes room for you. I'm smiling as I think about how our gifts will not only make room for us, but will also bring us before great men. Am I the only one shouting with a smile on my face?

Your gift *maketh* room for you. "Excuse me, making room here." And then your gift brings (brings being an active word, an active verb) you along with it as its making room. Okay, let me break it down like this. Your gift is not only making room for you, but it's grabbing you by the hand, grabbing some of you by your collar, and bringing you before great men. Wow!

I think about some of the people I've had the pleasure of meeting during my lifetime. Some of them have been known greats, but a lot of them are greats who don't have a clue who they really are. They have gifts and talents and purpose, but they think they are nothings and nobodys. And that's what they act like—like they're nothing and a nobody, when in truth: They're greats because God made them, and He has called them to greatness. Not to boast or to lord over others, but greatness to minister . . . to serve others.

I've been asked more times than I can count if I'm a minister. Well, yes and no. No, if you want to attach it to me as an official title. Yes, if you understand that the word minister means a servant of God, and I am indeed a servant of the Most High God.

May I have a "Word" with you? There is too much work to be done for you to continue playing small. God gave you a gift. Your gift will make room for you if you'll stop trying to sit your gift down, telling it how it doesn't look right for it to be up there trying to bring you from point A to point B. Your gift will make room for you, and you need to learn to go with your gift.

Allow your gift to do all God has placed in your hands to do. Allow your gift to make room for you, to bring you before great men, and to minister to and edify the body of Christ. "A man's gift maketh room for him, and bringeth him before great men."

Eyes have not seen nor have ears heard all that God has in store for those who are willing and obedient. Oh, the half has not been told.

"Excuse me, excuse me, please. Excuse me. I don't want to be late. We're just trying to get there." That's my gift talking.

So, tell me: What is your gift saying?

Remember Your History

S ome folks dread birthdays. Others who may celebrate it don't care to tell their age. Well, you should be honored to be on this earth yet another year. Be excited about your age and let the world know how good God has been to you.

I recall this one time hearing God, just as clear, say, "I WILL give you the desires of your heart." There my hands were wrapped around my turtle shell steering wheel, and it was as though God illuminated my hands to emphasize His point.

You see, there was a time when I had a desire for a particular car (Chrysler 300-C). I was specific with what I desired the car to have and not have, all the way down to the turtle shell steering wheel. God placed in my spirit at the moment He said, "I WILL" that He *had* given me the desire of my heart. And just like He'd done it with that desire, He would do it with my other desires.

Many of us don't have a problem proclaiming "God is able." "Yes, God can do anything but fail." "Child, there's nothing too hard for God." But the question is not *can* God do it? It's not is God *able* to do it? The question is: Do you believe God will do it for you?

Psalm 37:4 declares, "Delight yourself also in the Lord and He will give you the desires of your heart." Do you believe this or are you just being religious and enjoy quoting scriptures to show off?

God is looking for someone to show Himself strong. I've been on this earth for quite some years now. I'm proud of my years. I've been on the battlefield for the Lord a long time, and believe me: I have the scars to prove it. But the nice thing about having lived a life is that we have a history to look back on. I'm talking about a history like David had. You know, David the shepherd boy before he became king. When David heard of the giant called Goliath, he didn't have any fear because he had a history with the Lord. David remembered once when he was tending the sheep there was a lion that came to attack, then there was the time there was a bear. And God delivered him from them.

Because David knew what God had done for him, he had a history, he could boldly say, "Who is this uncircumcised Philistine who would dare come against our God."

Now that's me. I look back over my life, and I see how far God has brought me. I thank God for every one of those years because God truly has kept me. God raised me up. God promoted me. And God is not through yet. There's a song we used to sing. "How I got over."

May I have a "Word" with you? I don't have to wonder how I got over. It was by the grace of God that I'm here today. It is by the grace of God that I'm in my right mind, and I can sit here and type these words. It is by His grace that I live and move and have my being.

For sure, be excited about birthdays. And whether anyone tells you happy birthday or not, be thankful that God granted you another chance to let the world know what an awesome God you serve.

I still love a song entitled "Days of Elijah." The chorus says, "There's no God like Jehovah." For God so loved the world that He gave His only begotten son, that whosoever believeth on Him should not perish but shall have everlasting life.

Yes, you were born into this world. But when you're born again, that's when you begin to have life and life more abundantly. So on this day, why not tell God "Thank You." Thank You for saving me. Thank You for loving me. Thank You.

Let's Go Fishing!

atthew 4:18-19 reads, "And Jesus, walking by the sea of Galilee, saw two brethren, Simon called Peter, and Andrew his brother, casting a net into the sea: for they were fishers. And he saith unto them, Follow me, and I will make you fishers of men."

All my life, my father has loved to fish. I remember when I was a little girl; a group of them would go to Florida on Saturday deep sea fishing trips. Later, he started going to Mobile, Alabama. My father was known for catching coolers full of red snappers and groupers and what he called "Mother-in-laws." On Sundays, we'd go to church while the fish stayed under huge blocks of ice in the coolers.

After church, my siblings and I would do our part to help Daddy scale them, and he'd clean, then filet them. When Daddy wasn't deep sea fishing, you'd likely find him on a lake that generally took about an hour . . . hour-and-a-half to reach from our house. I didn't mind going fishing with him, but I must admit: I hated the long drive there and back.

Needless to say, my father was an excellent fisherman. He'd give us advice on what we needed to do to get a fish to bite. I never understood how the fish knew his fishing line from ours when we cast our hooks in the same place as his. But it sure looked like they did, since it was his line they seemed to always bite. I don't go fishing much these days, but sometimes I miss being on the boat with Daddy, casting my line with finesse and expertise, then waiting for that special tug, hopefully letting me know that my efforts and endless waiting were not in vain (as opposed to snagging a stick or debris).

Someone who had received an advance copy of my novel *Blessed Trinity* sent me a message. When you put a book out, you can never be certain how it will be received. But one thing that's always been important to me is that something I've written will bless someone else's life. I learned long ago that I have the Gift of Encouragement. God has called me to inspire, enlighten, and encourage His children to go higher in Him, and to live a life befitting of a King's child. So, for anyone who thinks I'm hung up on money and achieving material things, you really don't know me at all.

What I do, is recognize the position of being a parent. I recognize how often people judge a parent by their children. Sure, when children get grown they're responsible for their own actions. But with a dependent child, people have pretty negative thoughts and opinions of a parent dressed to the nines while their child walks around raggedy with dirty, smelly pampers.

Well, God is my Father, and as His child, people are looking at me. If you're His child, they're looking at you. I don't want anyone getting the mistaken impression that our Father in Heaven (who happens to be rich, for those of you who don't know) doesn't care about His children and lets us go out in public looking any kind of way.

I've been talked about (they don't know I know, but I do) regarding how well I dress. In their eyes, I'm just trying to get attention. I suppose I should care that some people don't like me because my Father wants me to look my best when I'm out bragging about being His child. But you know what? I really don't care, and they're just going to have to learn to deal with it.

Yet, I digress. We were talking about fishing and bait, weren't we? Here's what all of this has to do with fishing. If you're casting your line with your hook and what you believe to be the right bait but aren't catching anything, it's not the fishes fault. It could be that you're using the wrong hook or the wrong kind of bait.

I write books, mostly novels. I could write with nothing but drama and no substance, but Jesus called me to go fishing for those who aren't saved and those who are but may not be walking in all the power He's given us. The hook and bait I use just happens to revolve around my books. Your hook may be in your business. Or as a teacher or someone in the corporate world who can't necessarily talk about Jesus on the job. You may be living a life that causes a person to nibble at your bait, granting you the opportunity to eventually set the hook (that's a fishing term), and reel them in.

The woman, who read the advance copy of my book, left a note on my MySpace.com page that touched me. She said that God was not through with her yet. Then she quoted a scripture I used as one of my chapter headings (Psalm 53:2), "God looked down from heaven upon the children of men, to see if there were any that did understand, that did seek God." She then wrote, "Lord, I am a sinner. I want to be saved. Come into my heart, Lord Jesus. I believe in my heart and I confess with my mouth.". . . words she happened to have read in my novel *Blessed Trinity.*

Sometimes, I'm not sure if what I do truly matters. I write practically on a daily basis. I pen books that range between 85,000-105,000 words per book. What I don't want is to be doing something just to be doing it. I've always said if one person is blessed by what I do, then what I'm doing is worth it. I don't always know if someone has been blessed, so when I read this note, I couldn't help but give God the praises and the glory.

May I have a "Word" with you? Those of us who are saved, Jesus called us to be fishers of men. So what are you using to attract those who desperately need to know the Lord? What bait are you using? I'll make a deal with you. You catch them; the Lord will clean them.

Yes, Jesus wants to make you fishers of men. So grab your pole, rod, reel, and/or your net; and let's go fishing!

It's Not Always About Us

First Corinthians 15:58, "Therefore, my beloved brethren, be ye steadfast, unmovable, always abounding in the work of the Lord, forasmuch as ye know that your labor is not in vain in the Lord." Galatians 6:9, "And let us not be weary in well doing: for in due season we shall reap, if we faint not."

Isaiah 40:28-31, "Hast thou not known? hast thou not heard, that the everlasting God, the Lord, the Creator of the ends of the earth, fainteth not, neither is weary? there is no searching of his understanding. He giveth power to the faint, and to them that have no might he increaseth strength. Even the youths shall faint and be weary, and the young men shall utterly fall: But they that wait upon the Lord shall renew their strength; they shall mount up with wings as eagles; they shall run, and not be weary; and they shall walk, and not faint."

I know you may be tired. Tired of being mistreated, tired of folks talking about you, tired of trying and seemingly not get far (that's if you're able to get anywhere at all). Tired of having dreams and feeling like you're nowhere near where God said you'd be. What's taking so long, you ask?

God tends to show you the end at the beginning. But the awesome thing about God is that He watches over His Word. So when God gives you His Word in whatever form, and you tell Him what His Word says, He has promised it won't return unto Him void. His Word will come to pass. That's why First Corinthians 15:57 states, "But thanks be to God, which giveth us the victory through our Lord Jesus Christ." Don't be weary in well doing. In due season, oh yes, you will reap if you don't quit.

I thank God who always causes me to triumph. I spoke at this church and told them not to turn to their neighbors and tell them anything. I told them to say this out loud to themselves, "It's not all about me." This was not to put anyone down, but to lift those who were in attendance up. You see, when things are going on in our lives, we tend to think it's directed at us or it's against us. We think it's all about us. We don't see the big picture of how God uses what's happening in our lives for our good and for His glory.

It's not all about us. It's about God being glorified no matter what it is—good, bad, or in-between. When things are happening in your life, take comfort in knowing that God is right there with you. How do I know? Because God promised He would never leave nor forsake us.

If we believe this, then whatever we're going through we know that God knows. If He's allowing it, then He will use it for our good and for His glory. If He chooses to keep us from having to go through it, then it still will be for His glory. God is omniscient, omnipotent, and omnipresent so nothing gets by Him.

May I have a "Word" with you? When fiery darts are being hurled your way, take heart: It's not always about you. When people are trying to pull the rug out from under you, it's not about you. When people mistreat you or try to stop you from reaching what God has called you to do, take heart—it's not always about you. In the end, it's all to the glory of God.

You'll be able to tell somebody how God brought you through, how you made it over, how when Satan came in like a flood, God raised up a standard. So, no matter what's going on in your life right now, it really isn't always about you. You're part of the blessing of the Lord as somebody somewhere is watching you come through.

To Be or Not to Be?

Be ye steadfast and unmoveable, always abounding; be not conformed to this world but be ye transformed by the renewing of your mind; let love be without dissimulation; be found faithful; stand fast therefore in the liberty wherewith Christ hath made us free, and be not entangled again with the yoke of bondage. But if ye be led of the Spirit, ye are no longer under the law. Let us not be weary in well doing. According as He hath chosen us in Him before the foundation of the world, that we should be holy and without blame before Him in love. Be careful for nothing, but in everything by prayer and supplication with thanksgiving let your requests be made known unto God.

All of the above are scriptures. And when it comes to being what God has called us to be, we should be that. Children of the Most High God should be *His* children. Ambassadors of Christ should be ambassadors. The Word of God tells us to be led of the Spirit. We must be unmoveable even during those times when it looks like things aren't going the way God has promised. Yes, people will wonder what's wrong with you when it looks like you're sticking with a thing they feel is not working for you. But when God tells you something, you either believe the Word of the Lord, or you don't. There's no in-between. And when you really believe, then nothing or nobody can tell you differently. This much I know for sure.

The Bible says to be careful for nothing, that we are to trust God. Trust that God is Who He says He is. If God is for you, tell me: who honestly can successfully be against you? Yes, this is totally a mind altering thing. You have to lose your natural mind and take on the mind of Christ to be all God has called you to be.

To be or not to be?

May I have a "Word" with you? The military had a popular slogan years ago that simply said, "Be all you can be, in the army." Well, I say to you: Be all you can be in God's army. Don't worry about *how* God is going to do a thing. Just *BE*. When God says you're the head and not the tail, then *be* the head and not the tail. When God says you're above only and not beneath, then *be* above only and stop acting like you're beneath. When God says you're blessed, don't let anyone tell you that you're cursed. Tell me: Who can curse what God has already blessed? No one is bigger than God.

Jesus paid the price for you to *BE*. Before the foundation of the world, the Lamb was slain. Therefore, *be* victorious. *Be* at peace. *Be* in love. *Be* in joy. *Be* faithful. *Be* free! For whom the Son sets free is free indeed. *Be* all that God has called you to *be*.

To *be* or not to *be*?

First Corinthians 15:57 says, "Therefore, my beloved brethren, be ye steadfast, unmoveable, always abounding in the work of the Lord, forasmuch as ye know that your labor is not in vain in the Lord." Oh, yes, with Jesus and through His strength, you can do all things!

What's in Your Cup?

e often hear people say, "If it's God's will . . ." something either will or won't happen. I have been speaking a lot at various churches and one of the themes I spoke on was "Christian Women Accepting the Will of God." It came from Luke 22:39-42 where Jesus was in the garden right before He would be betrayed and taken away for a mock trial and later a crucifixion. At that time, God pressed on me to speak from the subject of "What's in Your Cup?" The focus being on the forty-second verse in Luke 22 where Jesus was talking to His Father in Heaven, "Saying, Father, if thou be willing, remove this cup from me: nevertheless not my will, but thine, be done."

At that time, I was led to speak on the cup, or more so, what was in Jesus' cup that He was speaking to God about removing from Him. I'll say here as I said on that Sunday: Jesus was not afraid to die. He knew: number one, this was what He came to this earth to do—to give His life for our sins. And number two, that God would raise Him from the dead as Jesus indicated when He said, "As Jonah was in the belly of the whale so shall the Son of Man be in the earth." It was what was *in* His cup that caused Him to make that request to God.

You see, Jesus' cup contained the sins of the world (past, present, and future) and here was Jesus who knew no sin now having to take on (drink) all that sin (just think about all the sin just you alone have done). My question to the congregation was: "What's in Your Cup?" In

175

other words: What are you called to drink that may not be all that great or pleasant as you're going through it, but you know God has called you to do a thing?

Many people believe that when God calls us to a thing, it's going to be a piece of cake, smooth sailing, a walk in the park, an advantage to everyone else just because God called us to it. Well, anyone who has been called to do God's Will can tell you that things aren't always easy when it comes to getting that thing done. I often say, "If it were easy, then everybody would do it."

This is where true action faith comes in. This is where I believe God can separate those who are for real from those who are not steadfast in their calling, or worse—those pretending. Here is where you distinguish the victims from the victors.

When God calls us, He gives us everything we need to accomplish that task. He promised He would never leave us nor forsake us. Generally, He shows us the end from the beginning without all (sometimes none) of the details in between (read about Joseph the Dreamer).

Sometimes when you're drinking it, it can be so bitter you want to say, "Can I have just a little sugar or something in this?" Many of you probably know something about this as well. You know, when things aren't going the way you envisioned them. People won't act right. You're not getting that much support not even from family and friends. People are talking about you. Some are laughing at you.

What's inside of your cup is not always easy or sweet, but drink it, and trust God.

May I have a "Word" with you? Luke 22:43 says, "And there appeared an angel unto him from heaven, strengthening him." In other words, when Jesus was praying about His cup, God sent an angel to strengthen Him. When you need it most, God will send an angel to strengthen you. I know this for a fact as I drink from my own cup.

Has what God called me to do always been easy? No. But when you look past what's in the cup, and you see how, in the end when it's all said and done, God will get the glory, then you can say just as Jesus did, "Nevertheless not my will, but thine, be done."

What's in your cup? If God has called you to it, then know that God has a plan, and God's plan is going to bless someone (if not a whole lot of someones). Drink it down with your eyes on Jesus, the author and finisher of your faith. Whatever God has placed in your cup, know that God is with you always.

During the Passover meal, three cups were passed around by the Jewish householder. The third cup was called "the cup of blessing." So as you drink from the cup that may be bitter, remember there's a third cup coming. And that third cup is your cup of blessing.

Bottom's up!

What Do You See?

hen you look in the mirror, how do you describe what you see? Think about it: how do you see yourself? This is a question that can prove to be important. I'm reminded of the story of twelve spies sent by Moses to Canaan to check out the land and its inhabitants. The twelve spies sent, went up and searched the land then brought back their report. They confirmed indeed the land flowed with milk and honey just as God had said.

Caleb, one of those twelve spies stilled the people and said as reported in Numbers 13:30, "Let us go up at once, and possess it; for we are well able to overcome it." There's a message in this verse if we will take the time to stop and look at it. Caleb didn't just say they could overcome the definite obstacles that for sure stood between them and the promises of God. Caleb said they were "*WELL* able." Now that's some kind of confidence.

As with anything God tells us, there will undoubtedly be a voice or two with a differing view. We see this in verse 31. "But the men that went up with him said, We be not able to go up against the people; for they are stronger than we."

Now, there was nothing wrong with these spies having a differing opinion and assessment of the matter. But this does show us why it's important that we take care about the people we let hang around us and ultimately speak into our lives. You'll find there will always be somebody more than willing to deliver a negative report they've gone as far as searched out to drop off at your doorstep.

But when God has told you something, you have to stand on His promises no matter what anyone else has to say. Don't be deceived: Much has to do with not only your trust in God, but how you see yourself. If you see yourself as victorious, and if you stay steadfast and faint not, then you're going to be victorious. However, if you see yourself as defeated before you even begin, then I suspect you're going to encounter defeat.

In Numbers 13:33, you'll find these words from those who were arguing for what couldn't be done. "And there we saw the giants, the sons of Anak, which come of the giants: and we were in our own sight as grasshoppers, and so we were in their sight."

First off, they saw those who occupied the land as giants. We can all identify with this on some level because I dare say that some of us have had to deal with our own giants in our lives at one point or another. Our giants are just identified by different names. Still, we've looked up and saw how big our giants stand before us.

The problem with those who were describing the situation was not that they saw them as giants; the problem was they saw themselves as grasshoppers. They then went on to say, "and so we were in their sight."

Did they interview these giants to find out how they saw them? No. At least it doesn't say that in the Bible. It merely says that because they saw themselves as grasshoppers, they concluded that they were grasshoppers in their enemies' sights.

So, how do you see yourself?

May I have a "Word" with you? You need to be careful about how you not only describe yourself, but how you see yourself. That's why it's important for you to search the scriptures and find out how God sees you, then see yourself as God sees you. When God's Word says you're fearfully and wonderfully made, then you should see yourself as fearfully and wonderfully made. When God says you're more than a conqueror, then why would you run from giants and say something contrary to God's Word?

How you see yourself is important, so important that God wants you to have a vision of yourself as He sees you. You are a designer's original, created by the Almighty God for an Almighty purpose to fulfill.

Are there really grasshoppers in the world? Yes. God did create grasshoppers, but he didn't create *you* a grasshopper. Let the real grasshoppers fulfill their purpose while you boldly fulfill yours—being fearfully and wonderfully made.

Lose the Weight

osing weight is generally always on many folks' list of New Year's resolutions. Weight can be a good thing when it comes to holding items in place you really want to hold. For example, weight used to anchor a boat. As big or commanding as a boat might be, weight used as an anchor will keep that boat in place. Some people use weights to keep papers in place. In fact, there's a thing called a paperweight. Paperweights are great in situations where a wind could come along and scatter papers you desire to stay put.

Weights are used when exercising, mainly to help pump up muscles. Muscles really are a good thing since they help burn unwanted fat. Still, even when lifting or carrying weights for exercise purposes, you have to be careful you don't pull or injure your body by having too much weight or lifting it the wrong way.

Then comes the weight too many of us may be familiar with. You know the weight that seems to sort of creep up on you. The weight you may not have noticed much at first (a pound here, five pounds there). That one slice of cake or pie that became two, and before you know it, cushions are forming all over your body. Weight that can somehow manage to shrink the clothes that used to fit loosely or so nicely before.

Let's face it—any of the weights mentioned above can slow down or put a stop to a thing. A boat looks like it's moving but it's not going anywhere. Paper may flutter, but it will remain put. If you're lifting weights, you need someone there to spot you or you might find yourself trapped, if not crushed (according to how much weight you thought you could lift before you learned you really couldn't). If you're carrying weight while walking or running, you can't go as fast as if you weren't. And if you continue carrying weight long enough, you'll find yourself tired or possibly wanting to quit altogether.

Hebrews 12:1 says, "Wherefore seeing we also are compassed about with so great a cloud of witnesses, let us lay aside every weight, and the sin which doth so easily beset us, and let us run with patience the race that is set before us."

What weight is holding you back or slowing you down? What weight is keeping you from moving forward? Weight can be a number of things in your life: worry, frustration, trials, the cares of this world. Now, if you picked up the weight on your own, then lay it aside. If someone is attempting to put weight on you, don't accept it; lay it aside. If you have unsuspectingly picked up weight that's continuing to follow you around no matter where you go, then start right now—lose the weight.

May I have a "Word" with you? Carrying extra weight makes it hard to run a race. Why carry the extra weight when you don't have to? Lay aside worry. Lay aside other people's troubles (tell them to do like you're doing with your own troubles and turn them over to the Lord— God can handle them). Lay aside the *weight* that's holding you down and pick up the *wait* on the Lord. Let's run with patience the race that is set before us.

Hebrews 12:2 goes on to say, "Looking unto Jesus the author and finisher of our faith." As you run this race, look to Jesus. Oh, can't you just see Him standing at the finish line with His arms opened wide saying, "Come on. You can do it! Victory is already yours! Come on, drop that weight and keep running until you cross the finish line."

Lose the weight, run with patience, and let's see what the end is going to be!

Looking in the Mirror

"Beloved, let us love one another: for love is of God; and every one that loveth is born of God, and knoweth God." First John 4:7. "If a man say, I love God, and hateth his brother, he is a liar: for he that loveth not his brother whom he hath seen, how can he love God whom he hath not seen?" First John 4:20.

When you say you love God while withholding love from another, whether you know it or not, in God's eyes, that's called hypocrisy. If you love God, Jesus commands us to demonstrate it through our loving of others. And it's not just those who do good to you, for where is the stretch in that? Our love should mirror God's love. Are you mirroring God's love? Or are you one who believes people should earn your love?

I'm talking about agape love—unconditional love. Not love that asks: What have you done for me lately? Not the love that says, "I'll love you as long as you're doing what I think you should." Not the love that says, "I'll love you as long as you're acting the way I think you ought." But love without condition. Love that says, "If you're doing right, I love you. If you mess up, come here, let me love you as I help you get up and do better."

God loved us *before* we were saved. How can I say this? John 3:16 says, "For God so loved the world, that he gave his only begotten Son, that whosoever believeth in him should not perish, but have everlasting life." First John 4:19 says, "We love him, because he first loved us."

God didn't wait for you to get right before he loved you. He gave His Son *while* you were messed up. In fact, the reason He gave His Son is so that you and I would have a way back to Him. And even when we mess up, He's still there. He promises never to leave us nor forsake us. So when there is a leaving, it's us leaving Him, not Him leaving us.

Are you mirroring God? God is love. I know it can be hard to love someone who mistreats you, use you, misuse you, abuse you, treat you as though you don't matter. That's why this love is not our own doing, but God's. He helps us to love outside of our normal selves. First John 4:18 tells us, "There is no fear in love; but perfect love casteth out fear: because fear hath torment. He that feareth is not made perfect in love."

You don't have to be afraid when you love. God's love is more than enough to fill you even when people don't return that love. Think about it this way: We don't always treat God the way He should be treated, but He still loves us. That's how we must mirror God's love. Love anyway, and in the process, you may win over a brother or a sister. In any event, God will be pleased.

May I have a "Word" with you? Jesus tells us in John 13:34, "A new commandment I give unto you, That ye love one another, as I have loved you, that ye also love one another." That sounds like a mirror kind of love to me. Jesus is saying for you to love one another *as* He has loved you.

Do you love others as Jesus loves you? Are you mirroring God's love? When people look into the mirror called you, what are you reflecting? Is it one that God can be proud of? Michael Jackson sang a song called "Man in the Mirror." When you look in the mirror, what's being reflected in your life?

God is love. Don't be afraid. Love the way God has asked us to do, and let God take care of the rest. Remember: What you do for Christ will absolutely last!

Threads of God's Wisdom and Love

J spoke once at a church where their theme was "Women Weaving Tapestry with Threads of God's Wisdom and Love." When we think of weaving, we do tend to think of women weaving. But men weave as well. The message God speaks applies to all. As I looked at their theme, what jumped out was not just weaving, but weaving tapestry which is more than a simple weave. It is a weave of artistic expression. In Exodus 39:1 it states, "And of the blue, and purple, and scarlet, they made clothes (woven garments) of service, to do service in the holy place (sanctuary), and made the holy garments for Aaron; as the Lord commanded Moses."

Have you ever thought about what clothes are made from? Yes, it's material (as we used to say back in my day, some of you know what I'm talking about), or fabric as is the more acceptable terminology. But what creates fabric? Most fabric is merely threads woven tightly together. Single threads interlaced, strengthened by both the process and the unity of those threads.

Allow me to give you a quick summary of weaving. There's the loom which is the device by which the process of weaving is held as it is being done. When I think of a loom, I think of life. A loom holds threads that are placed vertically (called the warp) tightly as threads being weaved horizontally (called the weft) are woven into those

185

vertical strands: two distinct yarns or threads coming together on purpose, for a purpose.

As we go through life, the relationship we have with God (vertical) is held tight. God is holding us tightly as the threads we are given are being weaved into our lives. Tapestry goes a step beyond just plain weaving. A vision, a blueprint, a picture of what the finished product will look like when all is said and done is required. With tapestry, the end product is usually envisioned by an artist of repute.

In our lives, God is that artist of repute. He sees us as we shall be. We are being held tightly by God as various threads are being woven into our lives, in the end, creating a spectacular tapestry. It does not yet appear what we shall be, but we know that, when we see Jesus, we shall be like Him.

Our vertical relationship with God has an effect on our horizontal relationships. It should have an effect on the way we interact with one another. As God loves us unconditionally (vertical), so should we love each other (horizontal). As God forgives us when we ask after our trespasses, we should forgive those who trespass against us.

Tapestry was very big back in the early centuries. Kings and nobleman had them. They were beautiful artwork hung on walls and used as rugs. They were portable and could be rolled up and easily taken from place to place. But tapestry was more than just for show. They were also used for insulation to keep out the cold—made for service.

May I have a "Word" with you? You were made for more than just show. Yes, there is a purpose for your life. People may see you and be encouraged. But just as tapestry in the days of old was more than just for show, so are you. You're made *of* service, to *do* service. So as various threads show up in your own life, take those threads and weave them into the appropriate places to form a beautiful picture. Don't get discouraged. Keep weaving God's wisdom and love in your life.

And know this: you were made for more than just show!

Make Me, Mold Me

Gold, iron, and steel. Actually, last week, I was awakened with steel on my mind. God showed me something that was so powerful; I knew I had to share it. It's nothing new (there's nothing new under the sun really), but I believe there are times when God wants to tell us things or remind us of things we may have heard or already know.

Most of us have heard of the Man of Steel—Superman. In fact, I saw that the very first comic book (Action Comics) where the "Man of Steel" was featured, sold for $317,200 in an online auction.

Steel is an alloy consisting mostly of iron. There is more to the process of getting to a state of steel than most of us know (or may care to know). But suffice it to say that it takes a lot of heat (and cooling just right) to get to a state of steel, and a lot of heat to make something out of steel, once you have it. We're talking over one thousand Celsius degrees of heat. That can be quite hot! But let's just concentrate on taking the steel and making and molding it into something to use for what is desired, after we have steel.

When man wants to use steel for a specific purpose, it's heated to more of a liquid form, then poured into the mold of what is desired. Even in the days of blacksmiths, metal that was being used had to be heated and molded or shaped into what was desired.

Well, some of us are like iron or steel in a cold state. We've been shaped into a certain thing, and left to cool, and this is where we are now. When God desires to use us for a particular service, He can work with us in our present state, but He may find that how we are, is not how we need to be for a particular use.

So you may find yourself going through a heating process. That's when things get really hot in your life. You know, when all kinds of stuff seem to be happening. And the more you try to get out of it, the hotter it appears to get. That's when things are just not feeling so cool no matter where you turn, whether on your job, at home, at church, with your family, your finances, or your friends. Yes, you're looking for some relief from the heat, but it feels like the more you pray—the more you have a little talk with Jesus—the hotter things seem to get.

Now, don't get me wrong. I'm not saying that all the heat happening in your life right now is coming from God. But contrary to what some of us want to believe, there are times when things are not just from the devil. And when it is the devil, I can hear these words, "What Satan meant for bad, God is using it for good." Some of the hot stuff you're in may have even come from something you've done. Still, God can use that heat and apply it to the steel in our lives. As things begin to melt, God can make us, mold us, and shape us into something totally different than what people may have originally seen.

May I have a "Word" with you? When you find yourself going through the fire, pray that God will use it to mold you even more for His service. Pray that He gets the glory in the end. Pray that He will make and mold you into an instrument of His peace, His joy, and His love.

Steel can be used for lots of things. It can be used to strengthen skyscrapers and highways. It can be used to reinforce that which would not be able to stand strong on its own. You may not be able to stop the heat, but you can sure pray that as you go through it, when it's all said and done, you'll be used as a man or a woman of steel in the service of the Lord!

Job (not job) Moments

any of us may have experienced a "Job moment" in our lives. A "Job moment" is when one thing after another seems to happen and you're left trying to figure out what's happening and why. Perhaps you didn't start out as a righteous man as Job was called by God.

Maybe there are things in your past that you know was (and is) flat-out wrong, and you can't see how even God could be so loving that He forgave you for it. But that's how God is. Maybe you grew up in church and you don't consider yourself a "bad" person, but you recognize you were a sinner who came to accept Jesus, and you're now saved by grace. You may really be trying to live right, but somehow Job moments have found a way into your life.

Job moments.

That's when you find that you're blessed, but before someone can tell you one bad news, here's someone else bringing some more bad news. It's having material things and finding something coming along that takes it away from you through no fault of your own. It's friends talking about you and concluding there has to be some sin (secret or otherwise) in your life causing all these bad things to happen to you.

A Job moment is when your physical body is being attacked and things don't seem to be getting any better. It's when you lose the people you love the most, when the person you have vowed to become one with gets so frustrated with your life that they tell you to just curse

God and die. A Job moment is when you find yourself crying out to God for help, love, and mercy as you expect any minute for things to turn around; only to find yourself questioning God on some level even though you know you shouldn't be questioning God on *any* level.

If I can bring this home to your doorstep, it's when you find that there is constantly more *month* left than *money*. It's when your children have turned away from the upbringing and teachings you've worked so hard to instill in them about God and responsibility. It's when you watch your children being hurt by the decisions they make, the people they choose to have in their lives, and you find there's nothing you can do to help or save them. It's when you pray that the few gallons of gas you put in the car will last like the oil in the lamps lasted for those who now celebrate it as Hanukkah.

It's when you pray that your credit card won't say "declined." It's when the people you have befriended and given so much of yourself to won't answer the phone and refuse to return your call after you leave a message. It's when that spouse you've sacrificed for and loved unconditionally leaves you because "something" or "someone" better came along. It's when you pray, confess, and believe, and you know you're walking in faith, but in the end, things still just didn't come out the way you desired.

A Job moment is when all is said and done, there is no one left but you and God, and the dialogue is only between the two of you.

After Job's "moments," he challenged God and, in essence, found that his arms were indeed not long enough to even attempt to box with God. From Job, chapter 38-41, God does what I often call "read Job." You know what it is to read a person? That's when you throw the book at them, and let them have it in terms they can understand.

In Job chapter 42, verses 1-6, Job fully submits to God. Verses 5-6, Job states, "I have heard of thee by the hearing of the ear; but now mine eye seeth thee: Wherefore I abhor myself, and repent in dust and ashes."

Job submitted to God and after that you see Job 42:12 where God blesses him. "So the Lord blessed the latter end of Job more than his beginning." His latter was greater than his beginning. Hallelujah to the Most High God!

May I have a "Word" with you? Submit fully to God, and you'll find you don't get as upset about the bad things that happen in your life. You can endure because you know that God is still in control. You know that when you fully submit to God, whatever Satan may mean for your bad, God is going to use it for your good. When you fully submit, you can go through whatever life brings with joy not because you're enjoying what's happening to you, but because you know that God sees and knows all.

You do know that the same God Who blessed Job will bless you after your own "moments," right?

Submit to God and watch Him do great things *in* and *through* your life!

Like a Tree, I Shall Not Be Moved

et's face it: Things don't always go the way we plan or want them to. Isaiah 61:3 says, "To appoint unto them that mourn in Zion, to give unto them beauty for ashes, the oil of joy for mourning, the garment of praise for the spirit of heaviness, that they might be called trees of righteousness, the planting of the Lord, that he might be glorified." That they might be called trees of righteousness.

This is powerful. You see, most trees grow deep roots—most, as deep as the tree is tall. A tree will stand in and through all kinds of weather and through the various seasons of life. When God plants you like a tree, you will truly be able to boast and say, "I shall not be moved."

Many times, I have used the example of a palm tree. If you've ever paid attention to a television news report during a hurricane, you'll see that many of those places are areas where palm trees are the dominant trees. What I love about a palm tree is: when the wind is blowing hard and the rain is beating down, a palm tree will stand tall and high. Its top always appears, to me, to be lifting up holy hands and praising God as it sways in the storm. A palm tree looks like it's determined to give God praises, even when in a storm. And you know what? You rarely ever see a palm tree uprooted after a storm.

I'm not going to say that it absolutely doesn't happen, but I've seen trees in other places after a storm, and it's a totally different scene. A palm tree stands strong in good times and bad.

May I have a "Word" with you? Let us praise God regardless of what's going on in our lives. I can tell you from personal experience that praise releases even more blessings of the Lord to flow into your life. A shout of praise has the power to bring down walls (remember the walls of Jericho?). Praise can lift up a heavy spirit and a heavy heart. Praise will take you to another level in the Lord. Praise takes the focus off the problem and places it on the One Who possesses the solution.

Be like a tree planted by the waters. Tell those who are looking for you to fall at any time that you're going to be like the palm tree, and you're going to praise God *anyhow*. Be like a tree planted by the waters, and declare with conviction, "I shall not be moved!"

Renewed Strength

At some point, all of us get a little tired. Whether it's something you've been doing all of your life, or something that you're beginning to do that seems to beat you down at times. It can be a physical tiredness, or one that comes from the inside. God gives us a way to recoup from the physical tiredness (sleep and rest), but what about the spiritual tiredness, the spiritual exhaustion we may experience?

Spiritual exhaustion. You know, when you know God told you to do something but it appears no one is responding to the work you're trying to do. Maybe you're a pastor and the congregation is fighting you on what you know, without a doubt, God has instructed you to do. Maybe you're a member of a church congregation with a gift God bestowed upon you (not a talent, and there is a difference), but a cap has been placed on what you're allowed to do. When you're capped, it doesn't matter who's doing the capping (the leader, fellow members, yourself, or the devil), capped is capped.

Maybe you feel like you've been fighting for so long, believing things were going to get better or help would come, and you're tired now. You put yourself out there to do the work of the Lord, but you're not sure if anyone is even receiving it. What do the tired do?

Isaiah 40:29 says, "He giveth power to the faint; and to them that have no might he increaseth strength." Without going any further than that verse, that's a Word right there for someone. God gives power to you when you're weak. And when you feel you can't take another step, he increases your strength. Isaiah 40:30 goes on to say, "Even the youths shall faint and be weary, and the young men shall utterly fall."

Strength has nothing to do with age. Young people get tired and weary, so it's not the getting up in age that makes one weary. When you try and try and try, and do and do and do, you're bound to get tired or worn out sometimes. However, Isaiah 40:31 declares, "But they that wait upon the Lord shall renew their strength; they shall mount up with wings as eagles; they shall run, and not be weary; and they shall walk, and not faint."

Wait upon the Lord! God will renew your strength. Renew means to make new again. If you renew a membership, you add the time back like it was when you first began. Just that should be enough to encourage you right now. But that verse goes even further by saying that you'll mount up with wings.

Can we stop here for a second? Where you were on your feet making it, now you're going to mount up with wings. Most of us know if we have a choice between walking, driving or riding in a car, on a bus or train, or to fly, we'd prefer flying. Face it, flying can get you there faster. When God renews your strength, He will put you on the fast track with wings. And not just any wings, but wings as eagles—a bird that soars with majesty and grace, and looks good while doing it.

And for those times when you must run, you'll run, but you won't get weary. If you have to walk, you'll walk and not faint.

May I have a "Word" with you? There's no god like our God. There's nobody like Jehovah. Nobody can do me like Jesus. God cares about you and every aspect of your life. So when you're feeling tired, beat up, beat down, or wondering why keep doing when it appears no one seems to care . . . when you feel like what you're doing is not making a difference, I say to you: "Wait on the Lord!" God is doing a supernatural thing in, with, *and* for you.

And your strength is being renewed daily.

Satisfaction Guaranteed

I was praying about what to write, and I was sitting there with my Bible. The wind from the ceiling fan flipped the pages. I flipped it to another page, and the breeze flipped it right back. I asked God what He wanted me to see. I looked down, and my eyes were directed to Proverbs 12:14, "A man shall be satisfied with good by the fruit of his mouth: and the recompense of a man's hands shall be rendered unto him."

"Ah, but I'm familiar with this verse," I say to God. "I've used it in one of my books." Then I hear in my spirit, "Satisfaction guaranteed." Wow, God! You are good!

Have you ever bought something and were told that if you weren't completely satisfied, you could bring it back? Or maybe during an advertisement to encourage you to purchase a thing or give a particular service a try, you heard, "Satisfaction guaranteed." Well, they don't know what real satisfaction guaranteed is all about.

According to Proverbs 12:14, you'll be satisfied with good by the fruit of your mouth. This tells us: In our lives, in our daily walk, that if things aren't going well, then the defect may be as close as under our nose. Literally, we might need to check our mouth, and see what's coming out of it. "Out of the abundance of the heart, the mouth speaketh."

How many times have you spoken negative things? Those classic hits like: "I told you I wasn't going to get that (you fill in the blank)."

"I said they'd give that promotion to someone else before they'd ever give it to me." Then there are some of Satan's favorites. "I don't ever seem to have any money." "Every time I try to get ahead, something always happens." "If it wasn't for bad luck, I'd have no luck at all." Oops, that's right—Christians don't use the word luck, right?

Okay, back to the list. "I'm so broke, it's not even funny." "The devil is busy." "I can't ever seem to win, I don't care what I do." "I believe I'm trying to come down with something." "Every time I take one step forward, I take two steps back." "If trouble ain't leaving me, it's on its way." "I can't do anything right." "I'm barely making it." "If it ain't one thing, it's another." I could go on, but you get the idea.

Some people call *thinking* it and *speaking* it, "The Law of Attraction." The Bible tells us, "A man shall be satisfied with good by the fruit of his mouth" which tells me that a man can then be frustrated with bad by the fruit of his mouth. I like to make it simple, and put it this way. "You have what you say." Yes, that's in the Bible several times in several different ways.

Mark 11:23 tells us that "Whosoever shall say . . . and shall not doubt . . . but shall believe . . . those things he SAITH shall come to pass . . . he shall have whatsoever he SAITH." If you think it and say it continually and long enough, you *shall* have what you say.

May I have a "Word" with you? Do you want real satisfaction, guaranteed? Then start speaking good things, Godly things. Start saying what God says. It's backed by God who inspired Isaiah to pen, "For as the rain cometh down, and the snow from heaven, and returneth not thither, but watereth the earth, and maketh it bring forth and bud, that it may give seed to the sower, and bread to the eater: So shall my word be that goeth forth out of my mouth: it shall not return unto me void, but it shall accomplish that which I please, and it shall prosper in the thing whereto I sent it." (Isaiah 54:10-11).

You want satisfaction guaranteed? Then check the label, and say what God says.

Pressing to Get the Wrinkles Out

ears ago, pressing or ironing clothes was a major job people would perform for others—charging a fee to do it even. Now with wash and wear, clothes dryers, and dry cleaners; we don't have to deal with this chore necessarily the way it was done in the past. Still, there are times we have to take out an iron and ironing board to get the wrinkles out.

And so it may be in our lives at times. God might find it necessary to take out the iron or use some form of steam to remove the wrinkles from our lives in order to make us straighter and more presentable.

Amos 3:13 states, "Behold, I am pressed under you, as a cart is pressed that is full of sheaves." None of us are probably fond of the idea of being pressed. But when you look at it, it's a way to ensure we're presentable and pleasing in God's sight.

In the natural, we understand how horrible wrinkles can appear to others (especially when the style wasn't meant to be worn wrinkled). Wrinkles can give the appearance of possibly not caring, neglect, laziness, or lack. So there will be times when God (as He looks at certain places in and on us, and to ensure that we're presentable) will take out the iron, and we'll find ourselves being pressed in order to get those unsightly wrinkles out.

Ironing can be a heavy thing, especially when some type of pressure is exerted. And even though steam can be hot, it can cause the process to go faster and be easier for all concerned. When you're being pressed, it may not feel so great, but just know: When it's all done, you'll be a lot straighter and even crisper looking. Personally, there's nothing I like better than seeing something wrinkled become transformed into something straight.

So if I may encourage you at all here, let me say: When you feel the pressure from the ironing process or the heat from the steam, just hang in there. I promise, after it's done, you're going to look and be so much better than before it began!

There will also be times in your life when you run into wrinkles — those things that make life crumpled and bumpy. Don't get frustrated or discouraged. Take out your iron (the Word of God) and just keep pressing. Philippians 3:13 tells us, "Brethren, I count not myself to have apprehended: but this one thing I do, forgetting those things which are behind, and reaching forth unto those things which are before." Forget about what it was like in the past. Press ahead.

May I have a "Word" with you? Philippians 3:14 says, "I press toward the mark for the prize of the high calling of God in Christ Jesus." Make up your mind that you're going to keep pressing even as you're being pressed. Then proclaim as Philippians 3:15 says, "Let us therefore, as many as be perfect, be thus minded: and if any thing ye be otherwise minded, God shall reveal even this unto you." God will show you the wrinkles if you'll ask Him.

And whether you're being pressed or allowed to be pressed by God so that you can truly be presentable as a Child of the Most High King, or you find yourself pressing through those things that attempt to make life unpleasant for you, remember: Pressing to get the wrinkles out is not always a bad thing.

And may I say: That looks *GOOD* on you!

The Right Word

As a writer, I realize the importance of using the right or correct word. I've seen people use the word *your* when the correct word is *you're, forward* when it was *foreword,* and *it's* when the right word should be *its* (and vice versa). The word "your" indicates possessive where the word "you're" is a contraction for "you are." And should you ever see the word "forward" being used in the front of a book, please know that the correct word and spelling is "foreword." And yes, there *is* a difference; and yes, it *does* matter.

Then there are my all-time favorites, the words *than* and *then.* In fact, these two words have been incorrectly used for one another so much, I had to make sure the definition hadn't changed and no one had informed the rest of us about it. My investigation proved that the word "than" is still used to show unequal comparisons, where the word "then" still has to do with time, in addition to, or consequences. Sure, I can almost hear some of you saying, "That was *then,* this is now. But spiritually speaking, does using the right word other than for my English class really make a difference?"

Yes, it does.

Proverbs 25:11 says, "A word fitly spoken is like apples of gold in pictures of silver." In eighth chapter of Matthew, there's a story of a centurion who came in search of Jesus. The centurion said, "Lord, my servant lieth at home sick of the palsy, grievously tormented." Jesus said to the centurion, "I will come and heal him." In the eighth verse,

200

the centurion said, "Lord, I am not worthy that thou shouldest come under my roof: but speak the word only, and my servant shall be healed."

Each time I think about this scripture, I absolutely love the words "Speak the word only." And I believe there's so much to latch onto inside this passage of scripture for those of us who are true believers. Speak the "word" only. Speak the WORD only.

No matter what's going on in your life, learn to speak the Word only. Say only what the Word of God says. Not what anyone else thinks or some cute little sayings that really have no power. But we need to write, believe, and *speak* only what God says about, over, and surrounding our many situations.

Just as there is a difference in using the wrong word when delivering a message, you can deliver the wrong *Word* when it comes to things concerning your life. Why continue saying wrong words like "I'm broke" or "I'll never win" when the Word of God advises each of us that life and death are in the power of the tongue? We should, like our Father in Heaven already does, "call those things which be not as though they were." In order words, make sure the words you use are the right words. You *have* what you say, so why continue using words that aren't bringing what you desire into your life?

Words . . . have . . . power!

Look at Genesis, chapter one verse three where God said, "Let there be light." Following that is the conjunction "and" which indicates there's more to follow. In this case, the word "and" is used to let us know what happened after God said, "Let there be light." And what happened? "*And* there was light." You see, God wasn't harping on what He saw (which was darkness), He spoke what He desired (which was light). Throughout the rest of that chapter, you witness God speaking, the Spirit moving, and things happening according to the words that were spoken.

Do you realize God's Word says that God can do exceeding abundantly above all we can ever ask or think? So what words are you using for God to work with? Are your words negative or are they the wrong words? Are your words speaking to lack and/or sickness, when God's Word tells you the right Word should speak to abundance and being in health?

May I have a "Word" with you? Are you using the word "their" when God uses the word "there"? As in Romans 8:1 where the scripture says: "There is therefore now no condemnation to them which are in Christ Jesus, who walk not after the flesh, but after the Spirit."

If you really don't believe using the right word makes a difference, then consider this example: No God, No Peace. Know God, Know Peace. See, there is a difference. Yes, using the right word can and will make all the difference in the world!

What Are You Waiting On?

hat are you waiting on to happen before you're satisfied? What are you waiting on to be happy? What are you waiting on to feel like you've made it? What are you waiting on to not only take out, but eat off your best china and drink out of your crystal glass?

So many people are waiting on something to happen before they're willing to celebrate life. Many people are waiting on certain things to happen before they can smile. People, God is so good. He's so good to us. Even when things don't seem to being going the way we think they should, God is still worthy to be praised. And when we walk around with our heads down, looking all gloomy because some things we thought would have happened already haven't, we're only cheating ourselves. We save our good china for company, waiting on outside things to occur before we'll allow ourselves to celebrate.

I'd like to ask you to do something for me for the next 21 days. Every day I want you to write down at least one thing you're grateful for. Every day, I'd like for you to look in the mirror and tell yourself something you're pleased or proud of yourself. And every day, I'd like you to purposely find at least one person and say something kind to them. And if you're not already doing it, one day a week, at least for the next three weeks, take out your best china with your best crystal and eat on it without having any outside company in attendance. Think of it as a date with the Lord—the Lord sitting right there with you.

Satan is beating up and beating down on enough of us already—we need to stop helping him. The Lord is speaking to me right now and telling me to let you know how much He loves you and wants the best for you. You're His child, and He wants nothing more than to come in and sup with you, to let you know how precious you are to Him.

You don't have to wait until everything is right in your life to celebrate God's goodness. Just being able to see another day should give you reason to celebrate! Not just because you're here, but because God so loved the world that He gave His only begotten Son. Celebrate because whatever is going on in your life, God is still right there with you as you go through it. You're not alone. I know you may feel like it sometimes, but you're not.

Maybe you don't hear much about how fearfully and wonderfully made you really are. But God is saying that you are fearfully and wonderfully made, and He loves you.

May I have a "Word" with you? When the apostle Paul was going through his trials and tribulations, he was still able to say in Philippians 4:10-12. "But I rejoiced in the Lord greatly, that now at the last your care of me hath flourished again; wherein ye were also careful, but ye lacked opportunity. Not that I speak in respect of want: for I have learned, in whatsoever state I am, therewith to be content. I know both how to be abased, and I know how to abound; everywhere and in all things I am instructed both to be full and to be hungry, both to abound and to suffer need." In a nutshell: content to celebrate!

When things are going great for you, praise God. When things aren't going so great, praise God. Why praise Him when things aren't going great? Because you know you're coming out. And just like the three Hebrews boys in the fiery furnace, there won't even be the smell of smoke on you or your clothes when you do.

What are you waiting on? You don't have to wait for the battle to be over; celebrate now. Shout now!

Glory!

Yet

any times people will want to know if what we prayed for or believed for has happened. Especially when some time has passed, in some cases years or possibly even decades. Many of us who've been told something by God really believed it was going to happen, then the time rolls along, and we seem to be just as far away from it happening as we were when we began. This morning when I arose, I heard the word repeat in my spirit like on a loop, "Yet."

One of the reasons I was thinking about that word is because when I tell people what God has spoken over my life, I will sometime add, "I know you may be looking and say that you don't see that to be the case . . . yet." Or I might say "It hasn't happened . . . *yet*."

Yet! A three-letter word, but it's a powerful qualifying word. I know my confession has been: "I am a #1 *New York Times'* bestsellers list published author," and many could say (and rightly so) that this has not manifested. To that, I will only add one small word—yet.

God showed me something one day when I was talking to Him about my confession (that incidentally *He* placed in my heart to begin speaking). He told me to take that confession and work it from the back to the front, right to left. He wanted me to see just how far He has brought me already.

So here goes. When I left my wonderful corporate-America job making good money and all of its fantastic benefits (which also included a nice lump sum bonus once a year), and I stepped out on faith, I couldn't claim the distinction of being called an author—yet. You see, I didn't have a truly completed book ready for publication. Sure, I may have thought I did. And I was working at my craft. But everything you write is not necessarily all that great and definitely not something a publisher might decide to acquire.

After I wrote a book that was ready, *that* qualified me to be called an author (the last word in my confession). I tried to get it published, but wasn't able to secure a traditional publisher in the beginning. I ended up publishing it myself. Still, here you can see the next word of my confession as we continue to move from right to left. I was now a published author.

And as only God can do a thing, one of the three books I published myself (*Promises Beyond Jordan*) was acquired by a mainstream, traditional publisher: BET Books as well as the rights to a second novel: *Wings of Grace*. Later, I would sign a three-book deal with Kensington (Dafina Imprint), and they released *Blessed Trinity*, *Strongholds*, and *If Memory Serves*. And then another three-book deal with them (in sets of three-book deals for a total of twelve published books in all).

One May 31st day, I opened an email announcing the BCNN1 Bestseller's List. Surprising to me (but not to God), the #1 Bestselling Christian fiction novel for their June report was *Practicing What You Preach*. My novels were hitting bestsellers' lists, fulfilling yet another part of the confession.

Little ole me, Vanessa Davis Griggs, from Village Springs, Alabama, and will you just look at how far God has brought me. And you know what? He loves you no less than He loves me. You just have to believe, be faithful, and act like the Word of God is true.

Next in line in this confession progression is *New York Times*, and then all that is left is #1 on the *New York Times*.

May I have a "Word" with you? I am not telling you this just to pump myself up. I'm telling you this to encourage you in your walk, in your dreams, in your goals. I don't want you to get discouraged when things have not manifested, and you begin to feel like you're failing.

Only you know what God has told you. Only you can continue to believe when it looks like it's *yet* so far away. So what if people laugh at you. Let them laugh . . . let them talk. Keep smiling. And when people don't support you; thank God for those who do.

As I sat here writing this, I ended up turning my Bible to a page where I had randomly stuck some of my bookmarks. It happens it was one of my favorite passages: Psalm 37. And then, the Word of God leapt off the page at me in verse twenty-five. "I have been young, and now am old; yet have I not seen the righteous forsaken, nor his seed begging bread."

YET.

Yet, have I not seen the righteous forsaken (even when it may look like it). *Yet* the righteous is not forsaken. Not by God.

Has your dream, your goal, your ministry happened the way God has spoken? Well, let me give you the proper and truthful way to answer that question from now on when it presents itself to you, and you can't answer with a resounding yes.

"No, it hasn't—**YET.**"

Praise God Through Your Storms

These past weeks, many have gone through a lot. My heart and prayers goes out to those who have lost loved ones and other things. Many people are hurting right now. People are dealing with a lot in their lives whether directly in the "storm" or not. People may not talk about it. You may even find yourself sitting next to someone hurting and never even know it. Others you may know but only know a fraction of what folks are dealing with.

Then there are the mental battles we face. Those promises God has told us specifically where reality doesn't seem anywhere close to what He told us. And yet, we know He said it to us. This is where family and friends usually come in and question our judgment or sanity. "If God told you that, then why are you having such a hard time bringing it about?" or "Maybe you just *misheard* God and what He really meant was _____ (fill in the blank)." Even you begin to question whether it was really God you heard or was it just your mind telling you something.

And if you let the devil see there's a crack in your armor, He will truly mess with you then. "If God really told you that then why are you having such a hard time? Why isn't God helping you more? You know: if I was you, I'd just quit. Why don't you stop and try something else?"

Someone knows exactly what I'm talking about. Things just don't seem to be lining up. Trouble comes and nothing seems to be working in your favor. You know God is with you, but you can't help but wonder why you have to struggle so hard, so much just to bring things about.

First let me say that when God tells you something, you know it's Him. There's something about God's voice, a peace and calmness when He speaks. God will settle things inside of you early on, so when you do find yourself in a place of questions, you can always reference back to that peace, tap into that calmness.

May I have a "Word" with you? You must learn to praise God anyhow. Praise God in the storm, no matter what form that storm may take. Praise God when you're up; praise Him when you're down. Praise Him when He's sending you the assistance and the people you need to get things done; praise Him when it looks like you're all by yourself. Praise Him when blessings are overtaking you; praise Him when you aren't sure how you're going to make it.

You see, Satan uses your down times as an opportunity to see just how steadfast you truly are. Anybody can praise God when things are up and going great. You find out when people are for real when things aren't going so great.

The bottom line: God is worthy to be praised! So praise God *anyhow*! That should be your mindset. Let me tell you a secret. I praise God even more when things aren't going great. You see: I know God is there with me and honestly, imagine how frustrating it is for the devil when you're praising God even more when he was expecting you to quit. That you have the *audacity* to praise God that much more when Satan thought he had you.

Saints, praise God anyhow! Praise Him through your storms!

Preserved

I really like fresh fruit and vegetables. Taking out a container of strawberries one day, God gave me a wonderful Word. Inside the container were various size strawberries. What caught my attention immediately was seeing a few of my beautiful strawberries were starting to go bad.

My first thought was to get the bad ones away from the good ones as quickly as possible. I knew the bad alongside the good would eventually cause the good ones to go bad, that much faster. For the fruit going bad, I understood I could cut off the bad parts and keep what was worth saving. For those too far gone, I'd have to just throw them away.

God spoke to me and said, "Just like the good fruit and the bad fruit here, that's how people must be attentive regarding who they hang around." You see, although good fruit was in there with the bad, the good fruit (as wonderful as it looked and was) could never turn the bad fruit back to good. But the bad fruit, if continued to be left around and with the good fruit could definitely infect the good fruit and cause them to go bad.

Many times those trying to live right . . . those producing good fruit believe they can hang with the infected, in their environment and on their terms, and change them. I'm not saying those who know the way shouldn't be witnessing and ministering to those who don't know that Jesus is the way, the truth, and the life, and that no man comes to the Father except by Jesus. What I'm saying is: If you're good fruit, you have to watch being around fruit that is rotten or rotting. Hear me again: Good fruit can't turn bad fruit to good; but bad fruit can affect good fruit in negative ways; and if left around and unchecked for too long, can turn good bad.

But there is Good News! The Holy Spirit is able to preserve and protect. And preserved and protected fruit can withstand being around bad fruit without being affected in the same way as good fruit that hasn't been preserved. Jude verse 24 says, "Now unto him that is able to keep you from falling, and to present you faultless before the presence of his glory with exceeding joy." This verse should have you shouting right about now.

Can't you just see Jesus presenting you as fruit, faultless, because all the bad parts have been cut away? He can present you faultless because you were "kept" . . . you are saved . . . you are preserved. And during those times you find yourself witnessing to or around bad fruit, you won't get infected because of "Him" that is able to keep you from falling!

May I have a "Word" with you? Don't be so arrogant as to believe because your fruit is good that *that* alone is enough to keep you from being affected by fruit that's infected. That's why good parents tell their children not to hang around certain people. They understand how other people's negative ways can rub off. You've heard, "One bad apple can spoil the whole bunch."

So when it comes to good fruit versus bad, good is great, but when you're preserved, you can withstand so much more. Just make sure God is with you and don't hang around bacteria-laced fruit too long to get infected.

Strive to be good examples for the Kingdom of God. And remember: the Word of God is sharper than any two-edged sword. Let God's Word cut away the bad parts in your life and the lives of others.

And when it comes to being preserved, know this—Jesus saves!

True Transformers

ransformers—more than meets the eyes." Okay, I had three boys, two of which happened to have grown up during the first time a toy called transformers hit the market. Children loved those robot-looking men called action figures that could turn into something else entirely like a car, an airplane, or an animal.

And when five of them became connected to each other, they were something even bigger than themselves. Those transformers had names like Optimus Prime and Megatron. There were the good guys (called the autobots) and the bad guys (called decepticons). The commercial selling those action figures would proudly sing, "Transformers—more than meets the eyes."

In real life, being a transformer can be a good thing or it can be bad. In a bad way, there are some who profess Jesus as Lord of their life while looking, being, and acting holy on Sundays, while changing into something else entirely during the rest of the week.

Question: When people see you, are they seeing the real deal or someone who's one way with some people or in certain places and another way with others?

The Bible has something to say about transformers, however it's more positive. Romans 12:2 says, "And be not conform to this world: but be ye transformed by the renewing of your mind, that ye may prove what is that good, and acceptable, and perfect, will of God." Stop trying to look like the world when you have been declared a peculiar people. Don't be copies popped out of a set mold with a worldly view of thinking and value system reflecting the world. You're not of this world. Become Godly, transformed by the renewing of your mind and taking on the mind of Christ.

First Peter 1:14 says, "As obedient children, not fashioning yourselves according to the former lusts in your ignorance." That's why Hosea says, "My people are destroyed for a lack of knowledge."

Holy Spirit-led transformers are truly more than meets the eyes. Godly transformers walk by faith and not by sight. They're not moved by what they see with their natural eyes, especially when it's contrary to the Word or promises of God. Godly transformers know that when you see them, there is more to them than meets the eyes.

May I have a "Word" with you? "Beloved, now are we the sons of God, and it doth not yet appear what we shall be: but we know that, when he shall appear, we shall be like him; for we shall see him as he is." (1 John 3:2) Those in Christ have already been transformed from sinner to righteous and yes, to children of the most High God. But even now, it still doesn't *yet* appear all that we shall be.

So don't get too upset when those who have confessed Christ don't always look and act the way you think they should. God is not through with any of us yet. He's still working on all of us.

No, I can't tell you what I'll look like when He finishes with me, but I do know that when Jesus does appear, I'm going to look like Him.

Godly transformers—yes, we're more than meets the eyes!

Vine and Branches

I witnessed something quite spectacular. My son called me to come outside to see a tree whose leaves were moving seemingly completely on their own. My first thought was a squirrel, a bird, or some other animal was the cause. Upon closer inspection, I saw that was not the case. Neither was it the wind. Suddenly as I stood there, almost every leaf on the branches of the tree began to spin or dance. We both agreed it seemed the tree was praising God—waving and spinning, giving God glory! I continued to stand in awe.

A few days before that, I'd looked out on a grapevine I'd bought a few years ago and planted. Two things came to my mind at that time. One: how that grapevine was merely a stick when I bought it. The second: how in John 15 Jesus described Himself as the True vine and we, as the branches.

Let's look at the first thing. Some of you may have been told you're "not all that" or that you're "not that much." Sort of like the grapevine I bought. It didn't look like it was all that much, and it certainly didn't look like the picture on the package. But I had faith, and I did as instructed. We planted it, watered it, and you know what? God gave the increase! Now that stick flourishes and is a thick green luscious vine stretching about six feet wide. It now produces fruit and looks like the picture it was advertised to be.

To those who act like you're nothing but a stick; let them watch and see as God gives the increase in your life. God already has a picture of what you're going to look like when you spiritually, fully mature. So fret not yourself about what people say about you. They don't have a clue who God has created you to be. They may see a stick; God sees a lush green vine producing lots of good fruit. You just need to be sure you're planted in the right place, and get growing.

Let me say it again: find some good soil and plant yourself in it. Get all the nourishment you can. Have the right PH balances (prophecy and Holy Spirit, meaning the Word with the Holy Spirit leading). If you need to be worked around to loosen things up, don't get mad, just allow it to take place. Endure the breaking up of compacted dirt realizing that you and your roots will be the better for it.

And yes, there will be times when you'll need to be pruned. Just know that it's being done to make you stronger, and to ensure you'll produce even bigger and better fruit in the future.

The other thing I thought about is how Jesus is the true vine and we are the branches. A branch cannot exist apart from the vine. If we (the branches) are rooted through Jesus (the vine), then we will produce good fruit.

The problem is when we decide as branches that we want to go off and do our own thing apart from Jesus. Let me say this as plain as I can say it. Jesus is the vine, you are a branch. There are other branches attached to the vine, so realize you're not the only one. And if you decide to cut yourself off from the vine, you will die. The branch cannot live apart from the vine. Period.

May I have a "Word" with you? Jesus is the True vine. Those of us who have accepted Jesus live, move, and have our being in Him. If you think you did something great because you've produced some really great fruit in the past, don't get the big head and think you can now go off and do your own thing.

I can personally say: Without Jesus in my life, what I do is nothing! He is the reason I do what I do. His love for the world and me doing what I've been called to do is what gives me so much joy.

Jesus chose us, we didn't choose Him. But you must accept Him into your life. We all have the opportunity to be part of His wonderful vine!

O taste and see how good the Lord is.

The Love of God

*P*eople at some point in their lives will ask the question, "Do you love me?" And if the answer is yes, the next question, whether asked or not, is "How much do you love me?" The thing is: everybody wants to be loved and to feel loved. That's how we're made. The hardest, toughest person out there, whether they admit it or not, wants to feel loved.

Not everybody will treat us the way we feel someone who loves us should be treated. And not everyone's idea of what loves is matches the other. There are also different levels in love. There is the parent/child love, the sibling love, the best friend love, the boyfriend/girlfriend love we also call dating. There is the love in marriage. Then there is the Love of God.

Oh, how my heart leaps when I think of the Love of God. John 3:16 tells us, "For God so loved the world that He gave His only begotten Son." Now, if God had just sent His only begotten Son to walk here on earth to show us how things should be done that would be a lot.

It's like when our wonderful, dedicated soldiers go to another place to give service on our behalf. I'm speaking specifically of soldiers that go to another state, many to other countries sometimes halfway around the world, and we eagerly look and pray for their safe return.

Well, God gave His only begotten Son knowing that He would be giving His life. God Who knew in advance, what awaited His Son when He got here.

This is why I tell folks who are feeling down or depressed because they feel no one loves them, they are loved so much. Think about it. God loved you so much that He gave His only begotten Son just for you. For you. Now, that's love that surpasses love!

Jesus came here knowing that He would die. Jesus often reminded people that He had to be about His Father's business. Not only did Jesus show us how to live our lives here on earth, but He was beaten for our transgressions; He was bruised for our iniquities. In other words, Jesus paid the price for us. It was charged to us, but Jesus paid the bill.

May I have a "Word" with you? Jesus loves you this I know. He was mocked for you. He was beaten for you. He was nailed to the cross for you. Jesus was pierced in the side . . . for you. That crown of thorns placed on His head . . . that was for you.

And every time you want to know how much you're loved, I want you to picture Jesus hanging high on the cross with outstretched arms saying to you, "Do you want to know how much I love you? I love you this much." Because that's how much He loves you. He loved you enough to give His life for you. There is no greater love than that. I'm talking about the Love of God.

As an author, I hate when people tell the end of the story. But I have to tell you: This is not how the story ends. Spoiler Alert: On the third day, the Love of God touched Jesus and raised Him from the dead. Jesus arose! And He arose with all power! You are loved so much that God desires for you to have the keys to the Kingdom so that you can loose and lock those things as they need to be done "on earth as it is in Heaven."

I'm talking about the Love of God: God the Father, God the Son, and God the Holy Ghost. If you don't know about this love, then you need to know. Because our God is an awesome God and the Love of God is powerful! Jesus gave His life for you.

Why would you not want to give your life to Him?!

How Long Will You Wait On God's Promise?

*A*nd, behold, there was a man in Jerusalem, whose name was Simeon; and the same man was just and devout, waiting for the consolation of Israel: and the Holy Ghost was upon him. And it was revealed unto him by the Holy Ghost, that he should not see death, before he had seen the Lord's Christ. And he came by the Spirit into the temple: and when the parents brought in the child Jesus, to do for him after the custom of the law, Then took he him up in his arms, and blessed God, and said, Lord, now lettest thou thy servant depart in peace, according to thy word. For mine eyes have seen thy salvation, Which thou hast prepared before the face of all people." Luke 2:25-31.

Has God told you something? Has God promised you something? Was something revealed to you by the Holy Ghost that has yet to come to pass? How long will you wait for it to manifest? How long before you quit? How long before you give up? How long before you become rational and start rationalizing, questioning what you may or may not have really heard from God, what you were told by the Holy Spirit? How long before you decide to "get real" and go another way because logic says standing and believing on this particular thing is not logical? How long will you wait on what God has promised you?

It's a legitimate question, and I dare say fair to ask you. I've asked it of myself on more than one occasion. We're all human. And honestly, most of us aren't that great when it comes to waiting. Oh, we think we are. "I'm going to wait until my change comes." But that's only if that wait is a reasonable time in our sight or those who are around us.

We're like children going on a trip (long or otherwise). They know there is a specific destination before they ever begin. They know they're due to get there at some time. But after a while, comes that all too familiar question. "Are we there yet?"

Simeon was an elderly man who had been promised a specific thing by God: that he would not see death before he had seen the Lord's Christ. Imagine him waking up every day wondering if this day would be the day that God's promise would be fulfilled. What I love about this account is the twenty-seventh verse where it says, "And he came by the Spirit into the temple." The Holy Spirit was leading and guiding him, but the blessed thing about this is that Simeon followed the leading. Many times the Holy Spirit is leading us in a certain direction but we decide to choose our own way. How many times have you missed an appointed time because you didn't follow God's lead?

What would have happened had on this day Simeon said, "I don't feel like going to the temple today. I'm tired. Why keep doing this?" People, it's so important to be in tune to what God is telling you to do and more importantly to be obedient even when it doesn't make sense to you . . . even if it doesn't make sense to your family or your friends.

May I have a "Word" with you? What has God told you? What has God promised you? Have you quit (for whatever reason that may have seemed legitimate and logical at the time)? Are you trying to stay the course but are tired, asking, "Are we there yet?" Don't be weary in well-doing. You will reap the promise God has made to you if you'll faint not. The question is: How long will you wait? Only you can answer this. Me? I'm going to wait until I see the salvation of the Lord.

I'm going to wait until the promises God has made to me are manifested. Trust God. Trust God's integrity. God is awesome!

Miracles

*J*udges 6:13 says, "And Gideon said unto him, Oh my Lord, if the Lord be with us, why then is all this befallen us? and where be all his miracles which our fathers told us of, saying, Did not the Lord bring us up from Egypt? but now the Lord hath forsaken us, and delivered us into the hands of the Midianites." The emphasis I'd like to focus on is, "and where be all his miracles?"

There was a popular song when I was younger. "I'm Looking For a Miracle." Many people are looking for miracles these days. Right now, someone's looking for a financial miracle. Someone may be expecting a healing miracle. Somebody may be praying for a miracle in their relationship whether it's between parent and children, spouse to spouse, another relative to relative, or friend to friend. Truthfully, few people are likely looking for the grand miracles referred to in Judges 6:13—parting of seas, raining down food from heaven, etc.

Then there was the first recorded miracle Jesus performed: Turning water into wine. No, we're not looking for anything grand. Most of us are happy with money coming from nowhere; cancer and other sickness miraculously showing no signs of ever being there.

Well, I want to direct you to some miracles you may have overlooked, or a better term might be, "taken for granted." Okay, lift your arm up. You can do that? Guess what—that's a miracle! Now, stand up. No problem? Praise God, it's a miracle! Tell someone something, anything, it doesn't matter what you say, just talk. You can speak? Hallelujah! It's a miracle. Okay, here's a biggie. Take in a breath, hold it a few seconds, now let it out. You were able to do that unassisted? It's a miracle! Oh, go on and shout; don't hold your peace!

I know you're probably thinking that I'm being facetious (definition: silly). But go visit someone who's had a severe stroke who has been left without the use of one side, and ask them to raise their arm or leg. See just how difficult, if not impossible it really is. Ask someone who is paralyzed from the waist down to stand. Ask someone who hasn't been able to talk, to tell someone something . . . anything.

But now here's where we see miracles. When these same people are able to do this again (should it become the case), we say, "It's a miracle! God is good!" Especially when the doctor has said they wouldn't be able to do it. The person on a respirator that's breathing for them—oh, how they'd love to take a deep breath on their own just one more time. Yet, we take these and so many other things for granted.

May I have a "Word" with you? Are you looking for a miracle? Then look in the mirror. You're a miracle no matter what's going on in your life. I wish I could go into all the intricate details of just how you're made. The detailed work God did when creating you. The fact that you're even here . . . surviving; what it took just for you to be born in the first place.

Then there are miles of tubing in your body carrying blood without you having to do anything, a heart that pumps, a liver that purifies, skin that protects (and some of you have the nerve to despise the color of that skin—oh, please!). No batteries or AC cord are required to keep you running—sleep and proper food being all that's needed to recharge you. All of these things are miracles.

If you can see, do you have any idea what it takes for that miracle to occur? Light reflecting off the back of lens inside your eyes as your brain flips the upside-down image so you can see things right-side up. Have you thought about what it entails just for you to hear, to smell, to think, to talk, to feel, to walk, to have the mind to do your job to make money, and then to have someone *pay* you for what you can do? It's a miracle, I tell you!

Are you looking for a miracle? Then look no farther than yourself. Now feel free at any time to thank God for miracles!

No God Like Jehovah

*H*ave you ever really stopped and thought about what an awesome God we serve? Look around at all that God—all by Himself—has created, and ask yourself: Is it really possible that all of this could have just happened all on its own? I scratch my head at those who believe that no God created this universe . . . that things just came together by science alone (so who created the scientific things then? I'm just saying!).

It reminds me of the tale of the person who found a watch just lying there. No, they may not have known exactly who created that watch, but they knew someone had done it. It just didn't appear out of nowhere or evolve from a rock into a watch.

I look at the birds that fly, and I say, what an awesome God we serve. Man created the airplane, but look at what all it takes just to get it off the ground. It's nothing like the ease in which the bird seems to do it. We take for granted the sun that we say rises every day, but imagine a God who put the earth into rotation to revolve around the sun like clockwork. From the ant to the elephant to the great white whale, God created them all. Meticulously, everything with a purpose whether we know that purpose or not.

If we just look at ourselves, see all that's created to work within us, that's enough for the world to know: There is no God like Jehovah. We also see how much God loves us. Yes, Jesus loves me. He cares about what's happening in our lives. I know sometimes we think we're alone, but God sees and knows all. God made us in such a way; I'd like to take a minute to point out some things so we can see just how awesome God truly is.

You have a hundred million receptors in your eyes so you can see. There are twenty-four thousand fibers in your ears to vibrate so you can hear. You have five hundred muscles, two hundred bones, and seven miles of nerve fiber that you probably didn't even know exists in just your body. God did it, and this only scratches the surface.

One of my favorite books (other than my own, of course) is called "The Greatest Miracle in the World" by Og Mandino. In that book, there is something called *The God Memorandum*. If you've never read this book, I would *highly* recommend reading it. In this *God Memorandum*, you get to see how awesome God has created you.

May I have a "Word" with you? There's no God like Jehovah! There's no God like our God. And He loves you. So child of the Most High, hold your head up. For you truly are one of God's finest creations, no matter what anyone else says about you.

God's Word – Never Out of Style

*I*n the beginning was the Word, and the Word was with God, and the Word was God. The same was in the beginning with God. All things were made by him; and without him was not anything made that was made. In him was life; and the life was the light of men. And the light shineth in darkness; and the darkness comprehended it not." John 1:1-5. "And the Word was made flesh, and dwelt among us, (and we beheld his glory, the glory as of the only begotten of the Father,) full of grace and truth." John 1:14. Hebrews 13:8 tells us, "Jesus Christ the same yesterday, and today, and forever."

We've had minis and maxis when it comes to our dress lengths. We've had bell bottom pants; platform shoes, pointy toes, square toes, round toes shoes. There was a time when if your pants were above your ankles and close to your shin you were accused of wearing high waters, told you were "flooding," and people laughed at you. Now they're called capris. Fishnets are in, fishnets are out. Tights are in, tights are out. Stockings are required; then who really needs to wear stockings anymore? Plaid is in, plaid is out. Three-piece suits are the rave. No, double-breasted suits are what's really happening.

Clothes may go in and out of style. Shoes may change from one season to another. But God's Word never goes out of style. The same

Word that kept the three Hebrew boys when they were thrown in their fiery furnace is the same Word that will keep you, be with you in your fiery furnace. The same Word that closed the mouths of hungry lions when Daniel was dropped down into the lion's den is the same Word that will keep you when people are roaring and looking hungrily at you.

King David wrote in Psalm 37:25, "I have been young, and now am old; yet have I not seen the righteous forsaken, nor his seed begging bread." God's Word, back in King David's day, is still relevant today.

King Solomon asked God for wisdom. God not only blessed him with wisdom but blessed him with riches. God's Word never goes out of style. You can still have wisdom from the Lord and still walk in God's blessings today. Joseph had a dream. He went through so much in his journey to that dream. But in the end, what God showed Joseph became manifested. What the devil meant for Joseph's bad, God turned it and used it for his good. So don't you fret: what the devil may mean for your bad, God will turn it and use it for your good. God's Word never goes out of style.

Paul, who is credited for so much of the New Testament, went through much as a Christian (the same Paul who once fervently persecuted Christians as Saul before His road to Damascus conversion). Paul was shipwrecked, bitten by a venomous snake that should have killed him but didn't, put in prison, placed under house arrest, and eventually crucified. And through all of this, in Philippians 4:4 we find him saying, "Rejoice in the Lord always, and again I say, Rejoice." Philippians 4:7 saying, "And the peace of God, which passeth all understanding, shall keep your hearts and minds through Christ Jesus." The same Paul who told us in Philippians 4:13 that no matter what is going on, "I can do all things through Christ which strengtheneth me."

May I have a "Word" with you? God's Word never goes out of style. Put on the Word of God. Wear the Word daily. You can sport God's Word in season and out of season. People of God, let me tell you this: God's Word never goes out of style!

Mission Possible

ow easy is it for you to say nice things to others? What about to yourself? I was thinking about how often we say negative things to or about ourselves. Our words have power. So, this week, I want you to take special notice to how often you say something negative either about yourself or to yourself. When you catch yourself saying something that doesn't build you up, or even worst, has the possibility to tear you down, I want you to say, "Lord, I thank You that I am fearfully and wonderfully made."

Become aware of the words you speak and the words you think. And when something is not affirming that you were created by God, the Master Designer Himself, not reaffirming to your spirit man that God is pulling for you to make it; I want you to stop right then and there and say, "Lord, I thank You that I am fearfully and wonderfully made."

Why am I asking you to do this? Because too many of us beat ourselves up and beat ourselves down. There are plenty of people who are happy to keep you down. Why must you jump on the bandwagon with them? Oh, I know, you don't think you're doing anything to yourself, but you are. This becomes an issue of the heart.

The Bible says, "As a man thinketh, so is he." If we continue with thoughts that tear us down and don't counter those thoughts, they get into our hearts. Luke 6:45 says, "A good man out of the good treasure of his heart bringeth forth that which is good; and an evil man out of the evil treasure of his heart bringeth forth that which is evil: for of the abundance of the heart his mouth speaketh." What you put in is what you'll get out. We need to deposit more good things so when things come out of our mouths, they will be good.

So here's your assignment for one week. Should you choose to accept this assignment, you're going to see a mission that becomes possible. You'll see joy come back; I don't care what's going on in your life. There's something about knowing that you are blessed to be a blessing. There's something special in knowing that God created you, that He created you for a purpose, and that God doesn't create junk. So *what* if people have told you that you weren't nothing. Who are they? So *what* if someone has said you're not going to make it. What do they know? So *what* if no one believes or subscribes to your dreams. God believes in you. God thinks you're worth it.

Yes, that's right. I said it. God thinks you're worth it. You may not be worthy of all His blessings, His love, His grace, and His mercy, but you are *worth* it. How can I say this with such assurance?

Because God sent His only begotten Son to die on the cross for your sins. He sent Jesus to save you from all your unrighteousness. Are you going to tell me that Jesus' life that was given for you is not worth anything? And if it's true that He gave His life for you, doesn't that mean He thought you were *worth* it?

May I have a "Word" with you? Yes, these are difficult times. The world has nowhere to turn to when they panic and get nervous about what faces us. But be of good cheer, for Jesus has overcome the world. The Word God has placed on my heart is to tell you to stop talking down and stop talking bad to and about yourself. Say what He says and quit tearing yourself apart. Speak life. Speak life to your body. Speak life to your mind. Speak life to your circumstances. This week, join me in a mission possible.

Speak words of life, love, and encouragement to yourself. Next, we'll expand the mission.

Mission Impossible

I love to play with words. Words are so powerful. That's why when growing up and we'd say that sticks and stones may break my bones but words can never hurt me, I didn't totally subscribe to that. Sure, words may not physically hurt you the way a stick or a rock would hurt. But words *can*, *do*, and *have* hurt a lot of people. Some who are messed up today at older ages or messed up because of what was said to them when they were young. Some of us have been hurt in our older ages by some things someone may have said to us now, yesterday, last week, last month, or last year.

When I was growing up, people used to tell me I had big eyes. That used to hurt me because I thought they were saying my eyes were ugly. Later I learned that my big eyes were pretty. I was taking my grandbaby's shirt off yesterday and she made the comment that she had a big head. I asked her who told her that. She proceeded to tell me which relative had said it, and I told her to tell that person the next time they say that, that she doesn't have a big head, and that her Nana said so. This was a relative who is supposed to love her saying this to the then three-year-old child.

Sometimes we may say things in jest, but even teasing a person can hurt, if we're not careful. We especially need to be mindful of the things we say to our children. Telling them that they aren't anybody, telling them they're nothing. Telling them we wished they'd never been born. Telling them they're not smart enough or pretty enough or talented enough. (If you're guilty of this, then repent and stop doing it!) Words can heal and words can hurt.

So, this week, your mission—should you choose to accept it—is to put a watch over your mouth and not say anything negative *to* or *about* anyone else. I called this article mission IMpossible because of the play on the "I" and the "M" in the word impossible. Think of impossible as being shorthand for "I'm possible." Whatever you desire to do in life, instead of looking at it as impossible, start seeing it as I'm possible.

May I have a "Word" with you? Nothing is impossible to him who believes. With God, all things are possible. We just need to do a better job with the words we use. Realize the power that comes with your words. Telling someone they are fearfully and wonderfully made is different than telling someone they are fearfully. Telling someone you believe in them and what they can do is vastly different than telling someone there's no way they will ever get something done, and that if they do, it will be a surprise to you. God created us in His likeness and His image. Well, God is awesome!

Begin to look into the eyes of His creations and appreciate His handiwork instead of putting people down all the time.

Snow that falls, do you realize that none of the snowflakes are exactly alike? Think about that. A snowflake falls from the sky, hits the ground and either melts or compacts with other snowflakes, and God thinks enough of snowflakes to ensure that each one is special and without a duplicate. How much more does he think of you and those He has created?

Build someone up with kind words. Go out of your way to find something to compliment someone on or say to them. Try it, and see just what comes back to you.

Faith Without Works

nyone who really knows me knows I am a woman who walks by faith. It's not a cliché for me. It's not a cute saying. It's not merely a scripture I use to impress anyone. It's the way I live my life. In fact, I know no other way to live.

Do you ever wonder if what you do really matters? Every now and then, I wonder whether the words I use here, or in the books I pen, or when speaking, really makes any difference. Inevitably, whenever I ask this, someone calls, emails, signs my guestbook, or tells me on Facebook or when they see me how much they enjoyed something I've written or said and how much my work blesses them.

I've received messages from people in places like England, Canada, the Bahamas, New Zealand and military people serving overseas telling me how much my books have blessed them. It's a blessing to know that my books are spanning the globe. What began as a dream has manifested into published books. Nobody *but* God!

Many of you have dreams, goals, and visions that Almighty God has placed inside of you. Maybe you don't have anyone cheering you on to "Go for it!" Maybe you have faith that God gave it to you, and perhaps, you have faith that it will happen for you "someday."

But please, let me tell you what the scripture says: faith without works is dead. Having faith is wonderful. But if you're not doing anything, then, I'm sorry, but that dream, that goal, that vision is DOA—Dead On Arrival. Faith without works is dead.

However, Jesus showed us how to resurrect dead things. He showed us that we must "do." Throughout Jesus' ministry, you saw Him being about His Father's business (doing something). Jesus told others to do things (go wash, rise up, take up, come). God gave Jesus His assignment just as He's given you yours.

If Jesus worked faith, then what makes you think you can sit around praying and crying all day without your having to do anything, still expecting something to just miraculously happen? Jesus went about doing good. So, what are you doing?

I've been extremely busy these past few years. Many times I feel like I'm meeting myself going. But I continue to do what I need to do because I realize that faith without works is dead.

May I have a "Word" with you? The Bible tells us that God will bless the works of our hands. But we have to have some works for Him to bless. If you've been putting off that dream, that goal, that vision because you're waiting on God to do something, then let me give you a jump-off right here (that's a vehicle term used for batteries that have gone dead for whatever reason).

Jump-off: God is waiting on you to do something! If you want to fulfill what God has placed in you to do, then by faith, do it! Just remember as you toil on, sometimes tired, sometimes frustrated, sometimes ready to throw in the towel: faith without works is dead. This tells me that the opposite of that must be true: faith *with* works is alive.

And I can truly testify: The just shall *LIVE* by faith!

A Future and A Hope

"For I know the thoughts that I think toward you, saith the Lord, thoughts of peace, and not of evil, to give you an expected end." (Jeremiah 29:11) Many of you may be familiar with this scripture. In another version it says "For I know the plans I have for you." God knows what's ahead. God is thinking of you even when you don't know it.

Over the years, God has told me many things pertaining to my life and my future. Truthfully, that's the only reason I've been bold enough to step out into so many unknowns in my life. There's hardly anything I do that I don't consult God before I do it. You see, I don't want to crawl out on a limb without having God there to back me up.

I remember when I was employed with the phone company and God called me to step out on faith and become a full-time author. Oh, sure, it's easy to take a leap when you can see the way already done, but I didn't even have a book contract at the time. My obedience to God's calling was totally stepping out on faith.

May I have a "Word" with you? God is faithful. When God calls you to a thing, He will be there with you. Sometimes you might feel like you're out there by yourself, but if God tells you something, He will keep His Word even when it might not feel like it. Hold on and don't let go. Don't quit. Don't turn around. The Bible tells us that God's Word will not return unto Him void, but it will accomplish that which He has sent it to do.

May I Have A Word With You?

I'd like to encourage you today. Get ready! Be in expectancy! Past years may have been years of chaos for you, but there is a time to be about God's divine order. Oh, if you only knew what great things God has in store for you, you'd be shouting right now!!! I see it. I see it! God has told me, and I believe Him. Oh, yes! You ain't seen *NOTHING* yet.

While it may have looked like you were losing, you were being set up for God to show out in your life! If your gift inside of you just leaped when you read this, then you know this Word is for you.

May I have a "Word" with you? There's nothing too hard for God. Whatever you have faced already or are facing, God brought you or He's bringing you through. Just hold on and don't let go of God's unchanging hand. Yes, it's been a struggle. Yes, it may be a struggle now. But the only way Satan can win is if you quit or start speaking negative things against the things God has said.

If you're sick, speak healing. If you're sad or depressed, speak of how the joy of the Lord is your strength. If things are crazy in and all around you, speak of the peace of God that surpasses all understanding. If you don't have enough money, speak your status as a child of God . . . the cattle on a thousand hills belonging to our Father thus belonging to you. Continue to speak into the atmosphere, "And my God *shall* supply all my need[s] according to His riches in glory."

May I have a "Word" with you? God has given you all you need to not only fight the battle before you, but to win. Life and death are in the power of the tongue.

Know that when God has you, He's thinking about you. God has plans of peace and not evil, to give you an expected end.

May God richly bless you!

God Knows

W hatever is going on in your life, whatever you're going through, whatever you're dealing with, I just want you to know that God knows. Whether you realize it or not, that's a great place to shout. Knowing that no matter what is going on in your life, nothing escapes God's knowledge. In fact, there are times when God may tell us before we begin a thing we're going to run into obstacles and resistance. That's why we shouldn't fall apart. God sees, He knows, and He's right there with you. Whether God takes you over, around, or through the situation, it really shouldn't matter to you. What should matter is that God is there.

In Ezekiel 2:3-5, God tells Ezekiel exactly what he could expect. "And he said unto me, Son of man, I send thee to the children of Israel, to a rebellious nation that hath rebelled against me: they and their fathers have transgressed against me, even unto this very day. For they are impudent children and stiffhearted. I do send thee unto them; and thou shalt say unto them, Thus saith the Lord God. And they, whether they will hear, or whether they will forbear (for they are a rebellious house) yet shall know that there hath been a prophet among them."

God knows when He calls us to a work that there will be opposition. God knows it won't be an easy road. Sometimes I think we'd prefer He made it easier. I know I have felt that way at times. But to be called by the Master to do a work in His service is an honor and a privilege. Of course people feel those who are doing the work and the will of God shouldn't find themselves in a fire. But thank God that if you find yourself in the fire, you're not in there alone. God will see to it that not only do you go through the fire, but when you come out, you'll be unburned without even a hint of smoke. God can take you through the flood and see to it that you don't even get wet. God can take you through what should have knocked you down, then out, and lift you up to a pure position of power.

May I have a "Word" with you? God knows what you have need of. And He knows exactly what you're going through. God knows those who are coming against you, trying to stop what He's called and placed in you to do. But do know this: even in the presence of your enemies, God will prepare a table before you. God knows, He cares, and He's there.

There is nothing that's happening now or will happen in the future that catches our God off guard. I'm talking about our God. And what a mighty God we serve!

So if you're going through anything, just know that you're not going through it alone, that God will even use the bad things that happen for your good. Know that as long as you trust God and walk according to the way He's telling you that God will bring you through. God knows and God cares. Thanks be to God Who has blessed us in the Heavenly places with every spiritual blessing in Christ!

God knows what you need before you even know you need it. Learn to trust God in all your ways and no matter what's going on in your life.

Rest in the assurance and just keep saying "God has this." Whatever it is: God has it. Whatever *it* is, learn to place your cares on the Lord. God can handle it.

God's *got* this!

God's GPS

L uke 24:49 says, "And, behold, I send the promise of my Father upon you: but tarry ye in the city of Jerusalem, until ye be endued with power from on high." Jesus spoke these words before His ascension. I was asked to speak at a women's conference at Mt. Pilgrim Baptist Church in Fairfield on "The Power of Prayer." God directed me to concentrate on the word power more so than the word prayer. You see many people already are praying. The problem is the POWER of the prayer.

Jesus said to behold. He said He sends the promise of His Father upon us. This promise, of God the Father, is upon us, that we be endued with *power*. And not just any kind of power, but *power* from on high.

In order to be effective in anything that we do associated with God, we need the Power of God. Sure, there are things you can do on your own power, but your power alone is not enough to go the distance, to do what needs to be done.

I bought a GPS. I had been traveling to various engagements using Google Maps and MapQuest. I like the portable GPS because you can take it from one vehicle to another when needed. I merely needed to decide which one. Portable is even great when you're walking somewhere. It can give you directions while you're on foot. See, that's the great thing about a GPS. It knows where you are because of the satellite that has zeroed in on your location. A GPS will let you know where you are, and once you have put in your destination, it will direct you which way to go, and the best way to get there.

Having a GPS is all well and good, but if you're not hooked into a power source, then you won't have any or much *power*. Granted a GPS has a little power to run on its own for a little while. But that doesn't last. And if you're not careful, you'll find yourself stranded somewhere, not knowing which way to turn or which way to go. You need to be hooked up to the power source.

Well, guess what? Just like a GPS knows where you are, God knows where you are. But God can tell you which way to go without you having to put in a destination. God has it like that. God sees the problems ahead, and He will tell you to detour before you get there. But you need to be hooked up to The Source. You need to study God's Word so you can know God so well, that you move when He moves (just like *that!*).

For here, I'd like to define GPS as this: God's Power Source. Real power comes from the Holy Spirit who resides inside of us. Real power comes from Jesus and what Jesus did on the cross and Him being raised up from the dead. Real power comes from Jesus ascending, now sitting on the right hand of the Father making intercessions for us.

May I have a "Word" with you? Don't leave home without GPS, God's Power Source. Don't try to do things without GPS, God's Power Source. Don't try to fight the battles that come your way without GPS. Be endued with power from on high.

Get wrapped up, tied up, tangled all up in God's Power Source! For you can do all things through Christ who strengthens you. You just need to be hooked up to the right power—Jesus, God's Power Source, our way to the Father. For the only way we can get to the source is through Jesus the Christ, our Savior. No other way! Jesus is our hook-up! And the Holy Spirit is the voice that gives us direction.

Doers of the Word

hen I was growing up, even now, there are plenty of people who would tell others to do something. They have all the answers to the problems. The problem is: When you look at their lives, what they are telling you, might not necessarily be what they themselves are doing. If anyone ever points out this fact, the person will likely say something to the effect of, "Do as I say, not as I do."

James 1:22-24 states, "But be ye doers of the word, and not hearers only, deceiving your own selves. For if any be a hearer of the word, and not a doer, he is like unto a man beholding his natural face in a glass. For he beholdeth himself, and goeth his way, and straightway forgetteth what manner of man he was." Granted, these scriptures refer to what we hear, then do (or don't do) after we hear it, for there are many who hear things but don't do them.

People go to various Bible services and hear the Word being preached and taught. They know what has been said. But when it comes to doing what they hear, they just don't do it.

Well, we've all likely heard that "Practice makes perfect." So I submit that if we would practice some of the good things we hear, it would assist us in becoming more perfect people. If we practiced the Word that we hear, our lives would greatly improve. If you were to practice being the head and not the tail, you would step up and be a leader instead of saying what you can't do. You wouldn't allow people to put you at the back of the line all the time. If you would practice being above only and not beneath, you wouldn't find yourself at the bottom of the pile when all is said and done. If you were to practice being blessed going in and blessed coming out, then both you and the world would see a great difference in your life and God becomes glorified.

I know many may think they have all this down pact. We can quote scriptures like a Bible champ. But when things begin to happen in your lives, do you really become a doer? When weapons are formed against you, you might be able to quote the scripture that "No weapon formed against me shall prosper," but are you truly a doer of that Word? Do you act like you believe it? Do you really believe it? Do you act as though weapons may be formed against you, but in the end, you know that whatever weapon is formed, it will not prosper?

May I have a "Word" with you? God has called you for such a time as this. God has placed inside all of us all that we need to do what we need to do. God needs us to work out our salvation. No, that doesn't mean work *for* your salvation. Jesus has already done what needs to be done for that. He died on the cross and rose with all power.

To "work out" means to start exercising in order to visibly bring out that which is already in you. Like a muscle builder. A muscle builder has the muscles there, but the person who desires big muscles, works out and eats right until that which was there becomes now seen. Muscles become visible because the muscle builder worked out.

When you're a doer, you don't just talk about what you've heard; you do what you've heard. So if you want to see positive and anointed results in your life, then become a doer of the Word and not just a hearer only.

Enough Said

"A fool's lips enter into contention, and his mouth calleth for strokes. A fool's mouth is his destruction, and his lips are the snare of his soul. The words of a talebearer are as wounds, and they go down into the innermost parts of the belly." (Proverbs 18:6–8) Okay, I'm just going to say it. It's great being able to talk. It's great to have the gift of speech. The Bible even tells us that life and death is in the power of the tongue. And with all of this, there are still times when some folks (not all) talk too much.

Then there are times when people are speaking death to themselves and their situations, when people are saying negative things and cursing their lives and the folks around them, folks who tell just enough for the devil to know how to come at them, and folks who—please forgive me for saying this, but it's in the Bible—talk like a fool.

You see, the Bible tells us that a fool will say there is no God. That's a fool. A fool is one who might say there is a God but their actions speak volumes that they don't bit more believe that, than the man in the moon! (Ooh, that was a throwback to my young days!)

In the scriptures quoted here, it says that a fool's lips enter into contention, a fool's mouth is his destruction, and his lips are the snare of his soul. A snare is a trap. If you don't use your lips in the right way, they can set you up to be caught. Then there are the words of a talebearer. You know: a gossiper, someone who slanders another. Some people love to run their mouth about other folks and business that doesn't belong to them! Well, I have two words for the people who are talking too much; talking about the wrong thing; speaking death over your finances, your life, your children, your spouse, your friends, the folks around you, your situation: Enough said!

In other words, hush! Shhh. Be quiet. You've said too much already. Button up, zip it, put a lid on it! If you can't speak the Word that God has sent to the earth for our benefit to cause you to win, something that can return to God and make Him smile about it because it's music to His ears, then hush your mouth! Shut up! Hold your tongue!

You wonder why you're broke. Check out your tongue. What has it been conspiring with your teeth and lips and putting out into the atmosphere? The reason is nigh thee, even under your nose. Yes, you spoke it. Why would you be against yourself? Don't you know that a house divided cannot stand? In your heart you want better, you want peace, you want joy, you want to be content. But then your mouth starts saying all these things like you're broke, you're sick, you're tired, you're sick *and* tired, nothing ever works for you, you know you're not going to get that job, you're not going to make it! Failure!

ENOUGH SAID!

May I have a "Word" with you? Stop speaking what you see if what your eyes see don't match up with the Word of God, and start speaking the Word of God until what you see lines up with God's Word. Be wise like our Father in Heaven. Do as God did when He created the earth. Look out into your darkness and your void and call forth what you desire to see! You remember: And God said, "Let there be light!"

Guess what? We marvel every day in God's light just because God said it, and it was so. Now, it's time for you to show the image of whom you have been fashioned to be. Are you the image of God or not?

I'm listening; the world is listening; God is listening. And should you find yourself veering off the path, learn to say to your own self: Enough said! Then change what you say, and speak God's Word!

Don't Tell Me What God Can't Do!

Yes, yes, I know. Some of you are saying there are some things God can't do. For one thing: God can't lie. Actually, God chooses not to lie. The Bible tells us that God is not a man that He should lie. Another thing people say is that God can't fail. Well, when my book *Ray of Hope* released; and I saw what God was doing, I continuously found myself quoting a line found in that novel: "Don't tell me what God can't do!"

When I look at the awesomeness of God, I tell you: God never ceases to amaze me. You see, I know what I have to deal with in my life just as I'm sure you know what you deal with in yours. We know, or at least have a good indication of, our limits and limitations—those we set, and those others try to set for us. But when it comes to God, there are no limits or barriers that can keep God from accomplishing that which He has spoken and set into motion.

When God says, "Let there be," He means let there be. That's why I love being in God's company, in His presence . . . being called His child and His friend.

God is doing some big things that only a powerful God can do. There is much to be said about the favor of God. I'm telling you: the favor of God will take you places you never thought you'd be able to go. The favor of God is like a master key to doors that can't help but open when it arrives on the scene. Yes, God can use who He wants, when He wants, and precisely how He wants, when He wants to. Oh, yes!

Sure, there are some people who think they can decide who God can and can't use. They'll say, "God can't use you because . . ." And after the because comes things like: You're too young, you're too old, you're not experienced enough, you're too experienced, you don't have the right connection, you used to be too much of a sinner, you don't know enough about what people deal with because you've not been through enough. I'm sure there are many more things you can think of here. But to all of this I say, "Don't tell me what God can't do!"

May I have a "Word" with you? Everything is moving by the power and hand of God! God is doing things in the body right now. We need to get out of God's way and let Him do His thing. But too often, we become the problem. We want to second guess God. We want to tell God how He should do things. When He tells us to do something, we want to argue with Him on why it can't work. Listen: I don't have a problem with you talking things out with God and bringing your concerns to the table (believe me, God and I have some great conversations when it comes to some things He has told me). What I'm saying is: if some time has passed and you're still trying to tell God your thoughts about the matter after He's told you, it's time for you to move on it.

I've been in this race a long time. As with many of you, I've had my good days and my bad. I've had plenty of ups and downs. There have been so many times when I've gotten tired and wondered what was the use . . . what difference does any of this make anyway.

But right now, I'm going to be like David in Psalm 37 and tell you this: I've been young; I'm a lot older now. But people, let me tell you this much that I know for sure: I have never seen the righteous forsaken, nor His seed begging bread. When I've not felt like there was anyone there to help me, when I've felt all by myself, God has touched someone to bless me as I was doing *His* work.

So I say to you: Nothing is too hard for God. Oh, and don't tell me what God can't do! God will make a way somehow.

End From the Beginning

How many of you have ever started something and, when you began it, you saw the end from the beginning? How often have you started something without fully counting the cost?

Isaiah 46:9-10 states, "Remember the former things of old: for I am God, and there is none else; I am God, and there is none like me, declaring the end from the beginning, and from ancient times the things that are not yet done, saying, My counsel shall stand, and I will do all my pleasure." One of the things that I love so much about God is that He knows Who He is, and He knows where things are going before He even begins a thing.

God is so powerful that He knew what we would be doing at this exact moment. Why? Because God is God! God is telling us in this scripture that He is God, and that there is none like Him. Then He goes on to let us know how He declares the end from the beginning. I said He *declares* the end from the beginning!

In seeing people chase various dreams, I know that many have seen the end at the beginning. That's why people will work so hard and put up with so much; they've seen the end before they ever began. Often God will show us the end at the beginning when He calls us into His service. Look, I'm going to be honest with you: had God not shown some of us what the glorious end looks like, some of us wouldn't have ever began. But by the same token, He doesn't show us the middle, and that's what messes with a lot of us. We know where we are at the time He called us. We see what the end will look like. But that middle part of struggles and disappointments; setbacks and letdowns; trials and tribulations; we don't see at the time. So when adversity and knockdowns show up, some folks start to question if they are even on the right path.

I'm sure Joseph the dreamer would say I'm right about this. I love that God allowed us to see into Joseph's life from the beginning to the end. How Joseph was shown that marvelous dream—revealed the end at the beginning. Joseph, like many of us when we see the end, was so excited. But when Joseph found himself in the pit with his brothers wanting to kill him, I'm sure he had to be thinking this looks nothing like the end God showed me. When Joseph found himself sold into slavery, I *know* that didn't look like the end God had shown him.

In prison, having people to tell him they would help after he helped them and then to be forgotten, that couldn't have looked like the end God had shown him. Having folks to lie on you when you're trying to do the right thing; that definitely couldn't have looked like the end God had shown him.

But God has assured us that His word would not return unto Him void. But it will accomplish that which He has sent it to accomplish.

May I have a "Word" with you? If God has given you a Word, if God has shown you the end from the beginning, I want you to believe God no matter what the middle looks like. I want you to have the attitude of gratitude that God is not a man that He should lie; and that what He has promised, He will fulfill.

Shout and give God praise when you're going through the valley of whatever name it might possess, *knowing* that God has shown you the end, and that end *will* come to pass. You just need to hold on, don't give up, and don't give out.

Who else but God can show you the end from the beginning and make it so?! There is none like God!

ASK! *Ask Seek Knock*

elight also in the Lord, and He will continue to give you the desires of your heart. This brings me to the word ASK.

A small word when you look at the number of letters it takes to spell it, but what a powerful word it can be. I've spoken in the past on how people are afraid to ask because they don't want to be rejected. Well, the Word of God tells us, "We have not, because we ask not."

As a young girl, I would quote, by heart, Matthew 7:7, "Ask, and it shall be given you; seek, and ye shall find; knock, and it shall be opened unto you." But what really amazed me was the secret that appeared to be hidden inside this scripture concerning the word ask.

The scripture began with "ask" which starts with the letter "A." The next thing you're told to do is "Seek," followed by "Knock." If you take the first letter from each of these words: Ask, Seek, Knock, you get ASK. That made the word "*ask*" even more powerful in my sight.

To ask is to make a request . . . make a desire known. If there's something we desire, we need to open our mouths and ask for it, whether it's to someone here on earth or to our Father in Heaven.

But asking shouldn't be the end. After we ask, we should seek, meaning to look for. Keeping with this theme, you should look for it to manifest. Many people may ask, but how many actually look for . . . expect it to show up? Then there's the final instruction: knock, indicating some type of action. But why knock?

The Webster's Dictionary defines the word "knock" as *1. To strike with a hard blow.* But I like the second definition better: *To affect in a specified way by striking hard.*

God has a way for us to achieve everything He's given us to do. But we must strike hard—put action . . . power behind our asking. And what greater power is there when getting things done than the Sword of the Spirit—the Word of God!

Yes, you can knock and wait for someone to let you in (note it didn't specifically say knock on a door, but knock and "it" shall be opened unto you). Or you can take the Word of God, mix it with faith and action, and knock (affect in a specified way by striking hard) your desires.

May I have a "Word" with you? Jesus said in John 14:13-14, "And whatsoever ye shall ask in my name, that will I do, that the Father may be glorified in the Son. If ye shall ask any thing in my name, I will do it."

So, what are you waiting for? Ask—A.S.K.—and let's get going! We have too much work to accomplish to be playing around.

What are you asking or have asked God for or to do? Are you thanking Him that's it's already done? Then do that now. Thank Him and start acting like you believe in Him and in His Word. You have not because you ask not.

Don't blame God; God is willing and ready to do His part. He's waiting on you to do yours. Ask, seek, knock!

Because of Who God Is!

No matter what's going on in your life right now, I've been sent to give you this word: It's not all about you! If good stuff is happening for you right now, it's not all about you. If bad stuff is happening, it's not all about you. It's for the glory of God!

I wrote something on my Facebook page. For those of you who aren't familiar with Facebook, it's a social networking online service. A lot of people were on MySpace and then the young people decided too many of the older people were there, so they left and went to Facebook.

As only we older people can do, we brushed up on what it was about and promptly followed. Personally, I like Facebook. It's simple to use and update without having to have fancy backgrounds and all the bells and whistles (update: that's all changed now).

I like it because it gives people a chance to connect. Many relatives and friends locally and in other states are part of Facebook and able to keep in touch. I've reconnected with classmates, and it's been a lot of fun. Christians are there also encouraging each other (although some use it as forum to just speak their minds on whatever is happening in the world).

I wrote on my Facebook page these words: "Exceedingly, abundantly, above all we can ever ask or think." I then proceeded to write what God was doing just in the next few weeks in my writing career.

After I listed things, I received a comment from the (then) director of Black Expressions book club (Carol Mackey) congratulating me letting me know that my novel *Goodness and Mercy* would be a featured selection with Black Expressions. Stay with me now, because I'm going somewhere. When I read her comment, I responded back to her, already knowing that this novel would be listed with Black Expressions, that because I only had 420 characters (back when they limited us), I had run out of room to receive all that God had blessed me with in this area. Yes, my books had been alternate selections before, so I thought it was nice that she was telling me it would be featured this way with my newest release.

But then the Holy Spirit told me I'd missed what she'd said. This is why it's so awesome to have a relationship with God where you don't just talk to Him, but He talks to you.

I have several things God has spoken over my life in this book writing business. Some of you know my biggest confession (I am a #1 *New York Times'* Bestsellers' list published author). Many of you also know that this confession was not even my idea, but God's.

What no one knew is that another confession and belief of mine was that one day one of my books would be what Black Expressions called their "Main Selection." The name was changed to Featured Selection. There are two books in each catalog granted this honor of being a Featured Selection, and the author/book receives a two-page spread.

After the Holy Spirit got my attention, I decided to clarify what director Carol Mackey had told me. Was it that my book would be featured, as in, just in the catalog being featured? Or would *Goodness and Mercy* be a real Featured Selection?

May I have a "Word" with you? I've often told God when He has spoken big things over my life that He must not know who I am and what I have to deal with. I've found myself reminding Him that I'm this little black girl from Village Springs, Alabama, in some cases you could say from Birmingham, Alabama, who doesn't have the connections or finances to do things like some others may have. And that's when God reminds me Who *He* is.

Oh, and that Featured Selection question with Black Expressions? I suppose you can say God "hooked me up!" *Goodness and Mercy* was one of the two Featured Selections in the December 2009 issue of *Black Expressions.*

Nobody *but* God!

So when you want to tell God what can't be done; shut up and let God show you just how, with Him, it *can* be done.

One more thing down; more big things to go!

Coming to Repentance

ut, beloved, be not ignorant of this one thing, that one day is with the Lord as a thousand years, and a thousand years as one day. The Lord is not slack concerning his promise, as some men count slackness; but is long-suffering to us-ward, not willing that any should perish, but that all should come to repentance. But the day of the Lord will come as a thief in the night; in the which the heavens shall pass away with a great noise, and the elements shall melt with fervent heat, the earth also and the works that are therein shall be burned up." 2 Peter, 3:8-10.

As far back as I can remember, I've heard the phrase, "We're in the last days." I know a lot of people who will be glad when this is all over and Jesus comes back. I would like to direct our attention to the scripture above, particularly verse nine where it states: "not willing that any should perish, but that all should come to repentance." John 3:16-17 tells us, "For God so loved the world, that he gave his only begotten Son, that whosoever believeth in him should not perish, but have everlasting life. For God sent not his Son into the world to condemn the world; but that the world through him might be saved."

God doesn't want any to perish, and He desires for us to walk in our called assignments. When we become saved, that should not be the end. Yes, it's great that you're saved. But we need to care about those who either have never heard about Jesus—His death, burial, and resurrection, or who have heard but haven't yet given their lives to

Him. God cares so much about us, all of us. He desires our hands, our voices, us, to do the work He has called us to do.

People say the world is coming to an end soon because of all the things that are happening these days. But we have been called to spread the Gospel. There are a host of saved folks, and with some of us, it appears our concern is too much about only ourselves. Our godly-walk should be more than just staying within the comforts of our four walls. It should be more than just attending worship services on Sundays and going home to enjoy ourselves, and that's all there is to it. Yes, it's more than just being saved and only being concerned about how "we" can be blessed or become *more* blessed.

May I have a "Word" with you? The Lord is not slack concerning His promise, as some men count slackness. But He is longsuffering to us-ward. God is not willing that any should perish, but that all should come to repentance. As you read this, I pray that you feel God's heart. How much He really loves the world. How He sent His Son, and even stronger when you consider this was His "only" begotten Son. Now that's real love.

Then Jesus came and walked the walk we walk, showing us how to live. He then laid down His life. No one took Jesus' life; He laid it down for us, then arose, and now He sits on the right hand of the Father making intercessions for us.

And what is God asking of us?

To not just keep this Gospel—the Good News to ourselves. To not just get ours, but to tell others. God wants us to do what we can with the gifts He's given us to bring others into the Kingdom. He's asking us to care about others the way He cares. To have His heart. So I challenge you to be willing to do what you can so that none should perish.

Share the love of God with others, and let's be about our Father's business!

The Garment of Praise

hen you get up and get dressed, you put on clothes. Some people make sure they are color coordinated. Some must wear some type uniform and really have no choice in what they wear. Some people wear suits; some more casual dress. Some wear things that are comfortable like jogging suits (even though they have no intention of ever putting the word "jogging" to use). But from a spiritual standpoint, what garment do you put on?

Isaiah 61:3 says, "To appoint unto them that mourn in Zion, to give unto them beauty for ashes, the oil of joy for mourning, the garment of praise for the spirit of heaviness, that they might be called trees of righteousness, the planting of the Lord, that he might be glorified."

I realize many of us look to Ephesians the sixth chapter when it comes to putting on the whole armor of God. But even before armor can be put on, there should be some other garments (underwear and other clothing) underneath it. Hence, the garment of praise.

You see, praise can do things that will boggle the average mind. Praise can make mountains low. Praise can raise valleys. Praise can make crooked places straight. Praise can bring down walls. Praise can win battles without a weapon ever having to be lifted. Praise can cause God's blessings to rain down. Therefore, put on the garment of praise.

Right now, I want you to make up in your mind that when you get up every morning and begin to get ready for your day, the first thing you're going to put on is the garment of praise. Praise God for Who He is. Praise God for another day. Praise God for where He has brought you. Praise God for keeping you over the years and even through the night. Praise God for what He's going to do for you in this brand new day—a day you've never seen before. Praise God that you're even able to praise Him.

May I have a "Word" with you? Let us put on the garment of praise daily—a fresh garment of praise. Thank God for His mercy, because He could have given us what we truly deserved. And I don't care how perfect we try to make people believe we are; we all have done something that if we got what we deserved—okay, somebody understands what I'm talking about right here (sins of commission and omission). Thank God for His grace—His unmerited favor. God blesses us to have things we didn't earn, but it's because of His grace.

So, even if you feel like things aren't going just right for you at this moment, put on the garment of praise, and praise God as He turn things around. If things are going well with you, then praise God. But let me warn you: there's something about putting on the garment of praise that causes you to praise, and that then gives you even *more* reasons to give God praise. It becomes a wonderfully, vicious cycle.

I thank You, Lord. For You are good, all the time; and all the time, You are good!

Put on the garment of praise!

A Friend of God

*L*ately people say and sing, "I am a friend of God" but what does being a friend really mean? I have many people who say they are my friend, when in fact; I know them but wouldn't classify our relationship as friends. John 15:15 says, "Henceforth I call you not servants; for the servant knoweth not what his lord doeth: but I have called you friends; for all things that I have heard of my Father I have made known unto you."

The great thing about this scripture is that Jesus is telling us we can go from being servants (not knowing what the Lord is doing), to being a friend (in a position to know all things). In the fourteenth verse of John 15, Jesus declared a stipulation for this position: "Ye are my friends, if ye do whatsoever I command you."

Here's the problem. Lots of people call others friends when all they seem to do is dump their problems and troubles but never ever seem to care about what's going on in their "friend's" life. Their conversation is all about them. Me, me, me; I, I, I.

Then there are the "friends" who are always asking for something: a favor, some money, a ride, or something else they need to borrow that may never find its way back to your possession. They are your friend as long as you're there for them. But if and when you need something, they're usually too busy to talk, to help out, to listen, to reciprocate. Most of us would agree, after you really notice a friendship like this, you'll eventually decide that person really isn't your friend, but more of a user (I said most—some folks never get it).

We say, "I am a friend of God" and sing "What a friend we have in Jesus" but here's a question: Is your friendship with the Lord one-sided? Are you always the one talking, always "telling Him all about your troubles," but never sitting or being quiet long enough to hear what God might want to say to you? Do you find yourself asking or begging Him for something every time you "call Him up," get down on your knees, or come before His presence? Are your thank You(s) and flattering words only because you need something, and you're trying to put yourself in a more favorable position to receive it?

In John 15:16, Jesus says, "Ye have not chosen me, but I have chosen you, and ordained you, that ye should go and bring forth fruit, and that your fruit should remain: that whatsoever ye shall ask of the Father in my name, he may give it to you." Jesus chose you. Jesus has ordained you.

And the commandments He's asked us, as His friends, to keep? There are two of them that all the other commandments hang on. One is to love the Lord your God with all your heart, mind, and strength; and the second is to love one another as Jesus has loved us. Love God, and love one another.

May I have a "Word" with you? Yes, you may be a friend of God's. Yes, you have a friend in Jesus. But can God say you're truly His friend? Does Jesus have a friend in you? Or, are you merely the type who uses your "friends" for all you can get? Do you truly have a relationship with God? Are you spending time with Him and in His Word?

Question: If God were asked about you, would His answer be like mine when I don't know or barely know a person who claims me as a friend? "Oh, I don't really know them; they're merely someone I met, was friendly with, helped out, or I'm acquainted with."

True friendship goes both ways. Don't just call God friend—be a friend. Love God and love one another.

Peace Offering

*D*uring a ceremony involving Moses and Aaron with his sons in the sacrificing of a bullock then a ram, the scripture tells us in Leviticus 8:23, "And he slew it; and Moses took of the blood of it, and put it upon the tip of Aaron's right ear, and upon the thumb of his right hand, and upon the great toe of his right foot."

People had certain type offerings they would bring to the temple for various reasons. I encourage you to read Leviticus to see what those sacrifices and offerings were. For this particular ceremony, a ram was brought—the ram of consecration—and Aaron and his sons laid their hands upon the head of the ram. That's when Moses took of the blood and placed the blood on the right ear, right thumb, and right toe of first Aaron, and then his sons.

In light of the blood that was shed, this was to show that someone who is truly serving God must, from the ear, be ready to hear the Word of the Lord; from the right thumb, do the work of the Lord; and with the toe, be ready to move at God's command.

May I have a "Word" with you? Even though this was for the priest in the Old Testament, we are now of the royal priesthood. Jesus is our high priest. There was a veil in the temple that separated us from direct access to God, in the holy of holies, but that veil in the temple was rent from the top down when Jesus hung on the cross, giving His life a sacrifice for our sins.

And now, after Jesus' death and resurrection, we can go to God for ourselves. Jesus' blood has been poured out on the mercy seat in Heaven for those who accept Him.

So let us symbolically take the blood of Jesus and touch our right ear, our right thumb, and our right toe and say: I consecrate my ear, so I can hear the Word of the Lord; my right thumb, so I can do the work of the Lord; and my right toe so I can go where God has me to go and do what God has told me to do.

The Bible tells us that faith without works is dead. So don't just say you believe in the Lord, put your faith and your actions to work. After all: It's all about Him! It's all about the Lord.

There is so much work to do. The harvest is truly plentiful and the laborers are few. So let's get outside our four walls and gather the harvest for our Lord.

Who Really Found Whom?

$\mathcal{I}$'ve heard people say, "I found Jesus!" Well, allow me to clear up any misconceptions here. Jesus was never lost—we were. For anyone who has not accepted Jesus into their life and heart, you still are. But God has made a way for you to be found and reconnected back to Him through His Son, Jesus. If you will confess with your mouth, the Lord Jesus, and believe in your heart that God has raised Him from the dead, you shall be saved.

Romans 5:6-8 tells us, "For when we were yet without strength, in due time Christ died for the ungodly. For scarcely for a righteous man will one die: yet peradventure for a good man some would even dare to die. But God commendeth his love toward us, in that, while we were yet sinners, Christ died for us."

If you've ever traveled anywhere and figured out that you didn't know where you were and you had no way of reaching where you were headed, then you understand the concept of being lost.

It is said that there's a difference between men and women when it comes to the discovery of being lost. Men don't like to stop to ask for directions (they just want to figure it out), whereas women would prefer stopping quickly (and as often as needed) to ask. I don't want to generalize anyone here (I happen to be a woman, and honestly, I prefer figuring it out as opposed to stopping and asking), but the bottom line is: When you're lost, you should want to get back on the right track quickly so you can reach your destination.

The first question that usually comes up when you're lost is: "Where are you?" Even with all our new technology like GPS systems, being able to go online to Web sites like Google, Yahoo, and Mapquest to get directions, you still need to know where you are in order to know which direction you need to take from there.

Jesus not only knows where He is, but He knows where you are and which direction you need to go. It was Jesus who came all the way from Heaven to earth to show us the way back to our Father. We were the ones who were lost; He found us. Jesus came to save us. He gave His life for our sake.

Luke 15:4-7 tells of the parable of the lost sheep. "What man of you, having a hundred sheep, if he lose one of them, doth not leave the ninety and nine in the wilderness, and go after that which is lost, until he find it? And when he hath found it, he layeth it on his shoulders, rejoicing. And when he cometh home, he calleth together his friends and neighbors, saying unto them, Rejoice with me; for I have found my sheep which was lost. I say unto you, that likewise joy shall be in heaven over one sinner that repenteth, more than over ninety and nine just persons, which need no repentance."

Jesus left the riches of Heaven and came and walked on the earth so we would know what to do as we walk this road. He then died on the cross to pay the wages for our sins (death) so we wouldn't have to. He was placed in a borrowed grave, went down to death, Hell, and the grave and conquered them, then arose on that third day morning with not just a little power, not just some power, but *all* power! And to the sons and daughters of God who have acknowledged Jesus as our Lord and Savior, we can walk in that power.

May I have a "Word" with you? I don't know if you truly understand this, but it was *AMAZING* Grace that saved us. And I, like the writer of that old hymnal, can proudly proclaim, "I once was lost, but now I'm found; was blind, but now I see."

No, none of us found Jesus. He came down from Heaven and found us. I don't know about you, but I think I'll stop right now and thank God for Jesus, and that He lives forevermore!

Praise break!!!!!!!!!!!!!!!!!!!!!!!!!!!!!!!!!!!!!!

Small Beginnings

nd he said, Whereunto shall we liken the kingdom of God? or with what comparison shall we compare it? It is like a grain of mustard seed, which when it is sown in the earth, is less than all the seeds that be in the earth: But when it is sown, it groweth up, and becometh greater than all herbs, and shooteth out great branches; so that the fowls of the air may lodge under the shadow of it." (Mark 4:30-32)

Technically, a seed is a small thing. And a mustard seed is a really small thing. When I was a little girl, my daddy always planted a huge garden next to our house. He would consistently plant greens (turnips and collards), and I was amazed at how much green seeds resembled tiny BBs. What was more amazing was what came from those little seeds.

In the book of Mark, especially the fourth chapter, you see much talk about seeds being sown. Mark 4:31 tells how the Kingdom of God can be compared to a grain of mustard seed—a small thing to some that may not appear to have much potential, but when it's planted and it grows, it becomes, as the scripture stated, greater than all herbs. Not only that, but great branches come from it that birds can lodge under the shadow of it.

What am I telling you? You may be doing things for the Kingdom of God that appears to you and even to others to be a small thing. Maybe you're just starting out in the ministry God has called you to.

Perhaps you've been on the battlefield for a long time and you're nowhere near where you thought you'd be by now. Yes, what you're doing may look small. Yes, you may even feel a bit discouraged because you've planted and watered but it's taking so long for anything to be produced worth mentioning.

May I have a "Word" with you? Don't despise small beginnings. What has been placed on the inside of you has more potential than you'll ever know. What you're doing has more greatness in it than people may see now.

As with the mustard seed, with the physical eye, no one can see the roots inside that seed. No one can see the green leaves that will spring up and out. No one can see the godly determination inside that seed to push past sometimes hard dirt, possibly obstacles like rocks and other things. But God has already placed inside that tiny seed all that it will need to do what it has been called to do, and to be all that it is called to be.

Inside that seed is fruit. Inside that seed is the potential for great things, possibly large enough for others to rest under its shadow. Inside the tiniest of seeds, eventually, you'll find even more seeds and more seeds inside of them.

So don't despise small beginnings. Celebrate the fact that God is so thoughtful and awesome that He has placed inside of you all that you need to do what you need to do. Inside of you rest great things, greater than natural eyes are able to see. I truly believe this with my heart.

Keep pressing even when things get tough. Push past the obstacles. God has already looked ahead, and He has already prepared the way for you. Small things, small beginnings can bring more than our natural eyes see at the moment. So much more!

Don't despise small beginnings. Stand still and *see* the salvation of the Lord!

Stand

J've done my best over these years to say and write things to encourage others. The books that I could write could have been geared toward showing more of a side of "church" and "church folks" that at times are true, but not always becoming. Those type books likely could have sold lots more books than the books I'm known for writing. But God impressed upon me this question when we were talking about it once: "How does people making fun of Christians and preachers who fall into temptation uplift the Kingdom?"

You see, whatever we do in words or deeds should reflect, point to, and uplift the Kingdom of God. There are many people out there in search of something better for their lives. Many of us who know the Lord, know that there's a peace with God that you can't find "out there" in the world. There is a joy in the Lord that can't effectively always be put into words or expressions. I'm talking about the joy of the Lord that becomes our strength.

There is a love from God that presses you not just to love those who do right by you, but to love those who want to harm you, talk about you, spitefully misuse you, and to love to see you get knocked down. There are people who are not saved who desperately need to be saved. But they're looking at those who profess knowledge of Christ and wonder why would they even want what *you* have if it doesn't seem to be working for you?

The books I write show people who have a heart for the Lord and are really trying to live for God. They are not perfect people by any means, because even Jesus said that there is none perfect but the Father. But the people and stories I write about point to Jesus, the author and finisher of our faith. They show what we need to do when we've been hit and knocked down . . . messed up, but are still working to stand and do right.

May I have a "Word" with you? There will be times when you want to quit. There will be times when you may just want to sit down. Then there are times when you get knocked down. Ephesians 6:13-14 tells us, "Wherefore take unto you the whole armour of God, that ye may be able to withstand in the evil day, and having done all, to stand. Stand therefore, having your loins girt about with truth, and having on the breastplate of righteousness." When you have done all to stand . . . stand.

When you get knocked down, pick yourself up and stand. When the devil is trying to tell you things that you know are going against what God is saying to you and about you, stand on God's promises and His Word. The Word of God calls you an overcomer!

So when you have done all to stand, let the last Word be **STAND**!

Stumbling Blocks or Stepping Stones?

saiah 57:13-14 says, "When thou criest, let thy companies deliver thee; but the wind shall carry them all away; vanity shall take them: but he that putteth his trust in me shall possess the land, and shall inherit my holy mountain; And shall say, Cast ye up, cast ye up, prepare the way, take up the stumbling block out of the way of my people."

I'm always in awe of how God works. When I awakened, I heard the Lord say to me, "Are some things in your way stumbling blocks or stepping stones?" Then, during church services, the pastor pointed out in his message that a thing being in a blind man's way when he was being led by another could be a stumbling block or it could be a stepping stone. Confirmation from God.

You see, there are times in life when people attempt to place stumbling blocks in your path. But God says what may have very well started out as a stumbling block when He is finished with it can just as quickly become a stepping stone. It's all a matter of how we see, how we name a thing.

Personally, I can share with you plenty of stumbling blocks I know that have been placed along my journey. We do need to look up as we go through life. Oh, I believe in lifting my head up. But one thing we should avoid is walking around with our noses in the air, thinking we're so high and mighty that we're better than everyone else. When your nose is in the air, you can end up walking upon a stumbling block and not even see it. Again, there's no reason to walk around with your head down, but truth is found in the heart. When you have the right attitude, the right heart, and put your trust in God as you walk; the Holy Spirit will lead, guide, and warn you in all your ways.

In other words, when you come upon a stumbling block, you'll not stumble. Sure, you could curse your stumbling blocks or you can use them. And it doesn't matter how big the block is either. With God, it won't stop you. God can and will use what Satan or your enemy was meaning for your bad, for your good. That block in your way can easily help you step up and give you an entirely different view of things. Now you can see things you wouldn't have been able to see had you not moved up a little higher. Maybe it even helps you to step up to a higher place you had no way of reaching before.

It's all a matter of perspective; how you look at things.

May I have a "Word" with you? Isaiah 57:13 says that he who puts his trust in God shall possess the land and shall inherit God's holy mountain. Putting your trust in God is a personal decision—no one can put your trust in God for you but you. Others can pray for you, they can intercede for you, but only you can make the decision to truly trust God.

You see, sometimes we're just looking at things wrong. We've traveled our God-ordained path. And when we've come to stumbling blocks, some have tripped and fallen, staying down—too tired to get up. Some have fallen and just stayed in that place, praying for God to help them up. But it's time to stop falling when we don't have to. Trust God to lead you. And when you come upon the stumbling blocks of life, possess a spiritual laugh as you thank God for showing you that block. Then, step up and use that block to take you to a higher level, or at the very least, to add a spring to your next step.

Stop seeing stumbling blocks, and start seeing how they can be used as stepping stones.

The Temple of God

ave you ever gone into a place and, out of respect, decided there were things you shouldn't do there? Like when we go to what some of us call church (although church really isn't a building even though we say, "I'm going to church.").

How often have you seen anyone actually smoke a cigarette inside the church? You may see them outside after church is over, but inside, you don't see that. I won't say people don't cuss in church (notice I didn't say curse, which can be an entirely different thing), but most people try to be careful of what they allow to come out of their mouths when they are "in church." Grant it, when some leave and are on their way to the car, getting in the car, or at home, that person might cut loose. But in the church building, most people want to be respectful.

"Know ye not that ye are the temple of God, and that the Spirit of God dwelleth in you?" That's in the Bible: First Corinthians 3:16. Uh-oh! You are the temple of God? You are the church? You're where the Spirit of God dwells? Does that mean when you're doing some of the aforementioned things, that—dare I say it?—God is there when you're doing it? Does this mean when you're smoking that cigarette, that God is there (inside) with that smoke? That when you're doing things you have no business doing, God is there?

There's a scripture that declares God does not dwell in an unclean temple. So the question now becomes: When you asked Jesus to come into your heart . . . your life, and the Holy Spirit—Who came in and took up residence in your temple to comfort, lead, and guide you—what are you doing when this Holy Presence is present *in* you?

When I see a person smoking for instance, I find myself thinking: "Can't you see the Holy Spirit being subjected to that smoke: coughing and fanning while you're smoking up the place where He is dwelling?" Truthfully, this applies to whatever you're doing that's defined as defiling the temple.

Romans 8:1 says, "There is therefore now no condemnation to them which are in Christ Jesus, who walk not after the flesh, but after the Spirit." I'm not trying to condemn anyone, just wanting to encourage. Don't walk after the flesh; walk after the Spirit. God has so many blessings He desires for us to have.

We, who are saved, are under grace; but can you please give reverence to the temple where the Lord dwells like you give reverence to the building you call church?

Are there things you can do to make the temple, where the Spirit of the Lord dwells, better? Is there any cleaning that needs to be done? I know this might be considered hard to do, but the Bible tells us, "I can do ALL things through Christ who strengthens me." You *can* do it! Oh yes, you can! Second Peter 2:9 lets us know that we are part of a chosen generation, a royal priesthood, a holy nation, a peculiar people.

May I have a "Word" with you? You are the temple of God. When you're the temple, you don't go *to* church—you *are* the church. That means where you go, so goes the church.

No condemnation here, only encouraging you to realize who you really are, and what your body is in Christ.

Seeing Beyond the Trees

There are a lot of people who have been knocked down and had a rug or two pulled out from under them at some point in their lives. I talk to Christians all the time who find themselves experiencing some type of frustration at some point. For anyone who may be feeling that no matter how much you try it seems there's always something trying to come against you or hold you back, allow me to say this: Be encouraged because God is still on the throne, He's faithful, and you can totally and completely trust Him.

Let me share some things with you about trusting God. You either believe that God is, or you don't. There's no in-between. And trusting God means that you may not know all the details of the "how" He plans to bring about a thing, but you do know that if God promises it, He's going to do just what He says. Scriptures explain that we have not because we ask not, that we can delight ourselves in the Lord and He will give us the desires of our hearts. This is a Word from the Lord.

Here's the problem as I see it. We ask God for something, and then we want to tell Him how He should bring it to pass. We further get upset when things don't go the way we think it should.

I'll say it again: either you trust God or you don't. The problem is we're too busy looking at the trees that are before us when in fact: God sees the whole forest and the world beyond it. You may want to tell God how He should do His thing, but He can see what you can't. Let God do what He's going to do, and you do what He's told you to do. When it's the devil coming against you, God will tell you. It's as simple as that.

This is where trusting God comes into play. If you believe God truly exists; if you believe He loves you; if you believe He's faithful to what He has promised you, then you should make your request known, and let God be God. The qualifying word here is "if."

The reason I can praise God and rejoice when things may not look like it's going the way I think it should after I've asked God for something, is because I do believe God exists, I do believe He loves me, and I do trust Him. Let me say this again: I trust God!

I trust Him to see down the road what I can't. I trust that He knows what He's doing. I trust that He loves me and wants me to have His best. So I rejoice knowing that *how* He brings a thing to pass is not as important to me as knowing that He *will* bring it to pass.

I've seen things that looked bad from my point of view where God used it to have me in place for some really great things. I'm reminded of Joseph the dreamer. I'm certain he would agree that the way things happened in his life was not the way he would have brought about God's promise to him. He would certainly have skipped being placed in a pit by his brothers. He would have foregone going to prison. He would have elected not to be a slave or lied on.

But everything that happened, in some way, positioned him for the promise of God. And how exciting was it for all of us to see that just as God had promised things would be, in the end, that's what came to be.

May I have "Word" with you? All you might be able to see right now are the trees; but be encouraged. When you trust God, you have to trust that he sees the whole forest, that He sees dangers you cannot see, that He sees blessings beyond your thoughts and imagination. Trust that whatever is happening, God sees and knows it all.

Yes, it may be that God sees some danger or something not in your best interest you have no idea about. You may encounter situations you label as being bad, but really ends up later having kept you from hurt, harm, and danger.

So when you give it to God, and you keep an open and continuous dialogue with Him; you can rejoice even while things may not look like it's going the way you think it should.

Second Corinthians 2:14 says, "Now thanks be unto God which always causeth us to triumph in Christ, and maketh manifest the savor of his knowledge by us in every place." Spiritually see beyond the trees, then thank God that He sees all, and that He always has your best interest at heart!

Under The Shadow of The Almighty

here were two things I considered writing on today. I was turning to the scripture for the one that was in my spirit, when I opened the Bible and went to another scripture. I started to write on that one but felt I should stay with this one. The scripture that my Bible flipped to was Psalm 122:1, "I was glad when they said unto me, Let us go into the house of the Lord." I paused and thought seriously about writing on that one, but I've decided to put it on hold and go with the one that first came to me: Psalm 91.

In Psalm 91:1, you find these words. "He that dwelleth in the secret place of the Most High shall abide under the shadow of the Almighty." Wow, wow, wow! What a power-packed scripture. God has a secret place. God is the Most High. And he who dwells; meaning you can linger, find a place, live there, but he or she who dwells in the secret place of the Most High shall abide under the shadow.

Okay, look at that. In order for there to be a shadow, certain factors must be in place. Number one, there must be that which casts the shadow. It can be a person or a thing. But just having a person or a thing there will not produce a shadow. In order to have a shadow, there must be some light somewhere, and that light has to be shone in order to create a shadow of what is there.

In other words, for you or I to dwell under the shadow, that must mean that the one who's making the shadow has to be close by! That means there is some light shining somewhere in order for the shadow to be produced. That means no matter what you're going through, as long as you're dwelling under the shadow of the Most High, God is there, and you don't have to worry because there is definitely light somewhere nearby.

People may wonder how you're able to make it, but they don't understand that you're dwelling in the secret place. Not everybody knows about this place, but *you* know. And not only do you know, but you know how to get there and how to dwell there. When God said He would never leave you nor forsake you, He meant what He said.

Our God is so awesome, so powerful, so omnipotent that even His shadow is a place of refuge. His shadow provides a fortress where the enemy can't even get in. I'm talking about just God's shadow. Just God's shadow is enough to provide healing, to provide protection, to provide joy, to provide a peace that surpasses all understanding.

We can declare that God will cover me with His feathers and under His wings I'm going to trust Him. God's truth will be my shield and buckler. In other words: When people are telling me who I'm not, God's truth is telling me who I am in Him. When people are saying what I can't do, God's truth is telling me what all I can do through Christ Jesus.

May I have a "Word" with you? You need to make your way under the shadow of the Almighty and learn how to dwell in the secret place of the Most High. That way when negative things come your way, light will be cast on it, and that negative stuff can't do anything but disappear. God will shine the light on some things. God will show you the way. And if you don't do anything else but follow the shadow of the Most High God, His shadow will lead you where you need to go.

That is some kind of Power right there! Just God's shadow is more than enough. He that dwells in the secret place of the Most High *shall* abide under the shadow of The Almighty!

To Be Present with The Lord

$\mathcal{M}$any of us have lost loved ones. It seems lately, a lot of people are facing this. People are leaving this earth at all ages: the young, the middle-age, and those who have lived to be ripe old ages. It's a difficult thing to say good-bye to those we love.

As a young girl, I remember when my Aunt Naomi would either visit us or we would visit her, she would always cry when it was time to say good-bye. She knew she had to go home or that we had to. Home is a place that most look forward to getting back to. In the "Wizard of Oz," Dorothy would say, "There's no place like home."

When I was little, I didn't understand why my aunt cried so hard when I knew she was looking forward to going home. I understood better as I got older: She hated to be separated from the ones she loved. She knew she would miss her loved-ones, and she didn't want to miss them. A few years back, we had to say good-bye to this awesome aunt one last time. And as many of us have experienced or will experience, we know this is part of life.

You see, I also understand that this is not our home. Yes, we're here on this earth, but this is not our home. We're travelers on a mission; missionaries on assignment. And to those who have accepted Jesus as our personal Savior, we're Ambassadors of Christ. This is not our home. We meet many while we're here. But there comes a time when it's time to go home. And as hard as it is to say good-bye, as much as we might cry (and it's okay to cry because when one leaves, we know we're going to miss them), what we who are in the body of Christ know are these words written by Paul: "To be absent from the body is to be present with the Lord."

May I have a "Word" with you? This is not our home. There is much work for us to do while we're here, but one day, we're going to leave this place and go to another place. We're going to go home. Being saved, there is rejoicing knowing that when we depart from here, we're Heaven-bound.

But let me encourage you in this: If you know someone who is not saved, if you know someone who has not accepted Jesus, has not acknowledged that He is the Son of God, that Jesus died on the cross, that God raised Him from the dead—if you know someone like this, then love them enough to talk to them about the Lord. Lead them in confession of the Lord Jesus.

Love them enough so that when it's time for them to leave this world, and even though you know you're going to miss them, you'll be able to smile, celebrate their life, as you say, "To be absent from the body is to be present with the Lord."

Yes, it's okay to miss them when they go. Miss their smile, miss their voice, miss their touch, miss their hugs, miss them. But then look to the hills from whence comes your help and think about that great day in Heaven when a great reunion will take place. When we take our final trip, and we see Jesus—face to face.

We're on a mission. Yes, houses are good, cars are good, money in the bank is good, and prestige is good. But to know that you're saved. And when you come to the end of this journey that you've done what you came here to do: Going into the hedges and highways and telling people about God the Father, God the Son, and God the Holy Spirit (which is your reasonable service), that's better than good!

And when it's our time to leave, we realize it's not death we're dealing with, it's merely going Home. And that to be absent from the body is to be present with the Lord!

When Is When?

"Therefore I say unto you, What things soever ye desire, when ye pray, believe that ye receive them, and ye shall have them." (Mark 11:24) I love this scripture because it has so much in it that we sometimes totally miss.

I was thinking on this scripture and I heard the Lord say, "When is when?" You see, we all have desires. Some of us have been waiting for what seems like a long time for our desires to manifest. But Jesus tells us first of all, that "what things soever you desire."

What things soever is a powerful Word mostly because it's not just limited to the spiritual things in life. Yes, it includes the spiritual, but it's not limited to only spiritual things.

Mark 11:24 is recorded right after the lesson from the withered fig tree. When Jesus saw the fig tree afar off, having leaves, and He had come thinking perhaps He might find some fruit on it only to find nothing but leaves. What was funny about this is that it wasn't even the time of figs. Mark 11:14 states, "And Jesus answered and said unto it, No man eat fruit of thee hereafter for ever. And his disciples heard it." Upon the morning as Jesus and the disciples passed by, they saw the fig tree dried up from the roots.

Peter pointed out to Jesus that the fig tree He had cursed had withered away. And Jesus' response was "Have faith in God." What things soever you desire!

Then in Mark 11:24 it went on to say: When you pray, believe that you have received them. The question then is: When do you receive what you desire? When is when? Is when *when* you see it become manifested in the natural?

No. *When* is *when* you pray. At the moment you pray, believe right then that you have received what you prayed for. The key word is "believe." Too many people are praying for "what things soever," but maintaining a stance of caution. You don't want to put yourself out there and look foolish by believing, so you're "cautiously optimistic." God doesn't need cautiously-optimistic Christians. He desires Christians who will boldly come to the throne, ask whatsoever you desire (as long as your "whatsoever" is not out of line with God's Word), then believe. But going a step farther, and acting like you believe.

Am I talking about name it and claim it? No. I'm talking about having faith in God, having faith in God's Word. Trusting that God is not a man that He should lie. Trusting that if God's Word says you can have it, you believe you can. Believing enough that you can tell others without feeling like God might not come through. Some of you know what I'm talking about. You don't want God to look bad so you give Him an out. Well, God doesn't need an out. He needs you to have faith, and act like it's already done!

May I have a "Word" with you? When you pray, you need to believe, at that very moment, it's done! You see, I don't have to wait to see it in the natural to give God praise for it. I speak the Word to God and say, "God, Your Word says in Mark 11:24 that what things soever I desire when I pray, if I believe I receive them, I will have them. Lord, I know that Your Word will not return unto You void, but that it *shall* accomplish that which You've sent it to do. I believe I have it now. I believe it's done now. Now! In Jesus' name I pray."

So when is when? When is not after you pray, but when is *when* you pray! Oh, yes! I believe I have it "when" whether you see it, believe it, or not!

What Kind of Fruit Are You Bearing?

The Bible tells us that people will know you by the fruit you bear. We understand this in the natural. Should we come across an apple tree, we expect it bears apples; a plum tree, plums; a fig tree, figs, and so on.

If we see a tree that's called one thing but it's bearing something other than what it's called, we think someone must have been mistaken in naming it or something is unnatural with it.

In your Christian walk (I'm addressing this to those who are called or call themselves Christian), what kind of fruit are you bearing? Do you think about how your actions (which are being watched whether you realize it or not) may affect others who might not know or have the full knowledge of Jesus Christ?

May I have a "Word" with you? What kind of fruit are you bearing? Are you living a life that demonstrates that no matter what is going on in your life, you have the victory? Or do they see defeat. Are you an overcomer? Are you showing the love of God, or are you playing a role, saying you're a Christian, yet there is no fruit to bear that out? Does it matter?

Yes, it matters to God. It matters to the Kingdom of God!

The Sacrifice of Praise

I love God. Do you hear me? I absolutely adore the Lord! And I have loved Him for as long as I can remember. In fact, even during those times when Satan has tried to tell me how stupid I was for believing God, when it looked like nothing was happening or that God wasn't doing things the way I thought it was going to be done, or that it was taking God too long to do what He said He was going to do (oh, you know what I'm talking about), even during those times, I learned to love God even more.

I love God not for what He has done for me, which I am so grateful for. I love God not for what He is doing for me right now, which I find myself standing in awe of His AWEsomeness. I love God not for what He is going to do, which has me smiling in anticipation right in this moment. I love God for Who God is.

Just for Who He is.

God is Jehovah-Jireh; that means: He is my provider. He is the source of my everything. God is Jehovah-Rophe; that means: He's my healer. The Lord is my Shepherd, I shall not want. Whatever I need, God has it. A cattle on a thousand hills belong to Him, and I am His child. Then God gave us Jesus, whose name is above all names. For all God is to me, for all God does for me, what can I give Him? What offering do I have for the Lord?

The sacrifice of praise. I can worship Him in spirit and truth.

Hebrews 13:15 tells us, "By him therefore let us offer the sacrifice of praise to God continually, that is, the fruit of our lips giving thanks to his name." To give the sacrifice of praise, you need to open your mouth and from the fruit of your lips, that sweetness that has come from a seed planted down deep, give God thanks!

Let me say this: praise is easy when things are going great in your life. Okay, you got that job you applied for. Of course, you can praise God. When you had more bills than money and somehow God showed up and made a way out of no way, sure you can bless the name of the Lord. But what happens when things don't appear to be working the way you thought? What happens when you don't get that job? What happens when the money doesn't come in on time? What happens when your children seem to be getting worse rather than better after you've prayed and believed? What happens when you feel all alone?

That's the time when you really need to press and praise. Praise God even more! Why, you might ask? Because God is still God, and He's worthy to be praised. But if you want to come at it from a natural standpoint, praise God because of His faithfulness and the faith you have in Him. You don't know what God is up to. You don't know how He's going to bring a thing to past.

When you praise God, you're saying, "Lord, I trust You fully and completely. I know You've got this. I recognize that You're in control, and You're going to do this how You want, when You want."

Rather than talk, your praise action alone demonstrates your faith in God. Faith works, but you have to work your faith.

May I have a "Word" with you? Daily, continually bring the Lord the sacrifice of praise. We no longer have to sacrifice animals for our sins. Jesus paid it all on the cross. When you wake up in the morning, give God a sacrifice of praise. Throughout your day, give God a sacrifice of praise. Before you close your eyes at night, give God a sacrifice of praise. Then I want you to see just how much more you're going to have to praise God for! You know it's true: when the praises God up, the blessings come down! Rain on me.

True Worshipers

*Y*e worship ye know not what: we know what we worship: for salvation is of the Jews. But the hour cometh, and now is, when the true worshipers shall worship the Father in spirit and in truth: for the Father seeketh such to worship him. God is a Spirit: and they that worship him must worship him in spirit and in truth." John 4:22-24.

God is self-existent. God is love. God is a Spirit. And they that worship Him must worship Him in spirit and truth. God is worthy of our praise and our worship. I love to praise God and to enter into His presence with worship. We may know people who do things to impress others. But one thing for sure: we can't fool or falsely impress God. He knows when we're sincere, and He knows when we're faking. They that worship Him must worship Him in spirit and in truth.

Second Corinthians 3:17 tells us, "Now the Lord is that Spirit: and where the Spirit of the Lord is, there is liberty." Being in a place of worship to the Lord puts us where the Lord is and that's an awesome place to be. From this scripture, we see that where the Spirit of the Lord is, there is liberty. It reminds me of the scripture that gives us the assurance: Whom the Son sets free is free indeed. Do you want liberty? Do you want to be free? Then become a true worshiper of God.

No matter what is going on in our lives, when we're truly worshiping the Lord, we come into a place where whatever is going on, it really isn't such a big deal. Oh, it may have seemed big before you came before the Lord. But it's nothing; it's minute when compared to our God and His power. I worship God because He is so good. I worship God because He first loved me. I worship God because when I am weak, He always shows Himself strong. I worship God because He is worthy of all our praise. I worship God just because He is God.

Worship is not something to be done for show. It's not something to be done to impress others. True worshipers look upon worship as a special time between them and the Lord. When I worship, I see myself standing and/or bowing before our loving and awesome God.

It's an honor to be able to worship Him. It's an honor to be allowed to come before His presence. It's wonderful to come before the Lord and being able to love on Him as He loves back on us. True worshipers get excited about worshiping God.

May I have a "Word" with you? When you have true worship experiences, you'll become like the woman at the well after she encountered Jesus. You'll leave your water pot (whatever you were carrying before you met Him), and go out and tell others, "Come, see a man, which told me all things that ever I did: is not this the Christ?"

People should be able to look at you and see something is different about you when you've been with the Lord. Are you having true worship with God? Have you spent time with the Lord, and I mean doing more than just coming to Him and asking Him for something?

Most of us love to be loved on. Have you loved on the Lord lately? Are you a true worshiper? Only you and the Lord know for sure.

Those Things Which Are Behind

"Brethren, I count not myself to have apprehended: but this one thing I do, forgetting those things which are behind, and reaching forth unto those things which are before, I press toward the mark for the prize of the high calling of God in Christ Jesus." Philippians 3:13-14.

New Year's means the year changes from one year to the next. You may have brought in the New Year in some special way with others or you may have brought it in alone. You may have merely awakened to the New Year having arrived during your time of slumber. I absolutely love these two scriptures. There's so much in them and so many directions one can go in after reading them. But for right now, I'd like to focus on "forgetting those things which are behind."

You see whatever has happened is behind you. It's what we call the past. There may be some good things that have happened, and there may have been some bad things. With the bad, people have a tendency to want to forget about them completely. With the good, we want to hold onto it as long as we can. We call it "reflecting."

But in both cases, it's still the past—gone from our present. And there is so much more God requires of you. You can't live in your past. So whether the past was good or bad, it's time to forget those things which are behind you. Reach for those things which are before you.

If someone hurt you in the past, forget those things. If things didn't go quite the way you envisioned them, forget those things. If you experienced loss (and there are many types of losses), yes, it may be hard to forget them, but you must reach forth and reach ahead toward those things God has set before you. Choose you this day!

You have dreams and goals. You have a calling and purpose. And the longer you sit back looking at what has already been, the more time you're taking away from what is now, and what you are to do in what you're being called to do.

We're human. We hurt. We want to quit sometimes because it's frustrating to continue when you feel you're not getting anywhere. But I often say that someone is waiting on your gift, your dream, your ministry to manifest. Someone is praying to God; telling Him they don't think they can hold on any longer. And what they are praying for may be what God has placed inside of you to give to the world. So when you want to quit, it doesn't always merely affect you. You must keep reaching forth toward the mark.

May I have a "Word" with you? Philippians 3:14 says, "I press toward the mark for the prize of the high calling of God in Christ Jesus." Look at all there is to mine in just that one statement.

To press, you have to push beyond what you feel like doing. "Toward the mark" is a specified goal, and in this case, the mark is "for the prize of the high calling of God." There is a higher calling than where you are now. Then the final part: "in Christ Jesus." That part takes me straight to Philippians 4:13, "I can do all things through Christ which strengtheneth me."

No matter what you've come through, the fact remains: you made it through. How do I know? Because you're reading or listening to this now. So forget those things that are behind you and reach forth. God has great things He desires to do using you.

You just need to possess the right mind and the right spirit!

True Givers

I was asked once what was my favorite scripture and why. This was a tough question because I have so many (Psalm 37, Ephesians 6). I absolutely love the Word of God. Now, you talk about life and life more abundantly—the Word of God is that and so much more.

When I was a young girl, I recall once being a little down, and I was looking for something to make me feel better. That's when I discovered the fourteenth chapter of John. The first verse began by stating, "Let not your heart be troubled: ye believe in God, believe also in me." That entire chapter was such a comfort for me—knowing that my heart didn't have to be troubled purely because I believed in God.

I love John 10:10 where Jesus says, "The thief cometh not, but for to steal, and to kill, and to destroy: I am come that they might have life, and that they might have it more abundantly." Jesus came so that we might have life and life more abundantly. John 3:16 tells us, "For God so loved the world, that he gave his only begotten Son, that whosoever believeth in him should not perish, but have everlasting life." God didn't just love the world; He *so* loved the world that He gave. Luke 6:38 declares, "Give, and it shall be given unto you; good measure, pressed down, and shaken together, and running over, shall men give into your bosom. For with the same measure that ye mete withal it shall be measured to you again."

True givers give from the heart. God showed His loved for the world by giving His Son Jesus. Jesus came to earth and gave His life so that we could be saved as well as walk in abundant life.

Jesus gave us the giving formula in Luke 6:38. In essence, whatever you give will not only come back to you, but it will come back to you good measure, pressed down, shaken together, and running over. This sounds like the abundant life Jesus was talking about in John 10:10.

May I have a "Word" with you? If you want friends, be a friend. If you want more joy, give joy. If you want more peace, give peace. Giving a smile will generally get you more smiles. Laughter, oh now that can be contagious. If you want more love, then learn to give love. If you give time to others, you'll get back time from others.

I've heard it said in different ways: "Give to others that which you'd like to receive." God gave His Son, and in return, more sons and daughters are coming into the Kingdom.

So the next time you find yourself desiring something in your life, give that, and watch it come back to you multiplied.

In truth, true givers don't really give to get. True givers give out of sheer love. But like a coin with a head and a tail, you can't have one without getting the other. If you give, you will receive.

Be a true giver—give from your heart!

Can I Get a Witness?

"And ye are witnesses of these things." Luke 24:48. When something happens, you'll often find someone looking for any witnesses to what occurred. Two people can see the same thing and each give a different account of what they saw. And if the incident goes to trial, a person may be called to testify as a witness. Question: If you were called to testify on behalf of what God has done for you, what would you testify to?

This is profound. Many people look at what's going on in their lives and become down, despondent, or in despair without remembering or regarding what God has already done in their lives. You know, recalling those times when you wondered how you were going to pay a bill only to have God prove just how much of a provider He truly is. I'm talking about witnessing God, Who can make a way out of no way.

You know, God, Who can call forth something out of nothing. God, Who can speak to the elements—earth, wind, and fire and the elements obey. God, Who set the earth in rotation and told it to continue as He'd set it. God, Who can speak to the wind, speaking peace and commanding it to be still, and it becomes still.

God, Who can tell fire to rest on a bush on a mountain, getting Moses' attention, while telling the fire not to consume that bush. God, Who commanded fire to get back when three Hebrew boys were cast into the furnace and demanded that not even smoke attach itself to their clothes.

If you were called to testify, as a witness for the Lord, what would you testify to about Him?

Do you know God as a healer? Can you testify on how you were given victory in spite of those who were hoping for your demise? Can I get a witness on what an awesome God the Lord is? Have you seen the Lord show up in times and places where you knew it wasn't anybody *but* the Lord?

May I have a "Word" with you? You are officially being called as a witness. It's time for you to step up and tell what you've seen, what you've heard, and what you know about the Lord. I can testify that God has truly been my provider. There have been times when I had nowhere else to turn except to the Lord. It may have looked like it was over, and I was done, but God! God stepped in the midst of it all, and said, "Oh, no. This is my child, and she's more than a conqueror. She is sealed with the Holy Spirit. She's above only and not beneath. She is rooted, built up, and established in faith. She's blessed going in *and* out!"

Maybe there was a time when the doctor called something a misdiagnosis or a wrong call when you know it was God Who said, "By Jesus' stripes, you are healed. Don't receive what that doctor has said contrary to this. That sickness is not My best. Speak My Word over your situation, and watch Me work."

And you did. Then you, as I once did, reported to your doctor what God said. My doctor looked at me like I was some poor misguided person in total denial when I told her a diagnosis I was given was not God's best. But I believed the report of the Lord. And when the end results finally came in, it was just as God's report declared.

You've been called to be a witness. It's time for you to tell others what you've seen, heard, and what you know about God! Can I get a witness? God is looking for witnesses to His goodness. Now, you are free to tell the truth, and nothing but the truth; so help you God.

You've been placed under protective custody!

The Word of God

I love the Word of God. Talk about life—the Word of God is all that and so much more. Need something to make you feel better, read John 14, "Let not your heart be troubled: ye believe in God, believe also in me. In my Father's house are many mansions: if it were not so I would have told you. I go to prepare a place for you. And if I go and prepare a place for you, I will come again, and receive you unto myself; that where I am there ye may be also. And whither I go ye know, and the way ye know. Thomas said unto him, Lord we know not whither thou goest; and how can we know the way? Jesus saith unto him, I am the way, the truth, and the life: no man cometh unto the Father, but by me." (John 14:1-6)

No matter what's going on, God has a Word that speaks to whatever situation you may be dealing with. His Word gives us comfort and assurance. John 14:27 tells us, "Peace I leave with you, my peace I give unto you: not as the world giveth, give I unto you. Let not your heart be troubled, neither let it be afraid."

No matter what you're going through, Isaiah 61:3 assures us, "To appoint unto them that mourn in Zion, to give unto them beauty for ashes, the oil of joy for mourning, the garment of praise for the spirit of heaviness; that they might be called trees of righteousness, the planting of the LORD, that he might be glorified."

When you're under spiritual attack, turn to Ephesians 6 to ensure you're dressed properly. If you want to know how much God loves you, read John 3:16, "For God so loved the world, that he gave his only begotten Son, that whosoever believeth in him should not perish, but have everlasting life." If you need strength in weakness, read First Corinthians 1:27. Looking to know more about God's grace? Read Romans 4:16, 9:16.

May I have a "Word" with you? Isaiah 55:6-12 says, "Seek ye the Lord while he may be found, call ye upon him while he is near: Let the wicked forsake his way, and the unrighteous man his thoughts: and let him return unto the Lord, and he will have mercy upon him; and to our God, for he will abundantly pardon. For my thoughts are not your thoughts, neither are your ways my ways, saith the Lord. For as the heavens are higher than the earth, so are my ways higher than your ways, and my thoughts than your thoughts. For as the rain cometh down, and the snow from heaven, and returneth not thither, but watereth the earth, and maketh it bring forth and bud, that it may give seed to the sower, and bread to the eater: So shall my word be that goeth forth out of my mouth: it shall not return unto me void, but it shall accomplish that which I please, and it shall prosper in the thing whereto I sent it. For ye shall go out with joy, and be led forth with peace: the mountains and the hills shall break forth before you into singing, and all the trees of the field shall clap their hands."

God is so good, He has a Word to comfort and give assurance in every area of our lives. We just need to find out what God has to say about it, and say that.

Count Your Blessings!

s a year comes to a close, it's a great time to look back over your life and count your blessings. When I look back over mine, I don't have to wonder how I have come to be where I am today. If it had not been for the Lord on my side, I know my life wouldn't be as rich and as blessed as it is. And rich is not always defined by money either. It's being in health (even when things seem to now creak, sputter, stall, or crack). Rich is family.

It's having a peace that surpasses all understanding. It's the joy of the Lord. It's being able to love and to be loved. It's having a purpose, knowing that purpose, and walking in that purpose. It's knowing that you're not alone and, with God, you'll never be alone.

Count . . . your . . . blessings!

Can you speak? Then count your blessing, and with your voice, give God praise. Can you lift your arm? Can you raise your hand? Then right now, give God a wave offering. Can you stand? Then pat your feet, stand up for Christ, even dance for the Lord.

Once I was leading Praise & Worship during a Sunday morning service. As I was praising God, I spun around dancing gracefully. I heard in my spirit, "You need to dance with the one Who brought you." I shared that with the congregation as I felt those words resonating in my heart and spirit. Yes! It was the Lord Who brought me—Almighty God. And He's brought me from a mighty long way.

How many times have we gone to a place where someone else brought us, but we ended up spending more time with the others in attendance, neglecting the one who actually brought us? At the time I was waltzing in glorious praise, I was hearing how special it is to "dance with the one who brought you." God brought me, and I am so excited about spending time with Him, and yes, dancing as I kept my thoughts on Him.

Take a few minutes (hours or days if needed) and write down some of the things you have to be grateful for. Often, we get so focused on what's not going right that we minimize what has gone right. When we focus so much on what we don't have, we actually diminish the importance of what we do have. Learn to appreciate what you have, and you'll find that it opens not only doors but windows for even more blessings to come.

I'm advocating for you get a facelift during this time. Smile. Yes, smile, and see how much younger your face will begin to look. You don't always need cosmetic surgery to have a successful facelift. Just smile. Believe you don't have much to smile about? Then smile anyway, and count your blessing that you are even able to smile.

How about doing some jogging? Too cold or hot to go jogging? Then do some inner jogging. Laugh. Yes, laugh. Laugh, and see how quickly your entire body gets in shape. Don't think you have much of anything to laugh about? Well, laugh anyway. Then count your blessing that you *can* laugh. Allow the joy of the Lord to permeate throughout. Laugh! "A merry heart doeth good like a medicine." Proverbs 17:22

May I have a "Word" with you? Proverbs 10:22 says, "The blessing of the Lord, it maketh rich, and he addeth no sorrow with it." Again I say: Count your blessings! Deuteronomy 23:5 tells us, "Nevertheless the Lord thy God would not hearken unto Balaam; but the Lord thy God turned the curse into a blessing unto thee, because the Lord thy God loved thee." No matter what's going on in your life, God loves you.

Know that God is for you. Count your blessings, and watch as more blessings make their way to you!

A Strong Foundation

or other foundation can no man lay than that is laid, which is Jesus Christ. Now if any man build upon this foundation gold, silver, precious stones, wood, hay, stubble; Every man's work shall be made manifest: for the day shall declare it, because it shall be revealed by fire; and the fire shall try every man's work of what sort it is." (First Corinthians 3:11-13)

Years ago, my husband and I had our house built according to our specifications. Growing up, I also watched my own father build our family home.

When you build a house, there's preparation work that should go into it before you ever even begin. There's the idea of what you want which includes the style and various rooms, among other things. From the idea, a blueprint is created which is ultimately what the builder will use to bring that home into a manifested state. But before anything is built, there has to be a foundation. Smart people understand that it should be a strong foundation, one that can hold up the weight and the rest of what's added onto it.

With our house, I chose two levels with a full basement, but I didn't want the house to be tall. Mostly, I just didn't want a lot of steps in order to enter the house. My builder recognized that meant our foundation would have to go deeper into the ground to accomplish my desire. We had to dig deep.

I remember going by the building site and seeing the foundation poured and being built up with cinder blocks. I was so excited. Working for BellSouth at the time, I went out of town on a business trip shortly after they began. Excitedly, I returned to the site expecting to see the first floor pretty much up. However, to my surprise, the foundation was being taken down. I called my builder to find out what was going on.

"Yes, the foundation is being taken down," my builder informed me. "There was a problem with the foundation."

The explanation he gave was: because we'd used dynamite in order to go deeper into the ground to break up the limestone rock that was too soft to dig out yet not hard enough to flip out, the foundation required steel be added, which hadn't been done.

You see the master builder knew that if the foundation wasn't right, no matter how beautiful and expensive everything else might be, in the end, there was going to be some serious problems later on. There would possibly be cracks in the walls, a shifting and a leaning of the house—costly and detrimental things that would most definitely have to be dealt with at a later time.

May I have a "Word" with you? If your life's foundation, your spiritual foundation is not right, there are going to be problems you'll have to deal with later. Jesus is the Master Builder. He is also the foundation in which we as Christian need to build our faith upon.

There's strength in Jesus. And just like my house's foundation required steel, so do we. We need the steel that only Jesus and the Holy Spirit can provide. We need a "peace be still." We need a "I'm *still* standing" steel; an overcomer steel. And you know, when Jesus says peace be still, even the winds and the waves obey.

When you build on the foundation of Jesus the Christ, the storms of life will not and cannot cause you to fall.

So build on a solid foundation, build on the solid rock. And that rock is Jesus!

Blessed—Not Cursed

J t is important that I say something just the way God spoke it to me. **I AM BLESSED**. I don't care who you are or what you try to do to back it up, you cannot curse what God has already blessed. My blessing does not come from my works. Because if they did, then I would most surely boast about what I've done. In fact, not only would I boast, I might even think I'm better than you because I feel I am a better person than you are.

Jesus came to set us free. We were in bondage of much, but thanks be to God who loved the world so much that He gave His only begotten Son that whosoever believed on Him would not perish but have everlasting life. I am free from the curse of the law. What is the curse of the law?

In short, there were 613 laws called the Mosaic Law—the Law of Moses. The rule was: if you messed up on one, you were guilty of them all. That meant you could keep 612 laws and miss one and be guilty of missing all 613.

In the book of Galatians (New Testament) it talks about the law. Galatians chapter 2, starting at verse 15 tells how justification is not of the law. Verse 21 tells us, "I do not frustrate the grace of God: for if righteousness come by the law, then Christ is dead in vain."

Jesus' grace (unmerited favor) has much value to me. The book of Galatians, chapter 3, verses 1-5 speaks on Freedom from the Law.

Galatians chapter 3 starting at verse 6, tells of God's Covenant with Abraham.

But here is why I refuse to allow anyone to tell me I'm cursed or that I will be cursed because of something I do or don't do. Galatians 6:13 says, "Christ hath redeemed us from the curse of the law, being made a curse for us: for it is written, Cursed is every one that hangeth on a tree." Okay now, the shouting verse is verse 14, "That the blessing of Abraham might come on the Gentiles through Jesus Christ; that we might receive the promise of the Spirit through faith."

Abraham's blessings are now for me (and for you)!

I am blessed because I believe, and I have faith in what Jesus has done. Period. I can't do enough to earn the blessings of God. I can't do anymore above what Jesus has already done. I love you because I love Jesus. Let me put it like this: because I love Jesus, I have to love you. I give because of Jesus. Because I love the Lord so much, it makes me *want* to give to the things He wants done down here on earth.

And let me say this: When I gave my life, I gave my ALL to the Lord. I love the Lord with all of my heart, mind, and soul. That means everything I have belongs to Him. I may be one of a few who feels this way, but 100% of everything I have belongs to God. I don't keep anything back for myself. That means my money is all His. This means I consult Him about every dime of my financial decisions because I see the money that He blesses me with as my being the steward of it for Him. God tells me what to do. Period. Not man—God.

Read into this however you choose. It's just that I know without a shadow of a doubt that where I am in my life has nothing to do with my education, with who I know, or with what I have.

May I have a "Word" with you? The only reason I'm where I am today is because of the Lord. People often say it's not *what* you know but *who* you know. Well, I will tell you this: The only person I know in high places is God the Father, God the Son, and God the Holy Spirit (Who dwells within me).

I am blessed because God has called me blessed. So when anyone tries to judge whether or not I'm blessed or cursed, or *when* I'm blessed or cursed, as for me I say: You have no authority! I don't care who you are or what your true intentions might be. You cannot curse what God has already blessed. And I refuse to allow Satan to trick me into believing and speaking anything different from what God has said to me.

I *am* blessed, and eye hath not seen nor hath ear heard what God is doing and about to do in this blessed woman of God's life. That's what I say. But I can only speak for myself. I do know this: Life and death is in the power of the tongue. As for me, I choose to speak life.

I choose to shout loudly and from the rooftops (if need be), I am **BLESSED** because God blesses me! And I thank God that I am free, and I won't allow anyone to come and try to put me back in bondage!

Nobody is bigger than My God.

Glory!

Established

"Commit thy works unto the Lord, and thy thoughts shall be established." Proverbs 16:3. Have you ever thought about something you'd like to do? Of course you have. That's how things get done, how things are created: it first begins with a thought. In fact, that's how everything we do gets done, it was first a thought. This applies to the good and bad.

You think you want to do well on a test, and things begin to line up for that to happen. You think about something you'd like to create, and steps are taken for it to manifest. Even people who find themselves in sexual situations they shouldn't be in (such as fornication and adultery), that action first began with a thought. Stealing—that was a thought first.

When I decide to write a book, there is first a thought about what that book will be about. If anyone has decided to start a business or have started it, it all begins with a thought. Thoughts are powerful, but a thought with no action behind it will remain just that: a thought. One scripture even tells us how our thoughts have an effect on who we are. "As a man thinketh, so is he." God has put so much inside of us.

Many of you have ministries that you're either already doing or thinking about doing. If you're doing what God has called you to do, you still have thoughts on things that need to be done. If you're thinking about what needs to done, these are still thoughts there with you.

301

Proverbs 16:3 tells us how to establish our thoughts. We need to commit our works unto the Lord. In other words, roll on the Lord your works, and the Lord will establish your thoughts. This lets us know that if you are committing your works unto the Lord, directing what you do toward the Lord, the Lord will establish your thoughts. God will give you thoughts you wouldn't have ever had. The Bible tells us that God will give you "witty inventions." God will direct your path.

I can't tell you how many times I have committed my works to the Lord as I was writing something, and He gave me something I *know* there was no way it could have come from me. That's how things go when you're rolling with God! I've written some things and literally had to stop to say to God, "God, that was good! You're awesome!"

Sure, I may get the credit for it when others read or hear it, but let me tell you: It's all God. It is *all* God!

May I have a "Word" with you? Commit . . . roll on the Lord your works. This battle you're fighting is not yours. The battle was never yours. It's the Lord's. Stop taking it all upon yourself when God is telling you that you don't have to. God is there with you *and* for you. He has shoulders that are broad enough to handle whatever you may have to roll onto Him. God's wisdom is infinite. He has answers for every question that may raise its head to you.

God is saying that if you'll commit your works to Him, on two fronts, He will *establish* your thoughts. First, the thoughts you have will be manifested and second, the thoughts you need in order to exceed anything you can ever ask or think will be given to you. God will direct your path.

Yes, do what you can do and are called to do. And allow God to do what God is going to do.

Even a Little Light Makes a Difference

My master bathroom doesn't have a window in it. Originally when we had the house built, I'd asked for a skylight in that room. My builder ordered it, but for some reason we didn't get the skylight put in. So at night, with the door closed and the lights off, that room would normally be totally dark, blackness. Except there's this blue light on a toothbrush charger that's there to let you know it's plugged in and being charged.

One day I was in there with what should have been total blackness when I noticed something interesting. I could still see when the main lights were turned off. With no other light, that little blue light was throwing off enough light to allow me to be able to see. Not all that well, but I could see well enough to know it wasn't dark in there and just where things were.

That little light made a difference in that room.

I know some of you might think that what you do is not all that important. You might think you're really not making that much of a difference. But just like that little blue light makes a difference in my bathroom (whether anyone is in there to witness it or not), your light, little or not, makes a difference.

Most of us have either heard or sang the song, "This little light of mine." As a child, I used to wonder why people enjoyed singing about a little light. Why not say, this light of mine?

First of all, most of us have a tendency to put what we do down as though it's not all that important. Notice I said most, because there are a number of people who, in my opinion, think more highly of themselves than they ought.

At this point, I'm not talking about those people who think that the sun revolves around them the same way they think the sun revolves around the earth. (Just a side note here for anyone who doesn't know this, but the earth actually revolves around the sun, not the other way around.)

Stop playing small. We serve a big God, an awesome God. The light you have does make a difference. Just like the blue light in my bathroom made enough of a difference to garner my attention, your light makes a difference.

That blue light on the toothbrush charger shines because it's plugged into the right source, and there's power in that source. You just need to be sure you're plugged into the right source, and that there is power in your source. Then you won't have to make your light shine, it will merely shine.

May I have a "Word" with you? It's time out for playing small. It's time to let your light shine. Shine, shine, shine! Somebody is in the dark. They don't have a clue which way to go or even where they are. With your light shining, it could make a big difference in the lives of others. Help someone else see not by trying to make them see, but by illuminating what's there. Even a little light can make a difference.

It's time to stop playing small. It's time to let your little light shine!

From This Day Forward

After being delivered out of Egypt, the children of Israel found themselves with Pharaoh coming hard and heavy behind them and nothing but mountains too high to climb and a sea too deep to cross on foot before them. In our day and time, we'd call that "Caught between a rock and a hard place."

So, what do you do when you find yourself in a place of Godly promise; and yet a place where you really can't go back, and it doesn't look like there's a way for you to move forward?

That was the question the children of Israel found staring them in the face. They'd prayed for deliverance. God sent Moses to deliver them. They were promised a land that flowed with milk and honey. But what they found was what appeared to be "no way out."

Where are you right now? There are some of you who've been toiling and believing, pressing onward in spite of what things look like, and now it looks like you're in a pickle—a jam. You're hemmed up between a past you can't or don't need to go back to, and a glorious future that awaits you with the exception of some obstacle you just can't see your way around. Hallelujah! This message is for you.

For others of you, things may be just fine right now. In fact, you may be saying, "Things couldn't be better, thank you very much." Well, congratulations! Hallelujah! This message is *also* for you.

Exodus 14:13-15 says, "And Moses said unto the people, Fear ye not, stand still, and see the salvation of the Lord, which he will show to you today: for the Egyptians whom ye have seen today, ye shall see them again no more for ever. The Lord shall fight for you, and ye shall hold your peace. And the Lord said unto Moses, Wherefore criest thou unto me? speak unto the children of Israel, that they go forward."

I say to you: from this day forward, go forward. Don't look back on where you've come from—fondly recalling only the good things; forgetting most of the bad. When you come to "no way," that's the time to learn firsthand that God is "a way" out of "no way."

When you've reached what appears to be impossible, that's when you learn: With God, all things are possible. After all, God told Moses to tell this same people before they ever even embarked on their own deliverance journey His name was "I Am that I am."

I get so excited about "I Am." There is so much ministering in those two words: I Am. I Am a deliverer. I Am a way maker. I Am a bridge over troubled waters. I Am bread come down from on high. I Am water from the rock. I Am peace that surpasses all understanding. I Am joy. I Am your healer. I Am your provider. I Am He that was, is, and is to come.

What are you in need of today? Well, God *is*. "I Am" is all that, and so much more.

Imagine standing before a sea of water and having God to tell you to go forward. You see, it takes real faith to move forward when logic and mind tells you that it makes no sense. Going forward in spite of, shows God that you truly trust Him. Moving forward takes faith further than mere lip service. Moving forward *anyhow* let's God know that even though you don't know *how* He's going to do it, you know *somehow* He's going to do it. And just as with the children of Israel, you'll end up crossing over on dry land.

May I have a "Word" with you? From this day forward, go forward. Don't look back. Quit trying to travel life constantly looking in your rearview mirror. Stop longing for what you had or how it "used to be" when you know some of "back then" wasn't nearly God's best for your life.

Rejoice in what God wants to do for you if you'll commit to move forward. Praise God when you find yourself at your Red Sea and Pharaoh's army fast approaching from behind. It merely means God has something better He's moving you toward. It means God is about to fight for you and show you something truly special.

From this day forward: Fear not, stand still, and *see* the salvation of the Lord!

Grace under Pressure

econd Corinthians 2:1 begins, "Grace be to you and peace from God our Father, and from the Lord Jesus Christ." Second Corinthians 2:8 declares, "For we would not, brethren, have you ignorant of our trouble which came to us in Asia, that we were pressed out of measure, above strength, insomuch that we despaired even of life." Grace under pressure.

Grace here is defined as God's unmerited favor. Favor: a gracious, friendly, or obliging unearned act, freely given. The definition for pressed I'd like to use is: to squeeze the juice or other contents from; to extract by squeezing or compressing.

Many of us know what it's like to be under some form of pressure whether it's at home, in personal relationships, or on our jobs. But have you ever really considered the benefits that can be derived from pressure?

If I have fruit, and I want that fruit's juice; then some pressure, some pressing will be required. Olive oil, which is marvelous in cooking healthy, is extracted from olives. Anyone familiar with "anoints my head with oil" will appreciate olive oil since that's what's generally used to do it. However, to extract juice from the fruit, to extract oil from olives, some pressure is required.

Pressure is known to cause some separating to occur. In the case with fruit, the hull, possibly seeds, and the meat of the fruit are being separated from the juice; for olives, it's the fruit from the oil—all for a specific purpose.

So when pressure comes into your life, don't become discouraged. Regardless of whether it was Satan who might have originally brought it for your bad, or God Who is now using it for your good, there will be some separating during this pressing process. How you view a thing or situation often will help determine what you can truly get out of it and ultimately end up left with.

Know that pressure doesn't necessarily feel good when it's happening. There was a song some years ago that asked, "When are we gonna get to the good part?" When you're under pressure, especially when there is grace with that pressure, know that a good part is coming. During this time, God may be removing pits. In some cases, pulp is being removed. Maybe it's impurities. But what's left after this pressing will be something of value; something special and anointed that can even be used in the anointing of others.

May I have a "Word" with you? I know there are times when you feel you're being put through the wringer. I know there are times when it has felt like things were coming at you from all sides. I know sometimes you think you just can't do this any longer. I know you're tired of folks mistreating you.

However, there's yet another "press." It's the one Paul speaks of in Philippians 3:13-14. "Brethren, I count not myself to have apprehended: but this one thing I do, forgetting those things which are behind, and reaching forth unto those things which are before, I press toward the mark for the prize of the high calling of God in Christ Jesus."

Forget those things that have happened to you and keep pressing toward the mark, even when you're being pressed. Keep your eyes on the prize of the High Calling. Know that as you're being pressed, in the end, there *will* be something special you'll be left with: An amazing grace—an anointed grace.

Oh, yes, there is grace even under pressure!

Grit in InteGRITy

I recall a few times I've made a commitment, and later; something greater came along. It appeared I had a choice to make. So what should a Christian do in situations like this?

Job 2:3 says, "And the Lord said unto Satan, Hast thou considered my servant Job, that there is none like him in the earth, a perfect and upright man, one that feareth God, and escheweth evil? and still he holdeth fast his integrity, although thou movedst me against him, to destroy him without cause." I heard someone say that integrity is what you do when no one else is around, when no one else is watching.

Many of us wouldn't dare go in a store and steal an item, but when you're at work do you take a few pens, maybe a pad for your personal use? Are you taking longer breaks than allotted? Do you arrive late for work and/or leave early? (Yes, this is a form of stealing whether you know it or not.) When you fill out your income taxes, do you fudge a little (honestly, some folks bake a whole three-layer chocolate cake)? You know, like claim you gave more to the church than you really did? Claim deductions you know you're not entitled to? Do you tell little "white" lies to keep from hurting someone's feeling or maybe to make yourself look better than you really are?

Would the Lord be able to say of you: "Have you considered my servant (insert your name here), that there is none like him/her in the earth?" Could God declare that you hold fast your integrity?

There's *grit* in integrity. Literally, "grit" is in the word inteGRITy. It takes real grit to stand up for your convictions regardless of what people say about you. It takes real grit to do the right thing, even if it means you might lose out on the other end.

Integrity is a big deal to me. In fact, I don't care to fool with people who lack it, mostly because I don't like and really don't have time to have to constantly watch my back. I have too much to do, and watching out for someone (and a friend at that) who says one thing and does another, is just not what I care to have on my daily to-do list. A person's action will usually tell you who they truly are regardless of what their words say. Personally, I look at what you do and not just listen to what you say.

I pray Psalm 25:21, "Let integrity and uprightness preserve me; for I wait on thee." Proverbs 11:3 says, "The integrity of the upright shall guide them." The Holy Spirit guides and deals in integrity. Now that's true grit.

When I give my word to anyone, it means a lot to me. God's Word to us means a lot to Him. And it's absolutely because of the integrity of God that I can do what I do with confidence. You see, I know if God says it, I can rest in it. I don't have to worry about God—God doesn't lie. God honors His Word.

May I have a "Word" with you? Proverbs 19:1 declares, "Better is the poor that walketh in his integrity, than he that is perverse in his lips, and is a fool." God deals with us with integrity. As His children, we need to look and act like our Father even if, in the natural, it looks like you may possibly lose out. The word grit can be found in integrity.

Yes, God keeps His Word. The question is: what about you? Do you have what integrity requires?

It matters to God; and yes, He sees everything.

311

Guilty

hat will the verdict be when we stand before the Righteous Judge? "Wherefore, as by one man entered into the world, and death by sin; and so death passed upon all men, for that all have sinned." This is found in Romans 5:12.

In the book of Genesis, we find that Adam was found guilty of sin. I have to admit something here. There was a time when I would hear how we all were guilty of sin because one man (Adam) sinned, and I'd wonder how that could be or truthfully, how fair that really was. I mean honestly, Adam was the one who did what he did, so why should the rest of us be charged and have to pay for *his* action? Essentially, we were "convicted" because of what one man did.

Adam, the federal head of the human race was also the seminal head. Seminal means seed. If you think about it, we all were a seed inside of Adam. I've often said that all of us are kin because we all came from Adam and Eve. So all of this racial division really has no validity since, should we trace our roots all the way back, we'd all end up with Adam and Eve as our fore parents. Adam was our seminal head so we were technically inside of Adam as seeds. When Adam sinned, we all sinned.

You may say, but I didn't do it so why should I be held accountable? Why must I be the one to pay? Why am I guilty of something someone else chose to do?

Consider this: your body is made up of many parts. There's your head, your hands, your feet, etc. Let's say your hand takes something that doesn't belong to you (that's called stealing by the way). They catch you, take you to court, put you on trial, and your lawyer argues that the rest of your body should be let off the hook because your feet didn't take the item, your head didn't take the item, and so on.

When you stand before the court, your mouth can plead all it wants that it had nothing whatsoever to do with this crime—that it was the hand that committed the offense. Your mouth may argue that it told the hand not to do it but the hand did it anyway. Your feet may say that it went there with good intentions and was shocked when that hand just reached out and took that item. The feet could even say it didn't have any say-so about what was happening and in fact, the brain should have intervened and put a halt to this crime.

Well, this argument won't fly! The judge might hear it, but in the end, you will be found guilty. The whole body will be sentenced, not just the hand that arguably committed the crime. It's the same with man (Adam). Man was found guilty of sin. Yes, he was found guilty! And the penalty for sin? Death. The whole of man would have to pay.

Then came Jesus. "Death?" Jesus said to the Righteous Judge. "Make Me a body, and send Me to earth. I'll pay the price." Jesus legally came to earth as a man. He offered Himself as payment for the sin that was committed by the first man Adam. Romans 5:15 says, "But not as the offense, so also is the free gift. For if through the offense of one many be dead, much more the grace of God, and the gift by grace, which is by one man, Jesus Christ, hath abounded unto many."

Through one man entered sin; through one man came the ultimate payment for sin.

May I have a "Word" with you? When Jesus paid the price, all that receive what Jesus did also received a full pardon. You see a pardon means that even though you may have been found guilty, even though you may or may not have paid your debt for that crime, that offense has now been wiped completely off your record. Gone! It's as though it never existed. Jesus paid the price, and we who accept Him receive a full pardon.

If you haven't already, accept Jesus and what He did in dying on the cross for your sins and Him being raised from the dead by God in order to transfer a pardon to your account.

Were you found guilty of sin?

Yes.

But Jesus paid it all!

Have You Lost Your Mind Yet?

*a*nd Jesus said unto them, Because of your unbelief: for verily I say unto you, If ye have faith as a grain of mustard seed, ye shall say unto this mountain, Remove hence to yonder place; and it shall remove; and nothing shall be impossible unto you." (Matthew 17:20) "Give, and it shall be given unto you; good measure, pressed down, and shaken together, and running over, shall men give into your bosom. For with the same measure that ye mete withal it shall be measured to you again." (Luke 6:38) "But I say unto you, Love your enemies, bless them that curse you, do good to them that hate you, and pray for them which despitefully use you, and persecute you;" (Matthew 5:44) "For if ye forgive men their trespasses, your heavenly Father will also forgive you:" (Matthew 6:14) "Therefore I say unto you, What things soever ye desire, when ye pray, believe that ye receive them, and ye shall have them." (Mark 11:24)

Wait a minute! I'm being told I can speak to a mountain, to tell it to remove from here to there, and it will be done? That if I have faith as a little old mustard seed, I can do things and nothing will be impossible for me? That to get; I should give? And that I determine what I receive based on how I give? I'm supposed to love my enemies? And not just love them, but bless those that curse me; to do good to people who hate me; pray for them that not just use me, but *despitefully* use and persecute me? I'm supposed to believe I have received *when* I pray?

Have you lost your mind?

When you hear things like this, the first thought is: "Okay, Jesus, I hear what you're saying, but maybe you don't quite understand. You see, if I start speaking to mountains, people are going to think something is wrong with me. And I don't understand quite how giving can get me more? And that love your enemies stuff: Why should I reward bad behavior with love? It just doesn't make sense. If I do just these things, not even looking at the other things in the Bible, people will truly believe I've lost my mind."

Philippians 2:5 tell us, "Let this mind be in you, which was also in Christ Jesus:" So again my question is: Have you lost your mind yet?

Losing your mind is: When everything that might make sense in the natural and to the world is being exchanged for the mind of Christ. You see, Jesus understands what we go through. He experienced these things when He was on the earth.

He knows what it is to have people who knew you, who grew up with you, not supporting you when you're doing things for the Kingdom. He knows what it feels like to be talked about, rejected, misused, persecuted, and hated for no reason, sometimes by people who really don't even know anything about you. To have mountains like doubt, jealously, envy, illness, and lack standing in the way. He knows what it is to be betrayed by those close to you. To be forsaken by those who say they'll be there with you through thick and thin.

And yet, while He was on the cross, He said, "Father, forgive them for they know not what they do." Forgive them? You mean not, "Father, get them!" But Father, forgive them?

Yes, that's what losing your mind will call for sometimes: forgiving people (whether family, friends, or foe) when they have wronged you. It's walking in the love of God regardless of how hurt or disappointed you may be.

May I have a "Word" with you? "Let this mind be in you, which was also in Christ Jesus." Losing your mind, many times, means flipping the world's script. So my question once again: Have you lost your mind yet?

As for me, let's just say: I'm losing my mind daily. (I'm just keeping it real here.) And as I continue in the Word, continue being led by the Holy Spirit, continue being transformed by the renewing of my mind, one of these days, I'm going to think and look *just* like Jesus.

Here Am I

ere, Johnny. Here, Patrice." When we want someone, we call them usually by their name. Maybe we want to tell them something. Perhaps we need to ask something of them. There are times when we may just want to be in their presence. But one sure way to get them to come is to call them. It even works with pets. When you call them, no matter where they are or what they're doing, if they can hear you, they'll come running.

I'm reminded right now of Isaiah in the sixth chapter where it begins, "In the year that king Uzziah died, I saw also the Lord sitting upon a throne, high and lifted up." In the eighth verse of that chapter we find, "Also I heard the voice of the Lord, saying, Whom shall I send, and who will go for us? Then said I, Here am I; send me." The Lord called. Isaiah heard His voice. Isaiah recognized who was calling him, and he answered.

First Samuel, chapter two tells of a child named Samuel who ministered unto the Lord before Eli. The word minister means "to serve." The prophet Eli was laid down in his place, his eyes began to wax dim; he could not see. Samuel had laid down to sleep. The Lord called Samuel, and Samuel said, "Here am I." He ran to Eli because he thought Eli had called him. Eli told him to go lay back down because he hadn't called him. The Lord called Samuel again. Samuel arose, went to Eli again, and said, "Here am I." Samuel knew he'd heard his name called, and that it couldn't be anyone calling him except Eli. Eli, calling Samuel son, told him he didn't call him so he should go back and lie down.

Because Samuel didn't yet know the Lord neither the word of the Lord revealed unto him, he didn't know who was calling him. We know since Samuel was in the temple with Eli that he had to know about the Lord, know of the Lord. But there's a huge difference in knowing *about* the Lord, knowing *of* the Lord, and knowing Him. You see, two are informational and the other relational.

When I was young and my mother would yell for me, I recognized my mother's voice. But what I find even more interesting is: twenty children can be somewhere, one child might cry out, "Mama!" and that child's mother knows her child's voice. The same thing with my daddy: I know his voice, and he knows mine.

Back to the scripture in First Samuel 2:8-9, "And the Lord called Samuel again the third time. And he arose and went to Eli, and said, Here am I; for thou didst call me, and Eli perceived that the Lord had called the child. Therefore Eli said unto Samuel, Go, lie down: and it shall be, if he call thee, that thou shalt say, Speak, Lord; for thy servant heareth. So Samuel went and lay down in his place."

May I have a "Word" with you? God is calling many of you to do great works. Are you listening? Do you hear His voice? Do you know Him, I mean really know Him? I'm talking about relationship, not religion. Are you willing to say, "Here am I"? Even more importantly, are you open to hearing what He's telling you to do and following His instructions? Can you say "Speak, Lord"? Or are you so busy trying to tell God how He ought to do a thing that God can't get a word in edgewise?

God is looking for some "Here am I" people who are not in it for themselves, but for His Kingdom. Are you one, or are you looking to man for your glory?

I say, "Here am I, Lord; send me!"

Just Do It

"And the third day there was a marriage in Cana of Galilee, and the mother of Jesus was there. And both Jesus was called and his disciples, to the marriage. And when they wanted wine, the mother of Jesus saith unto him, They have no wine. Jesus saith unto her, Woman, what have I to do with thee? mine hour is not yet come. His mother saith unto the servants, Whatsoever he saith unto you, do it." John 2:1-5

There is something about a mother. Now, I'm not taking anything away from fathers, because anyone who knows me, knows how much I pull for the fathers. But there's just something about a true mother. A true mother hears her children and knows their voices. A true mother knows what her child can do even when the child feels like he or she can't. Mary, the mother of Jesus, knew things about her son before others did.

Allow me to set the stage for these scriptures. Cana was a village west of the Sea of Galilee. Cana is the place where we see Jesus' first miracle—changing water into wine. Mary was at this wedding. Because we see Mary concerned about the fact that there was no more wine left, we know there was a deeper connection with her to this occasion. So being a mother who knew her son, she went to Jesus and told him the situation. Question: what impossible situations are you facing, and have you taken them to Jesus?

In the fourth verse, Jesus responded to His mother by saying, "Woman, what have I to do with thee?" Let's stop right here. On the outside looking in, some of us may find ourselves taken aback by these words. Jesus saying "woman" and not mother? On the surface, this appears disrespectful to His mother. But when you go deeper, you find the term woman in Greek is one of respect. Jesus was actually showing His mother much respect. The statement He was putting to her was about His time to reveal Himself was not yet.

Jesus knew He was headed for the cross. He knew what He was called to do. If He did things that drew attention now, it could mess up the order of things. Should Jesus, the Messiah, start doing things like what His mother was asking, then some would see something different about Him. Question: How many people know who you really are?

What I love about what happened next is that Mary didn't argue with her son. She didn't have a discussion with Him in the midst of the problem. She merely turned to the servants—those who were there to serve—and said, "Whatsoever he saith unto you, do it."

Wow, what a powerful Word. *Whatsoever*. If Jesus is telling you to do something right now, then what . . . so . . . ever He is saying to you, just do it. Don't try to reason it out. Don't argue with Him about how it doesn't make any sense to you. Don't try to tell Him how you would do it if you were doing it. Just do what He tells you to do.

May I have a "Word" with you? The Lord knows what He's doing. He knows what you need to do. It's time out for us being afraid or second guessing God. If God's Word says you're more than a conqueror, then start conquering some things. If God's Word says you can do all things through Christ Jesus who strengthens you, then get to doing what God has called you to do. You're an overcomer, then *be* an overcomer.

Whatsoever He says unto you, do it. Dip seven times in the Jordan River? Do it. Praise the Lord through your trials? Do it.

Just do it!

My Soul Looks Back

"And Moses went up from the plains of Moab unto the mountain of Nebo, to the top of Pisgah, that is over against Jericho. And the Lord showed him all the land of Gilead, unto Dan." Deuteronomy 34:1. "And the Lord said unto him, This is the land which I sware unto Abraham, unto Isaac, and unto Jacob, saying I will give it unto thy seed: I have caused thee to see it with thine eyes, but thou shalt not go over thither." Deuteronomy 34:4.

With God, all things are possible. When God gives a promise, that promise will move from a dream to manifestation. If you'll learn to wait on the Lord, don't worry, and faint not.

My soul looks back, but I don't have to wonder how I got over. I know without a doubt how we've come to where we are today. God is faithful to His promises!

I am so encouraged. There is so much more God has planned in our lives, individually and collectively, if we would only turn our focus toward Him and seek Him. God told the people of Israel about a land. A land He promised them, a land that flowed with milk and honey.

But there were people in that group who couldn't help but mumble, grumble, and complain throughout the journey. Yes, they were in the wilderness. Yes, things weren't going the way they may have envisioned it would.

I've talked with people that God has blessed so much where others are jealous of their success. And yet, they tend to only focus on what's not working, what they don't have, what's not going right in their lives instead of what *is* going right and being encouraged by how far God has brought them.

I thank God for everything in my life: the good, the bad, and yes, even the ugly. It is after the bad times that I can truly appreciate the good. It's the ugly that helps us see and be thankful for the beauty. When things have been tough in your life, you really do appreciate the times when things in life take flight. My soul looks back, but I don't have to wonder how I got over.

May I have a "Word" with you? When God makes a promise, learn to stand on that promise I don't care what things look like. God is not a man that He should or even needs to lie.

I'm so confident of God and His abilities that I will stand on what He has promised me. And personally, I don't care how many people laugh at what I'm doing. I don't care how many people talk about me, call me foolish for daring to believe.

Just as those who mumbled, grumbled, and complained died off in the wilderness without seeing the Promised Land, that's what will happen with the doubters of our time.

Then there are those who have given their all, given their lives for us to see God's promises. To and for those people, I stand and proclaim that the dream not only lives, but that God is faithful to bring it to pass.

So rejoice. We are where we are today because of God and those who bravely not only believed, but worked as *though* they believed. My soul looks back, and I thank God for bringing me over.

Thank you, Lord for continuing to bring all of us over.

What Say You?

*L*ife and death is in the power of the tongue. I am broke. I am sick. I am never going to win. I am tired. I am a loser. I am a nobody. Life and death is in the power of the tongue. I am rich. I am well. I am healed. I am more than a conqueror. I am strong. I am victorious. I am fearfully and wonderfully made. I am seated in Heavenly places. I am redeemed. I am a royal priesthood. I am an overcomer. I am redeemed. I am a child of the Most High God.

Life and death is in the power of the tongue.

Why don't we get this? God created us in His image. We see in Genesis, God created what He desired speaking words. You see throughout Genesis first chapter, "And God said . . . and it was so." There is power in the Word. God spoke it, and it was so. When you speak, you create. The reason I speak and write a lot about the words we use is because I want people to understand that life and death is in the power of the tongue.

Yet, many still speak words that are negative. We still speak words to ourselves and to others that lift up neither us nor others. Why do we do that? Do we not believe the Word of the Lord? Do we not believe that words spoken can produce life or they can produce death according to which words we choose to use and believe?

Yes, you may not feel well. The reality may be you really are sick. But why not speak words of life to the situation instead of saying what you see or feel? If you're not feeling well, if you've received a negative report from the doctor, instead of speaking words of death (I'm sick. I'm going to die.), why not begin vigilantly to speak words of life? It doesn't mean you're in denial. It shows you're using the power God has given you to speak life over the situation. That's the true act of faith at work.

I had a doctor decades ago give me a report I didn't care to hear. She said I had a B-12 deficiency, and that I would have to take a B-12 shot for the rest of my life. I looked at her and smiled as I said, "I don't receive that. That's not God's best." She in turn said that there was nothing wrong with me having to do this. What was going on with me was no fault of my own. I told her I would take the shot (which I did), but that I didn't receive what she was saying because it was not God's best. She looked at me like I was crazy . . . like I had lost my mind.

For two months, I went to her office and was given the B-12 shot. She asked me on the second trip was I not feeling better having taken them? In truth, I wasn't feeling any differently. But God had put something in my spirit that I told her is where I believed my problem was coming from. She had checked everything, but after I told her I believed there was something going on with my stomach because my thumbnails kept breaking in a funny way, she said there was one other test she hadn't done that she wanted to do.

They did it, and I was informed I had H-pylori, treatable by taking a series of medications for two weeks. After taking the medication, I went back to have my B-12 levels checked again. My B-12 was now higher than it should be, and I've not had to take another B-12 shot since.

May I have a "Word" with you? Life and death is in the power of the tongue. I said, "That's not God's best." God's best for me was: I am healed. I spoke what God said, and it was so. What say you today?

Is what you're speaking over your life God's best? If not, then why not use the power God has given you (the power of the tongue) and start speaking words of life no matter what it looks like. What say you?

Let's speak life!

Year of Redemption

As one year ends, another begins. People celebrate this ending and beginning in different ways. Some spend it quietly in the comfort of their homes. Some spend it at a church service in what we call "Watch Night." Some can be found partying with others. And for some, it's just another passing of just another day.

Leaving one year and going into another, think of it as stepping into a year of redemption. Even if you've never personally used one, most of us are familiar with pawn shops. It's a place where people take something valuable to exchange it for (most times) much-needed, short-term cash. I say short-term because the idea is to go back and redeem what has been left; to retrieve what was put into "hock."

Well, many are dealing with spiritual warfare pawn shops, right now—today. We've either voluntarily taken that which was of value and left it at the spiritual warfare pawn shop, or someone came in and stole what was ours, and pawned it. Either way, if something that means a great deal to you is pawned, you want to go and redeem it.

But to redeem something (which is to buy it back), is going to cost something. Even if it was stolen, it's going to cost something to get it back. You may have to give up something to prove it was illegally taken, to prove it was yours and, by right, shouldn't have ever left your possession. You may have to give up some time. You may have to take what you have, and buy it back. But whatever the case: it's going to cost something to get it back.

I came to tell you it's redemption time! It's time to get back what was lost, stolen, or pawned. That's how our Father in Heaven felt when it came to us. We were in need of redemption. But there was a cost associated with redeeming us. And honestly, that price was pretty steep. When God started looking around, He found that there was no one worthy to pay the price. So how do you redeem that which is of value to you when the cost is out of reach?

Glory to God, then Jesus stepped up and told the Father, "Make me a body. I'll go. You can use me to redeem those that are lost. My life for theirs."

So Jesus came legally. I say legally because you see, Jesus couldn't come down as fully the God we know Him to be. There is the spiritual, and there is the earthly. Jesus would have to come legally, born of a woman in the earth. So He was born, and He walked on this earth. He went through the things we all go through. Jesus understands what it means to be lied on, betrayed, forsaken, talked about, *and* mistreated. He knows what it feels like to ask God, "Why hath thou forsaken me?"

I'm talking about knowing God is there, but those times when it feels like you're all by yourself. Oh, Jesus knows. He knows because He became Who God used to redeem us. And because of Jesus, we now have a way back to the Father. Salvation is available because of what Jesus did.

May I have a "Word" with you? I know things may have been hard lately. I know many of you have lost much that was valuable to you. But let me encourage you. Let this be your year of redemption. It's time to go get your stuff back!

It's time to get your joy back. It's time to get your peace back. It's time to go get your children back. It's time to get that confused spouse back on track. It's time to go get your money back! Yes, I said it! It's time to have love back in the place it should be.

Let the redeemed of the Lord say so! Get your stuff back!

The Greatest Gift

*D*uring certain times of the year, it has become a tradition to give gifts. Hanukah and Christmas come to mind. People get and give gifts for birthdays, weddings, anniversaries, baby arrivals, Valentine's Day, Mother's Day, graduations, Father's Day, and the list goes on. There are times when people might give a gift because they were thinking of you or "just because."

Gifts don't have to be the most expensive to be the most cherished. I'm sure you've heard: "It's the thought that counts." I know this to be true.

I recall my parent's tenth wedding anniversary (I've known this couple like, all of my life). One might wonder why at age nine, I would remember that anniversary so vividly. My father had given my mother a present. My sister, Danette and brother, Terence, and I sat and watched as my mother began to open this huge box that we couldn't wait to see what was inside. She unwrapped the box, and lo and behold, there was another beautifully wrapped box.

She unwrapped that box, only to come to another smaller wrapped box. This seemed to continue for some time until I was beginning to believe her gift was merely wrapped boxes. She held up a small box, and when she unwrapped it, there inside was a velvet box. She opened the velvet box to the most beautiful watch I'd ever seen.

It wasn't diamond or anything, but it reflected rainbow colors because of the sterling silver band's diamond cut. It was gorgeous and different. I can still see it today: shining in all of its glory. My mother loved it. When I was older, I would pick it up, hold it as I looked at it, and that special feeling I had when I first saw it, always returned.

But what got my attention more than anything, was the time my father took to either wrap all those boxes himself (or get them wrapped in that way). Imagine the number of boxes, the time, and the thought put into that effort. I couldn't help but believe my father wanted this to be a special experience for my mother. (Then again, he may have just loved the idea of a good laugh watching her go through all of those boxes. I choose to believe he desired it to be special for her.)

May I have a "Word" with you? First Corinthians, thirteenth chapter speaks about faith, hope, and charity (charity to mean love). Most who know me, know that I am a woman of faith. To get to faith, I needed hope. The thing I, as many of you likely, strive for is the greatest of these things, which is love. To love others with an unconditional love. To love others as God loves us, as Christ loves us.

I think about the greatest gift I have ever received: the gift of Jesus Christ in my life. The gift of pure love wrapped expressly for you and for me. God's Love wrapped in swaddling clothes, wrapped in flesh in the name of Jesus.

Love nailed on the cross, placed in a borrowed tomb. Love that rose from the dead with all power and the keys to the Kingdom—power and keys that Jesus freely gives to us.

Now, don't you feel special?

We've been given the greatest gift of all. For God so loved the world that He gave His only begotten Son. If you haven't accepted this gift, why don't you do so today?

Jesus is The Gift Who keeps on giving!

Serving The Lord

hat has God called you to do? How are you going about doing it? In other words: what is your attitude when it comes to doing what you've been called to do? Do you think the spirit in which you do it in doesn't matter as long as you do it? Well, it does matter.

I smile a lot. I hadn't really thought about that until just now as I sit here writing this, and I find myself here with this big smile on my face. When my father-in-law was alive, he used to call me "Smiley." I liked that. Without me having thought about it, he had let me know how I was expressing myself to the outside world.

Last night and into the early morning, I was having a serious talk with a friend. She mentioned how I always seem to have joy. I've learned that people even believe nothing bad ever goes on in my life just because I smile, laugh, and always try to have a positive attitude about things.

Not that I want to brag here, but let me say that I do have my share of troubles. Things don't always go the way I would like for them to go. Things break down on me, need repairing, need replacing, and contrary to those who believe I'm rich financially, I am not rolling in dough . . . *YET.*

Notice I said yet, because I'm a firm believer that words matter, that words create—that words written and spoken today have an impact on our tomorrows. So even when my money is trying to act funny with me, I'm not going to say I'm broke. And for those who think things just come to me without any effort (just flows down from Heaven on a flowery bed of ease), allow me to set the record straight.

I know what it is to have to wait on the Lord. I know how to abound, and I know how to abase. So my smiling, my joy, my enthusiasm is not based on my situation, but instead, always based on My God.

I smile because I know that no matter what is going on in my life, God sees, He knows, and He's already worked it out. Yes, I could worry, cry, and even throw a tantrum, if I wanted. But none of that will change my situation nor will any of these things move God on my behalf. My smiling, my joy comes from my faith in God. And to be honest with you: I actually get a kick out of watching God work. He's just that awesome!

I have seen Him make ways out of no ways. I have seen Him open doors that man thought he had closed on me; close doors that might have been there to lead me in the wrong direction as He ushered me toward the right door. I've seen God promote me when others have tried to keep me down. I've seen Him fill ditches others dug and were watching and waiting for me to fall into. I've seen Him build so many bridges over troubled waters.

Based on what I know about God, why shouldn't I smile as I go through life? Why shouldn't I have joy as I serve the Lord, knowing that nothing that happens in my life catches God off guard? Knowing that God loves and cares for *and* about me? Knowing that no weapon formed against me shall prosper?

I can serve the Lord as Paul said in Acts 20:19-22 with all humility of mind, and with many tears, and temptations by the lying in wait of others, keeping back nothing that's profitable unto others, but showing, teaching publicly, and testifying repentance toward God and faith toward our Lord Jesus Christ.

May I have a "Word" with you? No matter what is going on in your life, you can't allow it to take your joy. I smile because I trust God to give me the strength and the wisdom to handle all things that might come my way. Acts 20:24 sums up perfectly the way I feel. "But none of these things move me, neither count I my life dear unto myself, so that I might finish my course with joy, and the ministry, which I have received of the Lord Jesus, to testify the gospel of the grace of God."

Let's serve the Lord with gladness. Finish our course with joy. Believe that no matter what is going on in the world or in our life, God has us completely covered.

You're in good hands with Almighty God. This knowledge alone should keep a smile on your face. I know it keeps one on mine.

Servant

$\mathcal{I}$ n Matthew, chapter 23, Jesus is speaking to a multitude and to His disciples. One of the things Jesus is talking about is the scribes and the Pharisees, and how they essentially were good at telling folks what to do, but weren't doing those things themselves. In verses 4-7 you find Jesus saying, "For they bind heavy burdens and grievous to be borne, and lay them on men's shoulders; but they themselves will not move them with one of their fingers. But all their works they do for to be seen of men: they make broad their phylacteries, and enlarge the borders of their garments. And love the uppermost rooms at feasts, and the chief seats in the synagogues, and greetings in the markets, and to be called of men, Rabbi, Rabbi."

When referring to phylacteries, that's talking about an amulet that consisted of parchment inscribed with certain portions of the Pentateuch (the law). This parchment was rolled and placed in a small metal cylinder inside of a square leather case. The cases were attached with straps to their foreheads and to the backs of their right hands as a literal interpretation of Deuteronomy 6:8-9. Usually these were to be worn only during prayer, but it appears the Pharisees wore them always and to make them conspicuous for all to see.

In other words, the Pharisees were just trying to show off; they merely wanted to be seen and elevated among the people.

Reading the verses that follow, you see Jesus speaking further on the matter. Then you see verse 11-12 and find a powerful Word to all of us. "But he that is greatest among you shall be your servant. And whosoever shall exalt himself shall be abased; and he that shall humble himself shall be exalted." Jesus said that the greatest among you shall be your servant. That sounds like one who serves and not the one who's being served.

Jesus had strong words in verses 13-14. "But woe unto you, scribes and Pharisees, hypocrites! for ye shut up the kingdom of heaven against men: for ye neither go in yourselves, neither suffer ye them that are entering to go in. Woe unto you, scribes and Pharisees, hypocrites! for ye devour widows' houses, and for a pretense make long prayer; therefore ye shall receive the greater damnation."

There were a few more woes that followed, but can you imagine Jesus calling someone hypocrites? Do you want to be that person Jesus recognizes as merely a hypocrite? Telling you that you shut up the Kingdom of Heaven against men, or in other words that you're putting stumbling blocks in the way of the sinner who's trying to come and repent and be converted. Jesus declaring that you extort money from the helpless, bringing folks into debt and bondage while making an outward show of religion.

People of God, the Lord is looking for servants. That's to all of us who profess Jesus—from the top to the bottom. We're all supposed to be servants.

May I have a "Word" with you? We often hear people talk about when they get to Heaven. We often hear people getting excited about hearing the words, "Well done, my good and faithful servant." My question to you is: How can you be told well done, my good and faithful servant, if you don't want to be a servant? How can you be called a servant if you haven't served? Remember this: Whatsoever you do to the least of Jesus' littlest ones, you do it unto Jesus.

Jesus is looking for true servants. Can He call you one?

Remembering Not To Forget

"And he spake unto the children of Israel, saying, When your children shall ask their fathers in time to come, saying, What mean these stones? Then ye shall let your children know, saying, Israel came over this Jordan on dry land. For the Lord your God dried up the waters of Jordan from before you, until ye were passed over, as the Lord your God did to the Red Sea, which he dried up from before us, until we were gone over." Joshua 4:21-23.

Many times in life, we forget just how *much* and *what* God has done for us. In fact, I believe some things we literally take for granted. We wake up in the morning and act like it's no big deal. But then, there was someone who went to bed the night before with plans for the next day who didn't wake up. We take for granted being able to get out of bed, but there was someone who got in the bed the night before who can't get out of it.

There's someone without a place to stay, without food to eat, and we scrape out food into the trash.

Then there are those big things God has kept us from: dangers seen and unseen. And even during those times when we've found ourselves facing our Red Sea with Pharaoh and his army hard and heavy behind us, God has made a way out of no way.

We need to remember, not to forget. Remembering, not to forget.

Remember those times when you didn't know how you were going to pay that bill, and God showed up with the full amount and then some? Remember when you were sick, and God showed His healing powers? Remember when you'd done something wrong and deserved for some awful thing to happen because of it, but God showed mercy— holding back the punishment deserved—and instead, gave grace— unmerited favor?

May I have a "Word" with you? David remembered not to forget. When he was facing the giant named Goliath, he began to remember the time when there was a lion and a bear. Believe me: these animals are nothing to play with for sure. But God helped David defeat the lion and the bear. And because David remembered how God had been on his side during that time, he didn't worry about Goliath. He knew God would be with him as he defeated this uncircumcised Philistine. David knew God was with him.

Do you know the Lord? Do you talk with Him daily? Does He talk to you? Do you know that God is with you no matter what you're going through? Can you remember a time when things looked hopeless or like they weren't going to work out, and God showed up and showed out— demonstrating the power of His might?

Are you remembering not to forget?

God is too awesome for you to shrink away from any challenges the world or the devil may bring your way. Remember what God has done for you. Thank God for what He has done. Then thank God for what He's *about* to do. And then I want you to stand back, and see the salvation of the Lord!

Everything is moving by the power of God!

It's in the Genes

enesis 1:26 says, "And God said, Let us make man in our image, after our likeness: and let them have dominion over the fish of the sea, and over the fowl of the air, and over the cattle, and over all the earth, and over every creeping thing that creepeth upon the earth." We see here God speaking to the Trinity and saying, "Let us make man in our image." In Genesis 2:7 it tell us, "And the Lord God formed man of the dust of the ground, and breathed into his nostrils the breath of life; and man became a living soul."

I was thinking about DNA and how interesting this science really is. People can tell so much about you just from your DNA. It has exonerated more than a few people who have been unjustly accused and imprisoned. DNA can tell you about your history as well as things that could impact your future. People are increasingly using DNA to know for certain whether someone fathered a particular child or not. Your DNA can tell things in your genes.

As I was thinking about DNA, I thought about God our Father, and my attention was drawn to the book of Genesis, a written record of the beginning of the world. Suddenly, I saw the word "genes" right there in the word "Genesis": Genes is.

When people are related, traits of that fact generally can be found; evidence of that fact, passed down. Evidence can be found in the genes. The question I'd like to pose is: Can people see where your spiritual genes come from? Do they see traits of God demonstrated in your life?

Does your DNA, certain things in your genes, point back to your Father in Heaven; or are you still in need of a blood transfusion?

Genesis 2:7 tells us that the Lord God breathed into man's nostrils. That tells us that, in the beginning, God's Spirit was breathed into man. If this is so, then traces of God's DNA should show up in man. People should see evidence. Yes, it's in the genes.

I just love how God works things. Genesis gives an account of how everything that is now first began. When it comes to mankind, Genesis tells how God breathed his breath into man. Looks like there should be traces of God's DNA passed down through the generations that first began with Adam to us. Regardless, with Jesus, there's hope.

May I have a "Word" with you? Being born again means the old man died and a new man has taken the old man's place. The transfusion of Jesus' blood saves when we accept Jesus as our Savior.

Can people look at you and see any resemblance to your Heavenly Father? Are your eyes like your Father's? Can you see what's beyond your physical eyes, see what presently might be invisible, to see things as God sees it? Are your ears different from the norm, meaning can you hear beyond what's being said to hear what your Father has to say? Children tend to know their parent's voice.

Do you hear your Father when He's talking to you? Do you walk like your Father? Do you talk like your Father? What about you can people trace back to your Father in Heaven?

If a spiritual DNA test was performed on you right now, would the results comes back and proudly proclaim, "God in Heaven, You *are* the Father!"? That's the results I'm excited about: when people can see God's genes in me.

What about you? Can people honestly say they see God in you . . . that they see the love of God flowing through you?

Let's face it: When it comes to family—naturally and spiritually—it's in the genes!

It Is Written

There are and will continue to be times in life when you'll find yourself either tempted or challenged. I've heard many people say, "If it's not one thing, then it's another." But knowing what the Word of God says about a thing and being able to use God's Word in your situation, makes all the difference in the world. You see, even though Jesus was the Word made flesh, we find Him using the Word when He faced Satan.

Matthew 4:1-4 states, "Then was Jesus led up of the Spirit into the wilderness to be tempted of the devil. And when he had fasted forty days and forty nights, he was afterward an hungered. And when the tempter came to him, he said, If thou be the Son of God, command that these stones be made bread. But he answered and said, It is written, Man shall not live by bread alone, but by every word that proceedeth out of the mouth of God."

Jesus had been in the wilderness. He'd fasted for forty days and night. He was hungry. And the tempter came to Jesus first off challenging who Jesus believed Himself to be. The devil will challenge you on who you believe yourself to be. "If you're a child of God, then you need to do this to prove that God really is with you." The truth is: you need to know who you are in God and not let anyone goad you into doing anything that is contrary to what the Word of God says. In this passage of scripture, the tempter (the devil) challenged Jesus to prove that He was the Son of God by having Jesus to command stones be turned into bread. But Jesus countered the tempter with the Word.

You see, what Satan didn't understand was that he was talking to the Bread of Life! Jesus knew Who He was. He didn't need to prove anything, especially anything to Satan. God had given Jesus an assignment, and Jesus was not going to be deterred from that ultimate goal.

May I have a "Word" with you? Has God given you an assignment? Are you standing firm on God's Word or are you too busy trying to prove things to those who challenge you?

Before you can tell the tempter or those who attempt to try you, what is written, you must first *know* what is written. And the only way you can *know* what is written, is you must study the Word to show yourself approved.

People, it's time to stop allowing our Bibles to be decoration or merely props in a religious narrative.

Realize this: The Word of God is rich. The Word of God is life to you. You can't tell anyone what is written if you don't know what is written. But when you know what God's Word has to say on the matter, and someone tells you that you're a loser, you can boldly declare, "No. I am victorious."

Read the Word of God. If you don't like to read, then listen to the Word on audio. But get the Word in you so that when the tempter comes to you with foolishness, you can say without blinking, "Excuse me. But *it is written*!"

IFs *With Promises*

he Bible has many promises, many of which are contingent on the word if. I wanted to remind each of us what is possible, IF we would merely heed God's Word.

"If my people, which are called by my name, shall humble themselves, and pray, and seek my face, and turn from their wicked ways; then will I hear from heaven, and will forgive their sin, and will heal their land." 2 Chronicles 7:14 (God will heal our land.)

"For he is our God; and we are the people of his pasture, and the sheep of his hand. Today if ye will hear his voice." Psalm 95:7 (God will take care of you.)

"If it had not been the Lord who was on our side, when men rose up against us." Psalm 124:2 (God is there fighting for you.)

"If I ascend up into heaven, thou art there: if I make my bed in hell, behold, thou art there." Psalm 139:8 (God is everywhere.)

"If I take the wings of the morning, and dwell in the uttermost parts of the sea; Even there shall thy hand lead me, and thy right hand shall hold me." Psalm 139:9-10 (There is nowhere God is not.)

"How precious also are thy thoughts unto me, O God! How great is the sum of them! If I should count them, they are more in number than the sand: when I awake, I am still with thee." Psalm 139:17-18 (God is thinking of you.)

"My son, if thine heart be wise, my heart shall rejoice, even mine." Proverbs 23:15 (Wisdom does a heart good.)

"If thine enemy be hungry, give him bread to eat; and if he be thirsty, give him water to drink; For thou shalt heap coals of fire upon his head, and the Lord shall reward thee." Proverbs 21-22 (With God on your side, there's no need to fight fire with fire.)

"If ye be willing and obedient, ye shall eat the good of the land." Isaiah 1:19 (God has good things waiting on you.)

"For if ye forgive men their trespasses, your heavenly Father will also forgive you." Matthew 6:14 (Forgiveness is more than a two-way street; it's a freeway.)

"Again I say unto you, That if two of you shall agree on earth as touching any thing that they shall ask, it shall be done for them of my Father which is in heaven. For where two or three are gathered together in my name, there am I in the midst of them." Matthew 18:19-20 (Agreeing to succeed.)

May I have a "Word" with you? These are all from the Word of God—IFs with promises used to encourage you in your walk with the Lord.

Let me leave you with Matthew 21:21-22 in hopes that IF you haven't tried any of these yet; you will. "Jesus answered and said unto them, Verily I say unto you, If ye have faith, and doubt not, ye shall not only do this which is done to the fig tree, but also if ye shall say unto this mountain, Be thou removed, and be thou cast into the sea; it shall be done. And all things, whatsoever ye shall ask in prayer, believing, ye shall receive." (God giving you the power to do more than you ever thought possible.)

If we would take these to heart, put them into action, we will reap the benefits of God's promises! Sorry, I must add one more. "And let us not be weary in well doing; for in due season we shall reap, if we faint not." Galatians 6:9. (Yet another promise we can count on.)

I Quit

There are times when you do your best. You give it your best shot. You give yourself that pep talk to keep going. You know some of those things we say. "If at first you don't succeed; try, try again." "Quitters never win, and winners never quit." And you continue on your journey to that place you have set in your sights.

But then you find that the more you try, the more things come against you. It feels like no one really cares one way or the other. People aren't supporting what you do. Not really. Oh, they talk a good game. They put on great fronts as though they're in your corner. But we know another saying. "Talk is cheap."

When it's time to put action behind that talk, where are they? Where are your friends who said they'd be there until the end? Where are the "blood that's thicker than water" group? Where are those who pushed you out there to do it, told you they would be there for you when you need them? Where are they? Where are they?

I write. And there are times when I wonder if what I do really matters. Am I making a difference? I write fictional books, and I've wondered why do I stick to the principles of how I've been called to write the fiction God has given me? I push and keep going despite all those who are selling books like crazy while I have the nerve to put scriptures in my novels. And sermons, oh, don't forget about the sermons. You'll most definitely find at least one sermon in my novels.

Why keep doing this? Why not be a sellout and do that thing which is sure to garner me lots of readers who'll spread the word about my writing like a virus unleashed into a network of computers? Instead, I write Christian novels. Christian: that which lifts up Jesus the Christ.

Preachers, ministers, teachers, business men and women, workers, laborers, mothers, fathers, political leaders, people with dreams, why do you keep trying when it feels like no one cares?

Why keep on going during those times when it feels like you aren't making a difference? When you feel like you're not getting any help. When it feels like you're wasting your time. Why not quit and do something altogether different, even though you *know* God has called you to this place? Why not at least change course? After all, it's possible you're on the wrong track.

Granted, some people are going in the wrong direction, and in those cases, I would definitely say it's a good thing to change course. But for those of you who *know* you're doing what God has called you to do, how He's called you . . . when you *know* you're in the will of God, that your steps are ordered by the Lord; then you're not included in the "change course" thought.

May I have a "Word" with you? The race is not to the swift, nor the battle to the strong. The race is given to the one who endures until the end. As long as you know God has called you to a thing, don't quit. Keep going. Keep the faith. Keep your eyes toward the hills from whence cometh your help. And your help comes from the Lord.

When family and friends forsake you, God is there. When you feel all by yourself, God is there. When you feel no one is helping . . . that you're not getting any support other than words spoken with little or no action backing it up, God is there. God will touch a stranger's heart to do what others *said* they would. God will provide what you need to do what He has called you to do.

Don't quit unless what you're quitting is truly not what you should be doing. Talk to the Lord about it. God will guide you. Don't quit. God is with you.

If It Had Not Been For The Lord

I f it had not been the Lord who was on our side, now may Israel say; If it had not been the Lord who was on our side, when men rose up against us: Then they had swallowed us up quick, when their wrath was kindled against us: Then the waters had overwhelmed us, the stream had gone over our soul: Then the proud waters had gone over our soul. Blessed be the Lord, who hath not given us as a prey to their teeth. Our soul is escaped as a bird out of the snare of the fowlers: the snare is broken, and we are escaped. Our help is in the name of the Lord, who made heaven and earth." Psalm 124:1-8.

There are songs that speak to some effect, "If it had not been for the Lord on my side, where would I be?" Think about that. We travel up and down dangerous highways. How many times have you been spared from some danger you didn't even know about? That's a question only God can answer.

Oh, and there are plenty of times where you may have been aware of the close calls you escaped; but how many are there that you didn't even know about? That's something to thank God for. How often have people set traps for you, wanting to catch you in a snare, but the snare was broken, and God gave you a way of escape?

God is so worthy to be praised!

I can't even begin to know where I would be if had not been for the Lord on my side. We all know things aren't always fair in this world. But that's the time when God will grant you His favor. You'll get things that will leave others to wonder how you could have possibly gotten them. I'll be the first to gladly acknowledge that I am where I am today, I am who I am today for no other reason than God's grace, His love, His mercy, the promises He made me, and His unmerited favor.

As much as we'd like to think it, God really is not all that impressed with our education (although education is a good thing to have, and He'll help you attain it), for God is able to do things with you whether or not you have what others may label as the correct degree. God is not impressed with who you know, because you don't know anyone until you really know Him. God is not moved by how much money you have in your bank account, your stock portfolio, or your 401-K because there are just some things money can't buy.

Money can't buy love. Money can't buy peace. Money can't buy happiness. Money can't buy good health. Money can't buy your salvation. Money can't buy God's favor. And unlike the favor of man: There's something truly special about God's favor.

May I have a "Word" with you? If it were not for God on your side, where would you be? I want you to really think about that. Blessed be the Lord, He is worthy to be praised! He has not given us as a prey to those who desire to do us in.

And our help? Our help comes from the Lord Who made heaven and earth. Our help is in the name of Jesus: Jesus our healer, Jesus our provider, Jesus our banner, Jesus our peace.

With that kind of help, what is there for you to worry about?

Okay, let me say it this way. If God is for you, who can be against you and succeed?

Release, Then Hold Fast

*H*ebrews 10:23 tells us, "Let us hold fast the profession of our faith without wavering; (for he is faithful that promised)." Verses 35-36 states, "Cast not away therefore your confidence, which hath great recompense of reward. For ye have need of patience, that, after ye have done the will of God, ye might receive the promise."

Patience. You need to be patient.

You see, God is saying to let go of the things that are holding you back and hurting you. To let go of trying to figure out how He will bring a thing to pass. But hold onto your confession. Hold onto the promise God has made you.

Many of us believe God, but we want Him to do a thing the way we think He should do it. And when it doesn't happen the way we envision it, then we start to panic, or worse: to lose faith. Doubt gets a foothold in the doorway, and the devil steps in and starts a conversation with us about whether God really said it, whether God really meant it that way. "Maybe God has left you out in the cold, and now you're looking all foolish because you still believe what you believe God said."

The devil's best trick is when he gets you to doubt you ever really heard God at all. "Maybe it was just you talking to yourself," he whispers in your mind. "That has to be the reason since nothing has happened toward that end in all this time." And you begin to believe what you're hearing and begin to doubt.

May I have a "Word" with you? The reason you need to let go of some things, specifically those people who have hurt you is because in Hebrews 10 verse 30 it reiterates what was written in Deuteronomy 32:35 and Deuteronomy 32:36. "For we know him that hath said, Vengeance belongeth unto me, I will recompense, said the Lord. And again, The Lord shall judge his people. It is a fearful thing to fall into the hands of the living God."

So let go of the evil that may have been done to you, I don't care how long ago or even how recent, and leave that to God to handle on your behalf. Let go of trying to make things happen when you think it should have already happened and allow God to work things on His own schedule. Believe me: God knows what He's doing. God sees from infinity to eternal. Trust God to do what He does, while you do what He's telling you to do, and do it *when* He tells you to.

Disappointment—let it go. Hurt—let it go. Frustration with folks who tell you they're going to do something, and they don't do what they say—let it go. Questions about what's taking God so long to bring your dream . . . that thing you've confessed and believed for—let that thought go.

But hold fast to your confession. Don't throw away your confidence. There's a great recompense of reward and guess what? It has your name already engraved on it. Engraved on it!

Hebrews 10:37 declares, "For yet a little while, and He that shall come will come, and will not tarry." Verse 38, "Now the just shall live by faith: but if any man draw back, my soul shall have not pleasure in him." I can hear some of you already singing that great song we used to sing years ago, "I'm holding on, and I won't let go of my faith."

Hold on. God is still God, and it's already done! Wait for it, wait for it, and give God the praise even before it makes its way to you!

Even in a Famine

I was thinking about how some people are struggling during certain times. Unemployment . . . layoffs . . . illnesses. You may be looking for a job right now or you may know someone else who is, and it looks like there's nothing out there to be had.

Even those who still have jobs may find that their money is not going as far as it used to. They're working so long and so hard until there's now a shortage of time with family and friends.

Don't get me wrong now; some people are doing wonderfully. But those same people may find their joy has somehow become scarce. The peace they once held close seems to be slipping through their fingers.

Maybe you've lost a loved one only to turn around to have someone else transition shortly thereafter. It's hard. I know it can be hard. My father went to be with the Lord on April 30, 2018, and I miss him.

All of these things could be considered a time of famine. But you know what? I'm so glad to report today that no matter what's going on in your life, God is God even in a famine. You may not be able to find a job, but God will ensure somehow you're provided for. You won't go hungry.

You might be dealing with all kinds of things trying to steal or that have stolen your joy. But God is God, and He will not only restore your joy, but He'll give you strength along with His joy. For the joy of the

Lord is my strength. When peace is trying to elude you, the Lord will give you His peace. And the wonderful thing about the peace of God is that His peace surpasses all understanding.

May I have a "Word" with you? Joseph the dreamer was put in charge by Pharaoh first *before* the famine, and then he was the one in charge to manage things *during* the famine. Did you catch that? God gave them what they needed before they ever even needed it. God put things and people in place before those who would need it, needed it.

Pharaoh had a dream. Joseph interpreted that dream. Pharaoh put Joseph over his house and the people of Egypt, with no one else being higher than Joseph except Pharaoh. But know that God was all in this.

It was God Who gave Joseph the interpretation of Pharaoh's dream. God granted Joseph favor in a land where he'd been a slave, had been imprisoned, was lied to and lied on. God elevated Joseph to the number two position in the land. God put someone in place that would later be a blessing to many, even in a famine.

And what came because of the famine? Joseph was eventually reunited with his family. His brothers were forced to go to Egypt to buy corn, "that they may live, and not die." (Genesis 42:2) And those same brothers who once plotted against him so many years earlier, found themselves bowing down to their brother and asking for help.

God's will was done, even in a famine. God will take care of you, even in a famine. God can elevate you, even in a famine. So don't fret about what's going on around you during a time of lack, of famine, and of downtime.

Trust in the Lord. Lean not to your own understanding. And watch God do what He does, even in a famine.

God's Will

We often hear people say, "If it's God's will . . . " something either will or won't happen. In the forty-second verse of Luke 22, Jesus was talking to His Father in Heaven where He told God "not my will but thine be done." We've also seen and heard "Thy will be done on earth as it is in heaven" in what we call "The Lord's Prayer." But I want to approach God's will from a different angle.

There are various definitions for the word "will" according to the way it's being used. There is the will used to indicate likelihood or certainty; the will that indicates willingness; the will used to indicate probability or expectation. A will can also be a desire, purpose, or determination. But the will I'm speaking of is a legal declaration of how a person wishes his or her possessions to be disposed of after death.

There are many who advocate those who have any possessions of value should have an up-to-date legal will (not just something you've written down on a piece of paper that likely won't hold up in a court of law). Far too many people still don't have a will even though they know it's wisdom to do it.

God has a will and those who accept Jesus become heirs and joint-heirs with Jesus Christ. Jesus died (yes, I know He also rose from the dead), and now we have a right to an inheritance. This means we now have a legal inheritance due us and a right to claim it.

Yes, God has a will, and God desires for us to have our part of our inheritance now. So let's look at some of the things in God's will.

In God's will, He desires you to have the desires of your heart. Psalm 37:4 tells us to "Delight ourselves also in the Lord and He will give you the desires of your heart." He wills that you prosper and be in health. Third John, second verse tells us, "Beloved, I wish above all things that thou mayest prosper and be in health, even as thou soul prospers." This verse also lets you know God desires that your soul prospers (I think some people gloss over or completely miss this part) that's why these things go hand in hand.

God wills that you be in peace, have a peace that surpasses all understanding, and know perfect peace. In God's will there is joy. For the joy of the Lord is your strength. In God's will there is fullness of life. In God's will there is abundance. An abundance of what, you might ask. An abundance of whatever you need. Philippians 4:19 says, "But my God shall supply all your need according to his riches in glory by Christ Jesus."

Oh, did I forget to mention that God is rich? Well, the earth is the Lord's and the fullness thereof; the world and they that dwell therein. The cattle on a thousand hills belong to Him. The silver, the gold, all the diamonds and other precious stones and metal, the oil—yes, all God's (I know people think they own it, but it's all God's).

May I have a "Word" with you? Just because you act like you don't have doesn't mean that's the truth. The truth is God's has already given you all that you need. What's happening is the equivalent of your being left an inheritance of millions of dollars and you not knowing about it as you struggle every day to make it. If you're in Christ, you are an heir and a joint-heir with Jesus, meaning you're entitled to the inheritance as stated in the Will of God.

So find out what's in God's will, then tap into your inheritance. If you don't have, it's not because God has not given it to you. Find out what you have in God, then begin accessing all He has willed to you.

Favor

 here are people who have access to all the money they need to do what they need to do. There are people who have access to others who can make things happen. By this I'm talking about the old saying: It's not always what you know but who you know. I grew up in a small community outside of Birmingham, Alabama called Village Springs. Our family was not wealthy, although I'll say that, as a little girl, I honestly thought we were.

As an adult, I've had to work hard for the things I've gotten in life. I could have used lots of things as an excuse not to accomplish what I needed, but I didn't. I worked at BellSouth for 18 years, then at the end of 1996, I did what some thought was absolutely crazy: I left that great paying job. I didn't retire, I wasn't laid off or fired—I walked away of my own accord. I left to pursue my dream of becoming a published author. At the time, I didn't have a book deal, wasn't in contact with any publisher who was even remotely interested in a deal with me.

In fact, I really didn't have a completed book worthy of a publisher making me an offer. All I had was a talk with the Lord about doing something that I knew I was called to do, and His assurance that He was with me.

I stepped out on faith and the belief that I was doing what God was leading me to do. So here I was out there without the money I might have needed to do some things or the people I needed to get it done.

But you know what I did have? I had the Lord on my side. And what you'll discover when you trust in the Lord and lean not to your own understanding is that it really is *who* you know.

Knowing the Lord has brought me into places I could have only dreamed of. *Knowing* the Lord has opened doors that man told me would be closed for me. *Knowing* the Lord has given me something that money can't buy and that's the favor of God.

You may have heard someone say "Favor ain't fair." Well, I don't know about all that, but what I do know is that the favor of God is fabulous.

May I have a "Word" with you? Psalm 41:10-11 says, "But thou, O Lord, be merciful unto me, and raise me up, that I may requite them. But this I know that thou favorest me, because mine enemy doth not triumph over me." You may not have the money you think you need, you may not know any famous people, but when you have the favor of God, when God favors you, you have all that you need to do what you need to do. The favor of God is the great equalizer.

Yes, it's great to have money, it's great to know people in positions, but honestly, I thank God for His favor. God's favor will take you places where no amount of money can get you into. God's favor will move people to do things for you they may not have even thought of doing.

So walk in God's favor, and see just how far God's favor takes you.

Good News!

I have some good news for you. Jesus was born! When exactly?

Well, I can't tell you the exact day and month although we celebrate His birth on December twenty-fifth. There are some who say it may have been in March; some who say it was likely in September (because shepherds were tending flocks in the field, and they wouldn't be doing that in the month of December). Honestly, the exact date is not as important as the fact that Jesus was born!

Matthew 2:1-2 tells us, "Now when Jesus was born in Bethlehem of Judea in the days of Herod the king, behold, there came wise men from the east to Jerusalem. Saying, Where is he that is born King of the Jews? for we have seen his star in the east, and are come to worship him."

In the past and still today, wise men seek Jesus. And Jesus had a star that was "His" star—a star that indicated the birth of a king. Numbers 24:17 states, "I shall see him, but not now: I shall behold him, but not nigh: there shall come a Star out of Jacob, and a Scepter shall rise out of Israel, and shall smite the corners of Moab, and destroy all the children of Sheth." Revelation 22:16 says, "I Jesus have sent mine angel to testify unto you these things in the churches. I am the root and the offspring of David, and the bright and morning star."

I have some Good News for you: Jesus was born, and wise men seek Him.

Matthew 2:10-11 further tells us regarding the wise men, "When they saw the star, they rejoiced with exceeding great joy. And when they were come into the house, they saw the young child with Mary his mother, and fell down, and worshipped him: and when they opened their treasures, they presented unto him gifts; gold, and frankincense, and myrrh."

When the wise men saw Jesus, they fell down and worshipped Him. Jesus, the King of kings who wasn't sitting on any throne when they found Him, wasn't wearing a crown, most likely at that time residing in a little rented house (yes, I know we've been told it was a stable, but this scripture reveals it was at a house).

These wise men (who weren't even religious people) recognized they were in the presence of a king, and they worshipped Him. Jesus, Who was sent from Heaven to the earth by an Almighty God. Wise men then and wise men now know He's King without any other proof than their belief. Good News, Jesus was born; Great News, Jesus died.

Yes, this is Great News. You see Jesus came to redeem us back. That's why He came to earth—to die for our sins. There is no greater love than a man who lays down his life for a friend. Oh, yes, that's love! The true *Christmas* gift! God gave us Jesus and Jesus gave His life. Good News, Jesus was born. Great News, Jesus died. Even Greater News, Jesus was raised by God from the dead!

If Jesus had just been born and that was all to it, that might have been good. But plenty of people have been born and did great things on the earth. And had Jesus merely died for our sins, that would have been great, but we can name many great people who have died. Jesus did something no one else has ever done. He rose from the dead with all Power, and that's even Greater News. He then gave that Power to the children and heirs of God . . . who have become joint-heirs with Jesus.

There's Good News, Great News, Greater News, but wait! There's more! The Greatest News of all. Jesus was born, died, arose, went to Heaven, and He's coming back again! He's coming back for those who seek Him (wise men and women), to take us to a specially prepared place. Let us examine our lives. Are you becoming more like Jesus?

Matthew 2:12 says, "And being warned of God in a dream that they should not return to Herod, they departed into their own country another way."

May I have a "Word" with you? When you have truly been in the presence of Jesus, you should leave a different way than the way you came. The wise men came one way, and having met Jesus, they left a different way than the way they had come.

Extra, extra, read all about it. There's Good News, Great News, Greater News, and the Greatest News—and thanks be to God, Jesus makes all the difference in the world!

Author and Finisher

I 've always loved a song by Natasha Bedingfield entitled *Unwritten*. The reason I love this song so much is because it sums up what I feel both from the standpoint of an author and life. The song says, "Staring at the blank page before you." As an author, I face blank pages prior to penning or typing words onto my computer screen—nothing but blank space and pages when I begin. But as I start doing something, what was once blank, fills up.

When we're born, technically, we were like a blank page. Each day we awaken to a new day, it's a blank page with every moment being written by our decisions and actions—good and bad.

Yes, I believe there are things that have been predestined by God. But I also believe God gives us free will; and that He cares about what we as His children desire in our lives. We, or others, choose things that daily fill up the pages of our lives.

As an author, I create characters with their own personalities and ways of doing things. People may get upset with me for not making my characters do certain things or do it a certain way, but I allow them to be and grow along their journey (albeit fictitious).

They may make mistakes, but I don't bash them or beat them down as they grow into, hopefully, what will be better people later in life. In fact, someone sent me an email telling me how much they've enjoyed seeing two of my main characters (Johnnie Mae Taylor and George Landris) mature and grow over the books they've appeared in.

So, you may be asking: What does this have to do with God?

Hebrews 12:2 says, "Looking unto Jesus the author and finisher of our faith; who for the joy that was set before him endured the cross, despising the shame, and is set down at the right hand of the throne of God." Jesus is the author and finisher of our faith.

In this scripture, the word "author" means originator and "finisher" means perfector. You see Jesus, the originator, has blazed the trail. When I was growing up, we would sometimes take a shortcut through a wooded area by creating a path. A path is rarely a paved place, but it's been traveled enough to be seen by someone else coming along. Weeds have been trodden down. And because of this, you can see your way more clearly when traveling a path as opposed to all woods.

The finisher—the perfector tells us that when we start this race, we need to keep our eyes on the finish line and finish our course . . . finish the race we've begun. A perfector polishes toward a glowing perfection.

Jesus is the author and finisher of our faith. When He hung on the cross, He said, "It is finished." Jesus has written it, edited it, polished it, and placed those all too familiar words most authors know all so well: THE END.

Now, if a storyline is good, we'll sometimes see a sequel. Well, Jesus said He's coming back. That was your clue that there will be a sequel—still more to come. But The Author declared this segment finished.

May I have a "Word" with you? Hebrews 12:1 tells us to "lay aside every weight, and the sin which so easily beset us, and let us run with patience the race that is set before us." We, who are in Christ, let us look to Jesus the author and finisher of our faith.

Allow the Lord to perfect your faith! And throughout the book of your life: the beginning, middle, and the end; you'll find that you win!

Giving Thanks and Not Just During Thanksgiving

Thank you. Yes, thank you. Thank you for taking the time to read this.

In your life, make sure you say thank you.

I can tell you when someone tells me thank you—it makes me feel good and causes me to want to do even more for them.

Now—how many people have you thanked lately? Has someone done something for you, and you took it for granted that they knew you appreciated them? Then right now, tell them, "Thank you"? And if right now is not possible, then do it as soon as possible.

Besides being good manners, why should you say thank you?

Because saying "thank you" takes you to a higher place. Think of it like putting helium in a balloon. If you put in a little helium, you may rise but not as high as you can when every inch is filled to capacity. Every time you say "thank you" it's like putting more helium inside of you and causing yourself to rise to an even higher altitude.

Write down or speak the things you're grateful for and watch how many more things start coming your way. Gratitude has a way of bringing you more to be thankful for.

If someone has blessed you in some way, tell them thank you. If God has brought you through something, tell God thank You. If you're going through something right now, tell God thank You. Thank You,

God for believing that, by faith, I can even handle this. Thank You for being with me as I go through this. Thank You . . . for I know I'm already victorious in this through Christ Jesus!

You don't have to wait until you see it manifested, by faith, learn to say thank You.

May I have a "Word" with you? Let's tell God, "Thank You!"

Made in the USA
Coppell, TX
23 August 2020